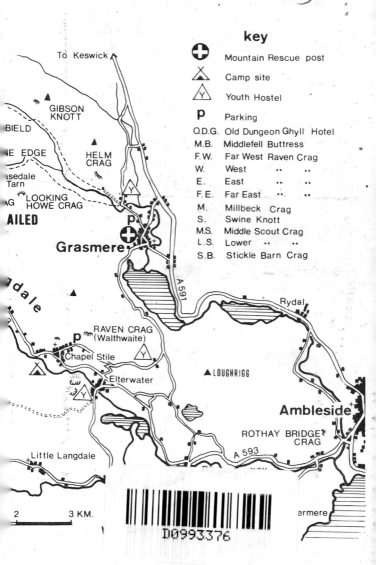

Lenartowicz

key

✚   Mountain Rescue post

△   Camp site

⌂   Youth Hostel

p   Parking

O.D.G. Old Dungeon Ghyll Hotel
M.B.   Middlefell Buttress
F.W.   Far West Raven Crag
W.   West   ..   ..
E.   East   ..   ..
F.E.   Far East   ..   ..
M.   Millbeck   Crag
S.   Swine Knott
M.S.   Middle Scout Crag
L.S.   Lower   ..   ..
S.B.   Stickle Barn Crag

To Keswick

GIBSON KNOTT

BIELD

NE EDGE

HELM CRAG

asedale Tarn

LOOKING HOWE CRAG

AILED

Grasmere

Rydal

dale

A 591

RAVEN CRAG (Walthwaite)

Chapel Stile

Elterwater

LOUGHRIGG

Ambleside

ROTHAY BRIDGE CRAG

Little Langdale

A 593

2   3 KM.

D0993376

ermere

The F&RCC and Rock Climbing Guides
to the
English Lake District

The Fell and Rock Climbing Club, founded at Coniston in 1906, published its first rock climbing guide in 1922 and since that date has produced a continuous series of guides which are accepted as the definitive series on Lake District rock climbing.

The guides are written and published by a volunteer team of members who update the text and check new climbs, many of which have been, and continue to be pioneered by club members.

Enquiries regarding the F&RCC and its guide books should be addressed to the current Club Secretary or Guide Books Editor, whose addresses are available from the BMC.

Climbing Guides to the
English Lake District

Langdale

by D. Armstrong, P. Rigby & J. White

Illustrated by

A. Phizacklea

Edited by D. Armstrong

Published by the Fell and Rock Climbing Club
of the English Lake District

© ISBN 0 85028 031 1

Previous Editions

1926   George Basterfield
1938   William Clegg
1950   Arthur Dolphin and John Cook
1967   Allan Austin
1973   Allan Austin and Rod Valentine
1980   Mike Mortimer

Present edition: Langdale 1989

British Library Cataloguing in Publication Data

Armstrong, D.
    Langdale. – (Climbing Guides to the English Lake District).
    1.   Cumbria. Lake District. Rock climbing. – Manuals.
    I. Title   II. Rigby, P.   III. White, J.
    IV. Fell and Rock Climbing Club of the English Lake District.
    V. Series
    796.5'223'094278   GV199.44.G7

    ISBN   0-85028-031-1

Prepared for printing by Synergy, Royal Oak Barn, The Square, Cartmel,
Cumbria, LA11 6QB.
Printed by Joseph Ward & Co. (Printers) Ltd., Wellington Road, Dewsbury,
West Yorkshire, WF13 1HR.
Distributed by Cordee, 3a De Montfort Street, Leicester, LE1 7HD.

CONTENTS

	Page			Page
Map – Langdale	IFC	Blake Rigg		166
		Side Pike		169
Map of Guide Book Area	RFC	Oak Howe Crag		172
Photographs	4	Spout Crag		175
		Upper Spout Crag		176
Introduction	5	Elterwater Quarries		176
Acknowledgements	9	Rothay Bridge Crag		176
Historical	10			
		Easedale		
The Climbs		Relief Drawing – Easedale		178
Langdale		Helm Crag		179
Relief Drawing – Langdale	24	Gibson Knott		182
Raven Crag – Walthwaite	25	Deer Bield Crag		183
Thrang Quarry	30	Slapestone Edge		192
Scout Crags	30	Eagle Crag		192
White Ghyll Crag	36	Blea Crag		193
Swine Knott	51	Looking Howe Crag		199
Stickle Barn Crag	52			
Millbeck Crag	53	Bouldering Areas		201
Tarn Crag	55	Climbing Walls		201
Pavey Ark	57			
Harrison Stickle	83	**Illustrations**		
Raven Crag	83	Raven Crag – Walthwaite		203
Far West Raven Crag	84	White Ghyll – Lower Crag		204
West Raven Crag	87	White Ghyll – Upper Crag		205
Middlefell Buttress	87	Pavey Ark – General View		206
Raven Crag Buttress	91	Pavey Ark – Central Area		207
East Raven Crag	101	Pavey Ark – East Wall		208
Far East Raven Crag	105	Middlefell & Raven Crag		
Far Far East Raven Crag	108	Buttress		209
Gimmer Crag	109	Gimmer Crag – South-East &		
Pike O'Stickle	133	West Faces		210
Bowfell	134	Gimmer Crag – West & North-		
Flat Crags	134	West Faces		211
Cambridge Crag	138	Gimmer Crag – North-West		212
North Buttress	139	Flat Crags		213
Bowfell Buttress	143	North Buttress		214
Hanging Knotts	148	Bowfell Buttress		215
Bowfell Links	148	Neckband Crag		216
Neckband Crag	148	Helm Crag		217
Crinkle Crag	155	Deer Bield Crag		218
Gladstone Knott	155	Blea Crag		219
Crinkle Ghyll	155			
Kettle Crag	158	Graded List of Climbs		220
Lightning Crag	159	First Ascents		234
Long Scar	161	Mountain Accidents		254
Black Crag	162	Index		256

Photographs

Pluto, Raven Crag Buttress   Cover
Climber – John Williams
Photo – Phil Rigby

Eastern Hammer, Gimmer
         Frontispiece
Climber – Steve Monks
Photo – Ron Kenyon

	Page

Elvis, Middle Scout Crag   24
Climber – Tom Walkington
Photo – Barry Rogers

The Crack, Gimmer Crag   121
Climber – Alexa Wightman
Photo – Steve Reid

Chimney Variant, White Ghyll   25
Climber – Dave Birkett
Photo – Barry Rogers

1984, Flat Crags   144
Climber – Alan Murray
Photo –Phil Rigby

Golden Slipper, Pavey Ark   96
Climber – Declon Doyle
Photo – Al Phizacklea

Mithrander, Neckband Crag   145
Climber – Unknown
Photo – Dave Armstrong

Fine Time, Raven Crag Buttress   97
Climber – Pete Kirton
Photo – Al Phizacklea

Deer Bield Crack   168
Climber – Steve Reid
Photo – Steve Reid collection

North-West Arête, Gimmer Crag 120
Climber – unknown
Photo – Ron Kenyon

Laugh Not, White Ghyll Crag   169
Climber – Steve Stean
Photo – Al Phizacklea

INTRODUCTION

This volume is the third in the seventh series of Rock Climbing Guides in the process of publication by the Fell and Rock Climbing Club of the English Lake District. This series will comprise five volumes as follows:

1. Buttermere and Eastern Crags
2. Scafell, Dow and Eskdale
3. Langdale
4. Gable and Pillar
5. Borrowdale

Ease of access, short approaches to the crags and a wide choice of routes of most grades (particularly easier climbs), has made this one of the most popular climbing areas in the Lake District. Combine this with the wide appeal that the area also has for walkers and tourists; the result is severe congestion and overcrowding particularly during the summer months, and Bank Holidays when it is best avoided.

This warning over, it must be admitted that Langdale does offer an excellent selection of first class crags, many with southerly aspects and with good rock predominating. I am sure therefore that people will be prepared to suffer the occasional queue's to enjoy the fine routes on offer if visits at off peak times are impossible. The more secluded Easedale crags can usually provide a welcome alternative from the hustle and bustle of Langdale and again can offer some first class routes of all grades.

The location of crags, which varies from roadside situations in the valley bottom to the most remote crags which lie high on the slopes of Bowfell, allow routes to be climbed at most times of the year.

Work on this guide has involved the metrication, complete revision and update of all descriptions, grades, stars etc. of the previous guide together with the inclusion of the tremendous number of new climbs on existing and new crags which have been developed in the past nine years.

In an attempt to provide a definitive guide, mentions or descriptions of many routes, not previously recorded (or subsequently omitted from later guides) have been included. Some that are poor have only been named, others which were omitted, sometimes because they were thought too short, (a problem which does not seem relevant these days when every micro route is recorded) have been described. This it is hoped will also help stop the continual recording of claims for routes already done.

I should like to thank Phil Rigby and John White for their assistance in tackling the daunting task of checking, writing and compiling this edition.

Excellent new diagrams have been prepared by Al Phizacklea for all the major crags, together with relief drawings for both the Langdale and Easedale areas. I am sure these will be appreciated as much as in past guides for the assistance they give in the location of crags and routes.

Special thanks are due to Alan Greig for his assistance in checking the manuscript and the never ending proof reading. Thanks also to other members of the Fell and Rock guidebook team and others who have helped with the production of this volume.

D. Armstrong, February 1989.

General Notes

Adjectival Grades
These give the overall grade of the climb, taking into account such factors as technical difficulty, rock quality and protection; and, of course, they assume dry rock. The grades are:- Moderate, Difficult, Very Difficult, Mild Severe, Severe, Hard Severe, Mild Very Severe, Very Severe, Hard Very Severe, Extremely Severe. The standard abbreviations are used for the grades in the text. The Extremely Severe grade is divided into E1, E2, E3, E4, E5, E6, to date. However, the system is open ended and E7 and above are available for the future.

Technical Grades
Included for each pitch of 4a and above on all routes of Mild Very Severe and harder (where known). This grade is an attempt to assess the problems to be encountered on each pitch and once again is open ended. The grades to date are:- 4a, 4b, 4c, 5a, 5b, 5c, 6a, 6b, 6c.

Aid
A few routes still require a limited use of artificial assistance and this is indicated in the description where appropriate. Many aid reductions have been made in recent years and routes are described in the most free style in which they are known to have been climbed and are graded accordingly.

Quality of Routes
A star system has been adopted to highlight routes of particular quality with three stars being used to indicate routes comparable with the best in the country. The absence of stars does not mean that a climb is poor, unless it is described as such, or receives a black spot.

Unrepeated Routes
Climbs which are not known to have been repeated, or verified by the guide writer, are indicated with a dagger (†) and their descriptions and gradings should be treated with caution.

Length of Climbs
The lengths of climbs and pitches are given in metres and this is abbreviated to m in the descriptions. Those who continue to think in feet will unfortunately have to multiply the lengths given by 3¼.

Location of Crags
The location of each crag is indicated by its Ordnance Survey grid reference. The aspect of the main faces have been included to aid the choice of crags. The altitude given is based on the Ordnance Survey datum, which gives mean sea level as zero. (The Old Dungeon Ghyll Hotel is approx. 100 metres above this level). The terms 'true left' and 'true right' are used to describe the position of a crag in a valley or ghyll relative to the direction of flow of the stream. The terms 'left' and 'right', unless otherwise stated, mean as the climber faces his climb.

New Routes

To aid future guide writers, descriptions of all new routes should be recorded in the New Routes Book in Rock & Run, Ambleside; the Log Book in Raw Head the F&RCC hut in Langdale, or sent to the Guide Books Editor. Information gleaned from magazines is not always sufficient to identify routes.

Comments on any of the information contained in this guide, whether thought to be inaccurate or misleading, would be welcomed for correction of future volumes and should be sent to the Guide Books Editor.

Conservation

The crags of the Lake District are an important habitat for wild plants. The lack of disturbance and the unique environment support the growth of rare species. In addition, some crags have become regular nesting sites for peregrine falcons.

To protect the natural environment, The Wildlife and Countryside Act 1981 makes it illegal to disturb nesting birds, such as peregrines, and to uproot any plant without the owner's permission. In designated 'Sites of Special Scientific Interest', which include a number of crags in the Lake District, any activity which damages vegetation or wildlife becomes an offence.

It is, therefore, important that climbers respect the natural environment and cause the minimum disturbance to crags to avoid future restrictions on access.

To avoid prosecution, climbers should avoid areas of crags where peregrines are known to be nesting and if, in ignorance, a peregrine is disturbed they should retreat from that area.

On established routes, climbing can proceed without conflict if the plantlife is respected. Generally, gardening of new routes should be kept to a minimum and avoided altogether in Sites of Special Scientific Interest. Before developing new crags, or gardening routes, environmental considerations should be taken into account and the Nature Conservancy Council consulted on the importance of the vegetation in that location.

ACKNOWLEDGEMENTS

Despite the unsavoury weather encountered during the recent summers, which has hampered checking on the rocks, the production of this guide is now nearing completion. It is now time to thank those who have assisted in this task.

This guide is a thorough revision of the previous edition but it is based upon the hard work of the writer of this, and previous volumes, to whom our thanks are due: G Basterfield; W Clegg; A Dolphin and J Cook; A Austin; A Austin and R Valentine and finally M Mortimer.

The F&RCC series of Recent Developments has also proved most useful in providing a record of new routes and their writers must also be thanked.

A fine new set of crag diagrams and perspective maps have been produced by Al Phizacklea for this volume. Thanks are due for his efforts which it is hoped will be appreciated by all users.

The assistance of friends in checking and climbing routes (many of which prove to be the more obscure, less popular or esoteric delights) whilst researching for the guide are much appreciated. Particular thanks going to John Williams, Alan Murray and Alan Greig.

The checking of grades and stars and compilation of a graded list has necessitated the assistance of many friends and fellow climbers, the following deserve special mention:- Martin Berzins, Bill Birkett, members of Carlisle Mountaineering Club, Steve Clegg, John Daly, Alan Davis, Rick Graham, Alan Greig, Dougie Hall, Mark Hetherington, Steve Hubball, Ron Kenyon, Howard Lancashire, David Miller, Stuart Miller, Alan and Christine Murray, Al Phizacklea, Barry Rogers, Leslie Shore, members of Ulverston Mountaineering Club, Tom Walkington, Bob Wightman and Stuart Wilson.

The task of word-processing the manuscript and repeated updating and correcting has been carried out by Jean and Les Ainsworth of Synergy. We would like to thank them for their friendly co-operative service.

Finally mention and thanks for their understanding and support, must go to our wives and families: Fiona, Paul, Iain and Katharine; Judy, Kate and Jane; and Gill who have endured the frequent neglect suffered by all climbers families, and particularly during the past few months when guide work has been most hectic.

Dave Armstrong, Phil Rigby and John White, February 1989

HISTORICAL

The history of any one climbing ground can never be regarded as a complete story in itself. Rather it is but one ingredient in the history of a whole district's climbing. Where, in the early days, a new climb, or even a new type of climb, was discovered on any one crag, that in itself showed the way to similar routes on other crags, or even to the exploitation of new crags where this newer type of climb was waiting to be led. And so the histories of all crags become but one all-embracing story. Nowhere has this been better demonstrated than in that excellent article by H. M. Kelly and J. H. Doughty in the *Fell and Rock Climbing Club Journal* of 1936. There it is shown how the original story of English rock-climbing is a story of summit seeking – of easy-way finding.

Langdale offered no such summits, no such easy ways. Langdale crags, Gimmer and Bowfell in particular, had their impressiveness – not one of broken, towering massiveness such as the Pillar and Scafell – but one of vast, airy smoothness, in no way inviting to the early pioneers. Little, too, was to be seen of the comfort of chimney and crack, beloved of the second group of our early climbers. But what little there was of this was duly noted by W. P. Haskett-Smith, most aptly named 'the prince of pioneers'. So in the 1880's he climbed the North-west Gully on Gimmer, the two Pavey Ark Gullies, and the North Gully of Bowfell Buttress. This was the real start of rock-climbing in Langdale, though Jack's Rake, probably known to shepherds from very early times, had been crossed within the previous decade by R. Pendlebury.

Perhaps, therefore, it would be unfair to say that Langdale lagged behind the other centres in its climbing history, although its first ascents came half-a-century later. More fairly one might say that Langdale took its true position in the story of English climbing, starting at the beginning of the 'Gully Epoch'. The remainder of the century completed this with the addition of the two Pavey Ark chimneys and a few outlying scrambles on Bowfell.

It was with the 'Slab and Wall' period that Langdale came into its own. The Langdale crags, Gimmer in particular, are perfect examples of this type. So, in the first decade of this century, the first climbs typical of Langdale began. H. B. Lyon and E. Rigby started the Gimmer alphabet. Bowfell Buttress climb and the Crescent on Pavey Ark opened up the two other main crags. From that time until the war, development in Langdale, though much of it was on outlying minor crags, went steadily ahead. During the war activity ceased.

Then came the great boom period, and in addition to his exploits on other crags, G. S. Bower quickly added a round half-dozen routes in this area. His ascents of 'D' on Gimmer and Crescent Slabs on Pavey Ark advanced Langdale climbing by almost one full stage in severity. H. B. Lyon returned, seventeen years after his original ascents of 'B' and Lyon's Crawl, to add Bracket and Slab Climb, Chimney Buttress, and White Ghyll Chimney to the list.

In 1924 the first of the 'very severes' came from J. A. Wray with 'E' route, and M. de Selincourt, in addition to four new routes (climbed solo), added the second with his ascent of the Right-Hand Wall of Bowfell.

Two years later G. S. Bower again looked round the North-west Side of Gimmer, which he had opened out in 1920 with Ash-tree Slabs, and added Pallid Slabs and Hiatus. Then in their 'laudable attempt' to put G. Basterfield's newly published Langdale Guide quickly out of date, A. B. Reynolds, H. S. Gross, and G. G. Macphee added another three 'very severes' on this side. Reynolds' final ascent of the Crack was the culmination of a very determined siege of a most noteworthy route. So came into being what, for a short time, was known as the 'Gentlemen's Side' of Gimmer, in comparison with the easier and now much be-touristed routes on the other faces. But not for long did the North-west Face merit this title, for Miss N. Ridyard quickly had them all ticked off.

By now Gimmer had a veritable network of routes on all its faces – there seemed little room for more – though never let it be said that there *is* no room. However, subsequent exploration has been concerned mostly with other crags. In addition to routes on minor crags, four new routes have been added on the Bowfell crags, and two 'very severes', Deer Bield Crack in Far Easedale, and Stoats' Crack on Pavey Ark, have added greatly to the quality and prestige of Langdale climbing. The girdling of Gimmer has also been completed.

Today rock climbing enjoys more popularity than ever before. The number of its devotees has grown enormously in recent years, and Langdale – so easily accessible from the civilized part of the Lake District, therefore becomes perhaps *the* most popular playground for the sport. What new climbs will this great influx of climbers add to our sport – what new methods – what new developments? The next new guide to rock climbing in Langdale shall tell.

Wm. Clegg, 1938

1938-49

Langdale remains as popular a centre as ever, as witness the fact that the number of recorded climbs in the area has more than doubled since the publication of the last Guide. Even during the war years activity was considerable, many finding the fells and crags ideally suited for precious leaves away from front-line England. Throughout this time the name of R. J. Birkett has figured prominently. His ascent of 'F' Route was probably the most notable achievement at a time when Gimmer still offered tantalising possibilities along natural weaknessess. Sydney Thompson and John Ashton, also contributed several fine routes here, but by the early 1940's interest almost inevitably began to be directed towards the further exploration of other crags. On Bowfell, the Buttress was 'girdled' but otherwise produced little of real merit.

Pavey Ark was rescued from its rather traditional status of a purely wet-weather cliff by the discovery of a number of good buttress climbs of all grades of difficulty, culminating in H. A. Carsten's magnificent Rake End Wall.

Despite this progress on the major crags, undoubtedly the most important feature of recent exploration in Langdale has been the development of White Ghyll and, to a lesser degree, of Raven Crag.

The former had already provided routes of quality in its classic Chimney and Slab climbs, but it was J. W. Haggas' epic ascent of the Gordian Knot which revealed the possibilities of the previously untouched, but extremely imposing, central mass. Five years elapsed before Birkett made the second ascent of this fine climb and then went on to pioneer a host of worthy routes along the entire range of the crag, of which Haste Not and Perhaps Not rank among the best and hardest climbs in the district. The opening-out of Raven Crag was due in the main to the industry of A Gregory, although Bilberry Buttress, perhaps the most attractive route here, was climbed quite early in the period by C. F. Rolland. The network of climbs now to be found on this crag is adequately justified by its extreme accessibility.

Among this spate of novelties the older routes have lost little of their warranted reputation. Established favourites, such as Gimmer Crack, may seem a trifle easier now that the trail is well blazoned; Right-Hand Wall has shed most of its legendary armour. The intrinsic difficulties of Deer Bield Crack, however, are as acute as ever, even if the most formidable problem in the district today is Kipling Groove.

In concluding his Historical note in 1938, Clegg pondered on the future of the sport in Great Langdale. Today the general standard of climbing is undoubtedly higher. New methods too (such as the carrying of pitons for use in emergency and a more scientific system of rope handling and belaying) have been introduced as safety measures, though they cannot be said directly to have influenced the recent exploration of the district. Future climbers will no doubt have their own story of further developments.

Arthur Dolphin and John Cook, 1950

1950-65

The most notable event of the post-war years was the first ascent of Kipling Groove. It was a remarkable lead for the time. Technically it was no harder than its contemporaries, but one faced the difficulties in a much more uncompromising position – and in those days there was no peg. At the time it seemed a fitting climax to a period of intense exploration.

Today we see it as the first of the big modern routes, a couple of years before its time perhaps, but setting a pattern for the future. It ushered in a new era and in the next few years was to be eclipsed by new developments in Langdale, and left far behind by the rapid rise in standards taking place outside the confines of the valley.

Nevertheless, measured by any yardstick, it was, and is, an outstanding climb, marking the emergence of Arthur Dolphin as possibly the finest leader of the period and opened the campaign that over the next few years was to make him a legend in his own lifetime.

This same period marked the retirement of another great climber. In White Ghyll, R. J. Birkett was closing down a fantastically prolific career, and for a brief period of two or three years the two men who had dominated the crags of the Lake District for so long raised the standard of Lakeland climbing to a level unequalled elsewhere in Britain.

The years following the appearance of the new guide were undoubtedly Dolphin's years. During this period extensive developments took place on most of the crags covered in this volume. The event of 1951 was the conquest – at last – of the famous central buttress on Deer Bield, thus solving one of the 'Last Great Problems' of the district, and at the same time producing a superb climb. Later in the year a visit was paid to Bowfell and Rubicon Groove appeared – a bold initial lead. In 1952 in spite of activities in other districts, time was found for several first-rate routes, notable amongst which was Dunmail Cracks, in which the lead was shared with P. J.

Greenwood. But best of all was a great route on Bowfell, the Sword of Damocles, comparable with Deer Bield Buttress. Again the honours were shared with Greenwood. The following year Arthur Dolphin, tragically, lost his life on the Géant thus bringing to an abrupt end one of the finest chapters in the history of Lakeland climbing.

The early fifties was also the time when East Raven enjoyed its burst of popularity. These little crags, stretching down from Raven Crag itself towards the New Dungeon Ghyll Hotel, had been by-passed by climbers of earlier generations. But now they became covered in a network of short routes reminiscent of gritstone climbs.

It is probably not true to say that the climbers concerned were alcoholics, but it is certain that the Old Hotel and its nearness to the crags was an important factor in explorations carried out at that time – and indeed, in climbing there today.

Climbing at the same time, but not directly concerned with the existing Langdale clientele was a new group of 'tigers' from Wales, the 'little men', the men of the Rock and Ice. In other districts these men proved to be the most formidable group of climbers ever to operate on British rock. In Langdale their offerings were less important than elsewhere – but notable for all that. Pendulum on Deer Bield was found, then Moseley returned with Whillans and the crag was girdled. Joe Brown led the unclimbed corner in White Ghyll and named it Laugh Not.

By far the most important event of the decade was the emergence of Pavey Ark as one of the most important climbing grounds of the Langdale area. This huge rambling mass of a crag, liberally endowed with heather and juniper, fostered an impression of decay. It was so different from the more obvious attractions of White Ghyll or Gimmer, but Pavey is big. It was easy to lose sight of a 200-foot buttress in this vast 800-foot crag. For many years both local and visiting tigers passed it by. It was left to the enthusiasts.

Arthur Dolphin was the first of the moderns to realise its possibilities. His activities elsewhere overshadowed his Pavey contributions and one tends to forget that he made four routes here. These additions marked the opening of the Pavey renaissance.

The next generation appeared in the persons of Brian Evans and Allan Austin. Over the next few years new routes on the crag were exclusively the work of these two. About this time Joe Brown made one of his sporadic visits to the Lakes and produced Eliminot in White Ghyll. As a route it has few attractions, but it is an exceedingly fine piece of climbing. On Pavey Ark explorations pushed forward, helped for the next couple of years by a new name, Eric Metcalf.

Astra and Arcturus were superb discoveries in this period, but new routes were becoming difficult to find. Gradually they became less frequent. Existing classics were no less popular, and well-blazoned trails no less attractive, yet the load began to spread a little. It was time to take stock!

During work for the guidebook several odds and ends were discovered, Poacher and Gandalf's Groove seemed worthwhile. Gimmer String was cleaned up and strung together, and so at last the guide.

Allan Austin, 1966

1966-72

The years during which the last guide book was written was a period of intense activity involving virtually every crag in the area. There was then a period of comparative quiet, until in 1969, Jim Fullalove climbed the right-hand arête of Stoney Buttress. This climb, The Hobbit, proved to be a major route, and an event of importance, since it marked the discovery of a buttress previously overlooked by the local experts and, without a doubt, the most serious crag in the valley. Two years later, Rod Valentine added his magnificent crack climb The Ragman's Trumpet, which was followed shortly by P. Livesey's Sally Free and Easy. These routes, together with Austin's attractive 'eliminate'-type extreme, The Bracken-clock, have advanced the development of Pavey Ark to such a pitch that it is now, without doubt, the major crag in the valley.

In White Ghyll, most of the obvious gaps have now been filled, two of them giving very hard pitches indeed: Paladin was led by R. Matheson, and the roof-crack above Haste Not was led by Austin to complete, at last, the true Haste Not Direct.

On the Neckband Crag, Gillette led by K. Wood completed a fine triptych. On Gimmer there has been little activity, although Carpetbagger is a worthy addition to the excellent routes on the north-west face.

As time goes by, it has become obvious that the average new route in Langdale is shorter than its predecessor, and it is unlikely that many more big classic lines will be discovered in the valley. What is certain, however, is that climbers of the future will continue to find untrodden places to exercise their talents, and that much that is good remains to be discovered.

Allan Austin, November 1972

1972-79

The most significant developments in climbing in Langdale during the seventies can be summarised very briefly. Namely, the confirmation of Pavey Ark as the major crag of the area, the intensive development of Deer Bield and that part of Gimmer Crag between The Crack and'D' Route, and perhaps most important of all, the acceptance of a strict code of ethics by most of those climbers active in the discovery of new routes.

The publication of the last edition of this guide was clouded in controversy concerning the decision to omit certain climbs. "It is no solution at all to fail, and then go round to the top and abseil down to place a fixed piton and hanging sling, which can be reached from below, in order to by-pass a particularly troublesome spot." This stand taken by Allan Austin and Rod Valentine, over the routes Peccadillo, The Graduate, Cruel Sister and Fine Time, received a considerable amount of criticism. Developments in Langdale and elsewhere have vindicated their position; in fact, climbing ethics have advanced to the point where the use of any sort of aid, pre-placed or otherwise is rejected by many of the best climbers. Moreover, almost every aid point in Langdale, including those infamous pre-placed slings, has been eliminated.

Most of the credit for this must go to Pete Botterill and Jeff Lamb, whose efforts have elevated these controversial climbs to a position of respectability.

If the explorations of Austin had established Pavey Ark as the single most important climbing area in the Valley, then the activities of Ed Grindley indicated the potential of the crag for big, hard climbs in the modern idiom. Grindley's determined approach produced a fine trio of routes on the East Wall, climbed without prior inspection and with the use of only minimal aid. Although Fallen Angel, in its free form, is quite definitely the best of Grindley's routes, his boldest effort was the ascent of Brain Damage, over two days. So sensitive was he to the threat of another party stealing the route, that he arranged for his second to be on guard at the foot of the route at six in the morning! Since then, still harder routes have been added to Pavey's repertoire, contributions being made by most of the Valley's activists: Martin Berzins, Ed Cleasby, Ron Fawcett, Jeff Lamb and Pete Whillance, each responsible for at least one major route.

Austin's very enjoyable Whit's End Direct marked the end of his explorations in Langdale; strangely, this was the first major new route on Gimmer for almost ten years and it heralded a phase of intensive development of this part of the crag. With the exception of Pete Livesey's Eastern Hammer, the routes of this period are not major lines, but they do give most enjoyable climbing on perfect rock and in superb settings.

A surprise to many has been the emergence of Deer Beild as a major crag; although only small, Deer Bield is packed with features, especially grooves and ribs, but also a number of very steep walls.

Pete Long pointed the way when he cast Pearls Before Swine, a bold and very fine effort; but it was left to Pete Whillance and Dave Armstrong to realise the true potential of the crag with the ascents of no less than five major routes, culminating in Take it to the Limit, the most serious lead in the area. Such is the pace of modern climbing, that this route received its second ascent within two hours of the first!

The other crags in the Valley have also received detailed scrutiny, but have not yielded more than a handful of really worthwhile routes. Cleasby has been particularly active; his best route, probably, being Warrior in White Ghyll, whilst the Berzins brothers have been busy eliminating aid and adding some new routes to Flat Crags, Bowfell. However, one of the best routes of recent years is to be found on the crag beloved by those whose climbing is regulated by the licensing hours; Lamb's modern version of the aid-route Trilogy gives high quality, high standard climbing, within 10 minutes easy walk of the Old Hotel.

What for the future then? Opportunities for good new climbs now seem to be drying up – 'though never let it be said that there is no room.' Certainly, there are still a few last great problems, not to mention a few esoteric corners of Langdale still awaiting development, but it is doubtful whether there are any really superb climbs awaiting discovery. Several recent climbs are eliminates or variants, very closely tied to existing routes and previously unclimbed only because they were considered unworthy of attention; no doubt, many more such routes will be "discovered." It is not easy to be optimistic about future development, but Langdale is such a superb place to climb that it will continue to be popular with all climbers, whether they are searching for new ways, or just content to follow familiar and well-blazoned trails.

Mike Mortimer, 1980

1980-88

This guide now contains information on over 700 climbs in the Langdale and Easedale areas compared with about 380 in the previous

edition. Information on lines previously climbed has been reintro-
duced to complete the picture but there are still over 250 new routes
recorded since 1979. This would appear to belie claims that
opportunities for new routes are drying up, however a more detailed
look at the worth of this vast number of routes is required before
jumping to this conclusion.

As observed by Mike Mortimer in 1980, "good new lines are drying
up", this I believe is a fact which cannot be denied. However since
this time a few of the 'last great problems' have been climbed; esoteric
corners visited and worthwhile routes developed; a number of superb
climbs discovered; several interesting variations and eliminates added
but most significantly many small crags and outcrops discovered,
cleaned and instantly worked out to give a mass of short routes from
the easiest to the highest grades and with a similar spectrum of quality.

A review of the last 10 years begins with the end of 1979 when the
addition of three variations of dubious merit to Gimmer Crag by Paul
Clarke and R Kidd served only to put the previous edition out of date.

The following year, inspired by the arrival of the new guide, gaps
were identified and new routes discovered throughout the whole area.
An early visit to Helm Crag by Pete Whillance resulted in a solo
ascent of Green Light (HVS) a pleasant route left of Beacon Rib.
This sortie also revealed a steep line which was to become Two Star
Red (E3) later in the year. The Ambleside team of Andy Hyslop,
Rick Graham and Bill Birkett visited White Ghyll Crag and squeezed
out two routes; The Fine Art of Surfacing a strenuous E3 and Dead
Loss G.G. a riposte to Gary Gibson's Dead Loss Angeles from the
previous year. Meanwhile the Berzins brothers took the long walk up
the Band to produce the excellent Close Shave (E3) on Neckband
Crag and Exposure (E4) on Flat Crags, a fine line which has
regretably been neglected and become rather dirty. Deer Bield Crag
yielded the difficult Limbo (E4) to Pete Botterill and Dave Armstrong
and later the even more testing Dynamo (E5) and the pleasant
Bravado (E2) to Pete Whillance and Pete Botterill.

The Watch (E5) on Raven Crag Buttress was linked together by Iain
Dunn and Rick Graham to give a difficult girdle of the main wall
whilst a mystery developed around the ascent of Kalashnikov, the
steep rib left of Trilogy. Members of the team reported to have
ascended it cannot remember doing so on the appointed day and no
one can be found to corroborate claims of a later ascent. Climbers
capable of leading routes for harder than the E3 grade given have
been repulsed and this has produced a reputation which has
discouraged most climbers from even trying. Would-be ascentionists
beware!

Because of the tactics employed on some routes 1981 turned out to be a controversial year. It began with Tom Walkington using two rest points (after repeated top rope practicing) to conquer the very steep Elvis (E4) on Middle Scout Crag. This he now admits was a misguided approach used on many of his early routes and which he now regrets. It was led free by Nick Dixon and Iain Dunn the following year with one preplaced nut runner. Tom went on to clean up the esoteric Millbeck Crag creating eight routes from Severe to E2, before returning with more bad habits to ascend Rudolf Nureyev on Side Pike. (He later managed to lead this free in 1983 after over 20 top rope practice sessions and numerous failed leads, producing a very technical (E5). Later in the year more rests on preplaced gear were used by Tom to climb The Beatles again on Middle Scout Crag. This had to wait until 1987 for Paul Cornforth to lead it free but then only after pre-placing a peg runner and top rope practice.

Rick Graham and Bill Birkett found two overlooked gems on Gimmer Crag with Crystal (E1) and Ash Tree Corner (VS). Bob and Martin Berzins meanwhile were battling with the fierce previously aided roof of Warlock (E5) down on East Raven Crag producing a difficult free pitch.

One of the most eyed lines in Langdale, the hanging pod on the East Wall of Pavey Ark was forced into submission by Messrs. Andy Atkinson and Ken Forsyth, using several rests on runners (although this was not thought worth mentioning at the time). When the truth came out, this incident angered many people who had looked, but left it for a better climber, or a better day. A better climber arrived in 1983 in the form of Chris Hamper; directed by Bill Birkett he climbed it in excellent style to produce a magnificent free route at a hard E5 grade. Although renamed Equinox, the original name of Sixpence has been retained.

During the summer, Ed Cleasby disappeared into the woods near Ambleside, found a crack, climbed it and christened it Crack in the Woods (E4). An excellent short pitch and an apt, though less than inspired, name! The year ended with a couple of pleasant routes on White Ghyll Crag. The Palestinians (E1) and Sahara (E2) were led by a visiting Penrith team. Not to be out done, the locals chipped in with Antarctica (E2), a fine, fingery, wall climb.

After all this excitement, a quiet year followed, with only twelve routes recorded, eight of which were easy lines on Scar Crag, Pike O'Blisco (all had been climbed previously, but not officially recorded). Tom Walkington was again found swinging off Middle Scout Crag; he finally managed to climb Abba and Blondie (both E3) without recourse to rests or aid. The best route of the year was an eliminate on Gimmer Crag, Midnight Movie (E4) an excellent direct line up the crag, starting just right of The Crack and finishing above Eastern Hammer, by Bill Birkett and Rick Graham.

This lull did not inspire renewed activity and 1983 proved to be another disappointing year. Fillers-in were found on Raven Crag, Langdale; Bryson's Flange (E2) and Campaign Crack (E1) by Iain Williamson, John White and Paul Cornforth; Muscle Wall (E3) and a number of routes on the East Raven Crags by Tom Walkington and friends. Finally a difficult roof problem on Middlefell Buttress became The Power of Imagination (E4) for John White and John Metcalfe. Sweeney Todd (E2) on Neckband Crag provided an excellent eliminate pitch up the slab left of Mithrandir for John White and Iain Williamson and Maggie's Farm (E3) on Pavey Ark could have done with more cleaning by Martin Berzins and Chris Sowden. Other routes in 1983 were distinguished only by their mediocrity.

Idle Breed (E5) on Deer Bield, the first route of 1984 was thought by many to be named as a skit at locals who had tried and failed, especially when given a grade of E3. Chris Gore denied this and claimed it was simply an anagram of the crag name! The secret development of Oak Howe Crag by Pete Whillance and Dave Armstrong resulted in nine difficult new routes the best of which are The Deceiver (E4), The Sting (E3), Crooked Crack (E3) and Going Straight (E1). During the same period Iain Williamson, John White, Paul Cornforth and Andy Tilney were hard at work scrubbing the left end of Blea Crag, Easedale to produce some fine slab routes; No Rest for the Wicked (E3) being particularaly fine and bold, Chameleon (E3) an awkward overhang and Erne (E1) a delightful thin crack line.

A Last Tango with Deer Bield Crag was enjoyed by Pete Whillance, creating a steep and technical E5 up the green wall right of Stiletto, before leaving the area for pastures new. Over on Pike O'Blisco R Greenwood, C Ensoll and Pete Donnelley did not realise what they were starting when they recorded a few outcrop type climbs on the excellent clean rock of Black Crag. This was another crag where climbing had gone on for years but no one thought the routes worth recording.

The most impressive route of the year must be Centrefold (E6) an audacious concept to climb directly up the centre of the blank main wall of Raven Crag Buttress. Unfortunately it was forced off right on a difficult traverse into Fine Time but nonetheless gives a very difficult and thought provoking pitch. After much effort it eventually fell to Bill Birkett with Iain Cooksey and Rick Graham.

Only one crag really featured in 1985; Crinkle Gill. It provided nine hard routes of steep sustained climbing with adequate protection to various combinations of Bill Birkett, John White and Paul Cornforth. The best lines are A Naked Edge (E4), Private Dancer (E4) and Bitter Days (E5) led by Bill Birkett and Crimes of Quality (E2) by John White. Rock Around the Clock (E3) an eliminate based on Bracken-clock on Pavey Ark which gave a pleasant climb for Martin Dale and Roger Brookes was the only other route worthy of note.

A major gardening session early in 1986 for Tom Walkington, Dave Bates, Barry Rogers and others resulted in fourteen routes on Far West Raven Crag typifying the modern approach to the new route business. Tom also visited other sections of Raven Crag filling in a few of the remaining gaps with such routes as Mythical M.M. (E2) and Pink Panties (E3).

A different though equally modern approach and tactics were being used on Deer Bield Crag where Paul Ingham was battling with the extremely steep thin crack in the wall at the right-hand end of the crag. Pretty in Pink (E6) was the result; regarded as the most difficult route in the guide it provides an excellent test piece for the modern hard man.

Talk of preparation for a forthcoming new guide spread and activity increased during 1987 with a total of fifty new routes being recorded. These were spread around the whole area but again the majority were due to the rapid development of small outcrops. Activity on Blea Crag moved to some slabs near the right-hand end and resulted in ten pleasant pitches. The best examples are The Ivory Wall (E5) a fingery wall with poor protection, Mussolini (E2) a thin crack in a slab and Asterix the Gaul (HVS) another pleasant slab. Whilst this was all happening Martin Berzins and Chris Sowden appeared on the scene to create Another Bleeding Controversy (E3), (their route name not my comment) and Offcomers Slab (E5) two good routes stolen from the locals who, whilst having a day off, had left ropes down the part cleaned lines ready to continue gardening operations next day. Unfortunately our Yorkshire friends are not put off by such things. Only the previous day the same pair had visited Neckband Crag and climbed Jagged Edge (E4) the aréte crossed by Aragorn and the very bold Razer's Edge (E5) up the overhanging wall left of Flying Blind, two lines part cleaned by others and left to await a return visit. The others, James Swarbrick and Phil Rigby had to be satisfied with Tonsure (E3) a route climbed during their gardening session.

The small buttress right of Walthwaite Gully on Raven Crag, Walthwaite received the modern treatment from Iain Williamson,

John White, Gill Hussey, Barry Rogers and others, this resulted in seven routes and no gaps. Bill Birkett had a return foray to Crinkle Gill this time with Luke Steer who led the steep and testing Deception (E3) while Bill satisfied himself with the more slabby Oberon (E1) and Titania (E1).

Blake Rigg the large vegetated crag overlooking Blea Tarn, an area designated as a Site of Special Scientific Interest (SSSI), to protect the plants and wildlife, was visited and two relatively clean buttresses developed. Keith Phizacklea and John Daly brushed up the Left-Hand Buttress for five routes then two more were found on a slanting buttress wall up to the right. Tom Walkington stepped in to say he had climbed very similar lines to these two in 1981 but hadn't bothered recording them. He has now.

The end of 1987 saw Tom Walkington, Dave Bates and Jim Cooper stepping into top gear with development on Black Crag, Pike O'Blisco. This continued well into 1988 with anything worthy of note or otherwise being recorded. The nearby Lightning Crag was also visited with Steve Hubbal and suffered the same treatment. Admittedly, some pleasant, and some very hard problems have been discovered, but also, a lot of the other. During this activity Tom found time to slip into Langdale to tick off a couple of small gaps left on Middle Scout Crag, Madonna (E1) and Elton John (E4). During checking for the guide a number of short routes were climbed on the extremities of Flat Crags; La Wally (E3) by Phil Rigby and Alan Greig; Moon Shadow (E1), Sunshine Crack (E2) and Edge of Darkness (E3) by Dave Armstrong and John Williams and finally Afterburner (E4) a bold eliminate up the centre of Flat Iron Wall by Dave Armstrong, Alan Murray and John Williams. Phil Rigby and Alan Greig also found the delicate and exposed Riboletto (E3) on North Buttress, Bowfell. During a visit to Blea Crag Martin Berzins and Chris Sowden took a wander across to the nearby Eagle Crag and attempted the prominent thin crack in the lower roof. A point of aid had to be used to pass this obstacle but the upper section still resulted in a difficult E5 with a reputedly horrible fist jam in a flared crack as the crux. An easier start was climbed the same day to produce a free route but the roof still leaves a morsel for some young Jackal to snatch.

Some mopping up was done on Blea Crag by John White and Mark Scrowston producing the fine Pam's Wall in the process. Al Phizacklea and John Lockley had a wet day wander, found Slapestone Edge and ticked off three short routes. Dave Birkett (the third generation of the family to lead new routes in Langdale) came Into

The Light with a difficult and poorly protected E5 on Raven Crag, Walthwaite but unfortunately only after extensive top rope/shunt practicing. Finally a mild spell at the end of the year enabled Keith Phizacklea and John Daly to climb three routes on the Crescent Slabs area of Pavey Ark.

It will be seen from the above that in recent years development has centred on the more readily accessible small crags with less and less appearing on the major crags. Whilst this can continue for a little while longer these too must run out and a return be made to the hills in search of any unclimbed pieces of rock. There are still some major lines to climb which will provide difficult challenges for the future. It is hoped that a lack of ethics will not result in these being bashed or bolted into submission. The variations and eliminates will no doubt continue, becoming more and more difficult to distinguish them from the parent route and the flow of mini routes continue. Regard must also be paid to existing routes when making these variations, for example the peg placed to protect the crux of Perfect Head on Middlefell Buttress is on an existing route – Armalite, and thus alters the commitment required to climb this route. One cannot deny anyone the right to try and make his mark on climbing history, as long as it does not spoil the rock for others, but one cannot help but feel that black marks will be the reward for some of the routes created. It should always be remembered that the vast majority of climbers can have a more rewarding days sport searching out some of the many fine though often neglected lines which have already been recorded in this guide rather than grovelling for the scraps which remain.

Dave Armstrong, February 1989

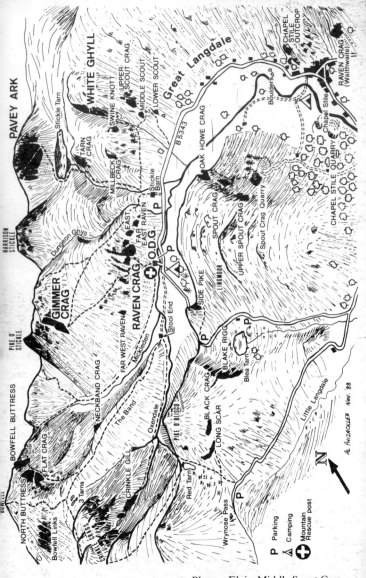

Photo – Elvis, Middle Scout Crag

LANGDALE

Great Langdale lies 6 kilometres due west of Ambleside and runs in a west to east direction. The B5343 branches from the main A593 road from Ambleside and runs along the north side of the valley as far as the Old Dungeon Ghyll Hotel, and is the route of a regular bus service.

Little Langdale lies just to the south of Great Langdale. A minor road runs the length of the valley from the A593 near its eastern end to Wrynose Pass at its head. The Blea Tarn road links this road with the Great Langdale road at the Old Dungeon Ghyll Hotel.

For the motorist free official car parks exist at the Old Dungeon Ghyll Hotel, (285 061); near the Stickle Barn (295 064) and adjacent to the road opposite the Stickle Barn (296 064). These can not cope with the large number of visitors and fill up rapidly at busy times. Roadside parking is very limited and controlled by yellow lines along most of the valley.

The crags are described in an anti-clockwise direction starting from Chapel Stile at the eastern end of Great Langdale proceeding along the north side of the valley and returning along the southern slopes with a brief excursion into Little Langdale.

Details of the easiest approach are included under the introduction, for each crag. Some minor crags have only a grid reference and location described, the best approach being left for the individual to determine.

Raven Crag, Walthwaite (325 058)   Alt. 180 m   South Facing

This is the only crag of any size on the hillside to the north-east of Chapel Stile, above a part of the village known as Walthwaite. Access is from the road leading from Chapel Stile up onto Red Bank, limited parking is available here in a small lay-by below the crag. A small path leads up to the crag in 5 minutes. A descent is available on either side of the crag.

Though only small, Raven Crag, Walthwaite is well worth a visit, especially as a poor weather alternative or for an evening visit. The rock is usually good, but there are some loose areas to watch out for, these are noted in the descriptions. The routes are described from left to right.

Photo – Chimney Variant, White Ghyll

Main Buttress

★ Route 1 22 m S ✓

Pleasant, on good rock but without a generous helping of protection.
Start at a holly at the left end of the crag.

Climb the slabby wall above the holly direct to the top.

The next three routes start from a ledge reached by scrambling up
and right from the holly.

Hardup Wall 22 m MVS

Start midway between Route 1 and Walthwaite Crack.

(4b). Scramble up to the foot of a groove and climb it to a resting
place. An awkward move leads to easier ground.

Walthwaite Crack 25 m VS

The prominent wide left facing corner crack 10 metres right of Route
1. Start at a small holly.

(4c). Climb the crack which is fortunately not as steep as it
appears.

● Walthwaite Chimney 27 m Hard Very Vegetated

Definitive black spot climbing up the jungle filled gully to the right
of Walthwaite Crack. Start at the holly below Walthwaite Crack.

Climb the vegetation to a large holly at the top.

Cliff at Christmas 25 m HVS   1988

An eliminate route up the clean rib right of Walthwaite Chimney.
Start at the holly below Walthwaite Crack.

(5b). Climb the rib and continue awkwardly until a move left leads
to a thin crack just right of the chimney. Climb this, resisting the
temptation to join the chimney.

Alfresco 33 m MVS   1954

Start a few metres right of and below Walthwaite Chimney.

1   9 m. A short vegetated wall leads to a belay on a glacis.
2   24 m (4b). Climb the wall trending right until the wall steepens
    and becomes a cracked bulge. Climb this with care to a junction
    with Route 2. Follow a short open groove to the top.

★ Route 2 42 m HS ✓

An excellent route. Start at the lowest point of the crag.

1   15 m. Climb a groove and move onto a rib on the left which leads
    to a ledge and belay by a large block near a large tree.

2   27 m. Climb a shallow chimney on the left of the ledge to some
     good pockets. Traverse right and up across a slab until a couple
     of short grooves lead leftwards to a swing onto a rib on the left
     and a final awkward chimney.

Meson   36 m   HVS   1968
Start as for Deuterus.
1   10 m. Pitch 1 of Deuterus.
2   26 m (5a). Climb the wall left of pitch 2 of Deuterus for 3 metres,
     then up and left to an overhanging crack with a flake in it.
     Surmount this trending slightly right and continue up the
     overhanging crack to a rib. Up the edge of this to the top.

Deuterus   40 m   E1   1947
A serious route with some loose rock and poor protection. Technically
low in its grade. Start just right of Route 2.
1   10 m. Climb the wall right of Route 2 to the ledge and block belay.
2   30 m (5b). A problematical scoop on the right of the ledge leads
     to easier ground and a junction with Route 2. Traverse right and
     up on reasonable holds but with rather poor protection, round a
     corner to finish with both better holds and rock.

★ **Protus**   30 m   HVS   ✓   1947
Good climbing marred only by the proximity of the large elm tree.
Start about 10 metres up and right of Deuterus at a large holly.
1   10 m. Climb up and rightwards via a bulge to the elm tree.
2   20 m (5a). Descend a little and traverse left then go up a couple
     of metres into a groove via a rib. Go left and up to leave the
     groove, passing a small overhang, and ascend a wall to a recess
     and a junction with Deuterus. Finish by moving right to good
     holds.

Olympus   28 m   E1   1980
Start 5 metres right of Protus at a wide corner crack.
1   10 m. Climb the crack to an elm tree on a large ledge.
2   18 m (5a). As for Protus to start but instead of going left, climb
     straight up for 5 metres to a ledge on the left. Move back right
     and up just right of the edge. Make a difficult move right to good
     holds and finish via a scoop.

Into the Light   22 m   E5   †   1988
Start 2 metres left of Walthwaite Gully.
1   10 m (4b). Pitch 1 of Out from the Darkness.

2   12 m (6b). Climb up to a small pocket left of Out from the
Darkness. Follow the flake leftwards with difficulty and then make
a very hard move to gain better holds on the wall above, which is
followed to the top. Protection is limited to a friend in the pocket.

Out from the Darkness   22 m   E2   1987
Start 2 metres left of Walthwaite Gully at a crack.
1   7 m (4a). Climb the crack to the large ledge and trees.
2   15 m (6a). The groove just left of pitch 2 of Walthwaite Gully is
quite vicious to start but the finish is easier.

Walthwaite Gully   27 m   MVS   1957
The damp and rather grotty looking corner which has its fair share of
trees in close attendance.
1   10 m (4b). Climb the corner crack to a ledge.
2   17 m (4c). Climb the flake crack and fine yew to the top.

Variation   Left-Hand Finish   17 m   E1   1987
2a 17 m (5c). Climb pitch 2 to the flake, bridge left and make a few
moves diagonally upwards.

The Girdle Traverse   90 m   VS   1953
1   30 m. Climb Route 1 to 5 metres below the top. Move right from
here and cross Hardup Wall to a stance and belay on the right
edge of Walthwaite Crack.
2   25 m. Over blocks and descend the vegetation of Walthwaite
Chimney until a few more vegetated moves right lead to a stance
on Alfresco.
3   14 m (4b). Traverse right again and join the rightwards traverse
of Route 2 to gain a poor stance on Deuterus.
4   21 m (4b). Continue traversing to join Protus and finish up this.

Right-Hand Buttress

To the right of Walthwaite Gully is a short steep wall. A number of
good pitches now exist here, unfortunately the central ones are often
rather dirty due to soil being washed down from the top of the crag.

Porcupine   33 m   MVS   1968
Start as for Walthwaite Gully.
1   10 m (4b). Pitch 1 of Walthwaite Gully.
2   23 m (4c). Traverse delicately right past a dirty groove and
continue until a concave wall is reached after 3 metre. Up this to
the top.

Riverboat Gambler   25 m   VS   1987
Start 3 metres right of the hawthorn at the bottom of Walthwaite Gully at a slabby wall which is often wet and looks rather dirty.
    (4c). Climb the slab and some grooves over a bulge to an easier finish.

Swing to the Left   17 m   E1   1987
There is an obvious square cut roof in the centre of the wall 10 metres right of Walthwaite Gully. Start directly beneath this.
    (5b). Gain a small ledge a couple of metres up and move left into a groove. Follow this to the left end of the roof and surmount this with a short wall to finish.

Swing to the Right   17 m   E1   1987
    (5b). Gain the small ledge as for the start of Swing to the Left. Climb to a short groove below the centre of the roof. Pull onto the arête on the right and climb a short wall to the top.

Rhythm Killers   20 m   E2   1988
A route which pinches bits that have already been climbed, but is still worthwhile. Start below a small downward pointing spike below the right side of the overhang, 2 metres right of Swing to the Left.
    (5c). Climb a short groove with difficulty and move right to a rib. Gain the centre of the roof and climb directly to the top.

Party Animal   20 m   E1   1987
Start 2 metres right of Rhythm Killers at a dirty wall.
    (5b). Rock up on small holds until easier climbing gives access to a thin crack on the right of the overhang. Move up with difficulty to good holds and a finishing groove.

Proportional Representation   20 m   HVS   1987
Start just right of Party Animal on top of a block pedestal below a groove and spike hold.
    (5a). Move up and left into a short groove. Exit left and finish up another groove.

Militant Tendency   18 m   HVS   1987
A poorly protected route which starts below an area of knobbly black rock just right of Proportional Representation.
    (5a). Climb up a groove rightwards to the knobbly rock and enter a short groove. Up this to the final wall and either finish up moving slightly right to the top or, equally worryingly traverse left to an easier finish.

Marginality   16 m   HVS   1987
Start at a right trending ramp at the right end of the crag, 5 metres
right of Militant Tendency.

(5a). Climb the ramp to its end and swing left onto a bulging
section of rock. Over this with a stiff pull to easier ground.

Thrang Quarry   (320 057)   Alt. 130 m   South East Facing

A small outcrop type crag which lies close to old quarry workings just
outside Chapel Stile. It can be clearly seen from the road and is
recognizable by an obvious left to right slanting ramp line. Approach
the crag either by traversing the fellside above the church until the
crag can be seen at the first sight of quarry workings, or by walking
up a small road which leads from beneath the church leftwards (west)
into the area beneath the crag.

Recount   16 m   HVS   1983
Takes the conspicuous corner/pod on the left side of the crag. Start
below a steep wall left of an easy ramp.

(4c). Climb up to a loose break on good holds and continue up
the jamming crack in the corner above.

Pollster   16 m   HVS   1983
Takes the central line of the crag. Start at the foot of the easy ramp.

(5a). Climb leftwards along the ramp to a break in the overhangs.
Climb this, following cracks to a flared chimney finish.

Bryson's Picnic   19 m   E2   1983
(5c). Takes the good looking ramp which rises to the right. Start
up Pollster and then gain the ramp. Follow it delicately to its end
and finish direct.

Scout Crags   (299 069)   Alt. 160 m to 275 m   South Facing

These crags were previously regarded as an area for beginners but
following the development of Middle Scout Crag, there is now plenty
for the hard man. The crags are situated between five and ten minutes
walk up the fellside behind a barn which is a few hundred metres east
of the New Dungeon Ghyll Hotel. All the crags can be approached
by a path which leaves the road near the barn. The Lower Crag is
reached first and the boulders at its foot provide some excellent sport.
The prominent crack on the rear of the lower boulder, usually feels
a little hard for its original grading of Severe!

Lower Scout Crag

This crag is very popular with organised groups and beginners. The rock is therefore highly polished and can be dirty after rain due to washout from the eroded ground on top of the crag. Though short, the routes are very good.

The climbs are described from left to right.

Basher's Bulge   10 m   E1   1978
>   (5b). The overhang on the left side of the crag is taken direct.

Variation   S
>   An easier alternative avoids the roof on the right by an airy little traverse.

Cub's Groove   13 m   VD
Start a couple of metres left of the crack which splits the centre of the crag beneath a holly.
>   A right slanting line of polished holds leads to ledges below the tree. Climb carefully past this and exit either direct or to the left.

Cub's Crack   13 m   S
The steep crack in the centre of the crag gives a good, though slippery introduction to jamming.
>   Climb the crack and finish up past the holly direct.

★ **Cub's Wall**   13 m   VD
An excellent route starting just right of the crack.
>   Climb up for a few metres until it is possible to traverse left onto a ledge system. Climb direct past the tree on magnificent holds.

The New Partnership   15 m   E1   1984
Start just right of Cub's Wall.
>   (5b). Climb direct to finish through the final overhanging nose.

Oh Heck Direct   14 m   HS   1968
A poor route which is often dirty.
>   Climb the prominent corner on the right of the wall.

The Slab   12 m   S
A route up the glossy slab which lies at right angles to the main crag.
>   Start on the left and work rightwards to the arête. Climb up until a move back left leads into a triangular niche. (This used to be the home of a 'chockstone which rocked alarmingly'). A tricky move up leads to easier ground.

The steep wall to the right has a couple of routes.

Short Man's Route   15 m   E3   1988
    (6a). Climb the wall a couple of metres right of the rib via an obscure hold and a long stretch up to the right for a small hold, which allows a pull over to an easier section. Climb to the small overhang, surmount this and climb easily to the top.

Confidence Trick   15 m   E1   1988
Start a couple of metres right of the last route.
    (5b). A fault line leads delicately to the roof. A brief but exciting layaway leads over this to huge holds.

Middle Scout Crag

The black, steep-looking crag above and to the left of the stile above the Lower Crag. A large hawthorn at its base provides a useful landmark. Although the routes are short, they are strenuous and sustained and in the summer often remain dry, even during rain. Most routes are difficult to protect, this has resulted in the use of the crag as a popular top-roping venue.

The routes are described from left to right.

Skinhead   10 m   E4   ÷
The slab (or at least it looks like it) at the left end of the crag and set at an angle to it.
    (6b). Desperate moves up an incipient crack system lead past at least one in-situ wire.

Abba   16 m   E3   1981
Start immediately left of The Beatles.
    (6a). Reasonable holds lead to a difficult move left to a hidden sidepull/pocket. Reach up for a flat spike, stand on it and continue up sound but poor looking rock above.

The Beatles   18 m   E6   ÷   1981
A peg about 7 metres up the crag and a couple of metres left of the hawthorn tree marks the line of this serious route.
    (6a). Climb strenuously to the peg, past the occasional reasonable hold and a runner at 4 metres, and make difficult moves past it, mainly on sideholds. Reach better holds up to the left, from where another long reach up to the right leads to easier ground.

★ Elvis   18 m   E4   1981
Start a short way right of the hawthorn beneath an obvious undercut
flake. A really good route which gets progressively harder.
>   (6a). Climb to the flake, past one hard move. Undercut left to a
>   thin crack and follow this on poor layaways to a final difficult
>   move.

Blondie   18 m   E3   1982
>   (6a). As for Elvis to the undercling. Traverse right then up to a
>   semi-resting place at the foot of a corner. Pull out left and follow
>   a small groove to an overhang. Over this to the top.

Tenderfoot   15 m   E3   1981
Harder than it looks. Start 6 metres right of Elvis under a prominent,
wide and blocky-looking groove.
>   (6a). Good holds are followed by some wild layback moves which
>   lead into the corner. Up this to the top.

Elton John   15 m   E4   †   1988
Start just right of Tenderfoot.
>   (6b). Climb up to a small tree. Move up to a peg runner and make
>   a long stretch up to the left to a flake in the overhang. Continue
>   up strenuously.

Madonna   15 m   E1   1988
Start just left of a yew at the right side of the crag.
>   (5b). Commence on big holds and move left after a few metres to
>   the deceptively steep crackline which leads to the top.

There is an excellent low level traverse here, along with some good
problems on the steep wall immediately left of the main buttress.

Upper Scout Crag

The largest and topmost of the trio, reached in ten minutes from the
road. The crag is easy angled and can be climbed anywhere at a low
grade – pitch mixing is common here. The rock is excellent and well
supplied with good holds and pockets, but protection can be difficult
to find at times. The ascent of a route on Lower Scout and then Upper
Scout provides a good way of reaching White Ghyll Crag, which can
be approached from the highest point of the Upper Crag via a rising
leftwards traverse across the fell. The best descent is to the left, via
a well worn scramble ending in a short crack down some slabs which
leads into the easy descent gully.

The climbs are described from left to right.

Some pleasant short pitches lie up the gully on the left of the crag, on some slabs close to the descent route.

Route 2   55 m   VD   1922
Start at a short buttress lower than the bulk of the main crag and on its left-hand side.
1   10 m. A deceptively awkward stepped groove leads to a large ledge.
2   13 m. Climb a wall and move up past a tree to another good ledge.
3   13 m. Traverse right for 3 metres and make some interesting moves up and just left of the overhangs to easier ground and another stance.
4   19 m. Move left and climb the gradually easing rib.

Variation   32 m   1950
3a. Traverse left to a nose and ascend direct, up the black streaked slabs.

★ **Route 1.5**   43 m   VD   1947
A line between Routes 1 and 2, which has a dirty and often wet start, but improves higher up. Start at the foot of a grubby groove midway between the starts of Routes 1 and 2.
1   13 m. Climb up into the mossy V-groove and follow it for 4 metres, when an exit right can be made. A short ascent leads to a spike belay.
2   11 m. Avoid the overhangs above on the left and belay as for pitch 2 of Route 2.
3   19 m. An easier finish up the slabs between Routes 1 and 2.

Variation   The Ramsbottom Variation   13 m   S
3a. Climb through a gap in the roof on the right and pull through a bulge to belay at the top of the arête on Route 1.

★★ **Route 1**   50 m   VD   ✓   1922
The best route on the crag, following the line of the rib above the large holly. The second pitch is one of the best of its grade in the valley. Start below the large holly.
1   14 m. Climb a short left slanting slab and follow some well marked grooves which lead to a good block belay just before the arête.
2   36 m. Traverse right onto the arête and ascend this in a delightfully exposed position, using some excellent pockets, to a ledge. Continue up past flakes and easier slabs to chipped flake belays at the end of the difficulties. Easier alternatives lie just left of the arête

Zero Route   50 m   VD   1939
Start 3 metres right of the start of Route 1, at a steep little wall.
1   14 m. The 5 metre wall with a small ledge halfway is followed by
     slabs to a flake belay. This pitch is often wet.
2   36 m. Climb a shallow groove on the left to a junction with Rt. 1.
     Finish up this.

Rambler's Hangover   47 m   VD   1948
A less frequented route than the others, but quite pleasant. Start
below a small and often wet overhang at the foot of the crag, some
15 metres right of the start of Route 1.
1   13 m. Surmount the overhang, or the easier chimney to the right
     and continue up slabs to a copious ledge.
2   17 m. Climb the diamond shaped wall to a ledge, pull over a bulge
     and traverse left to a recess at the foot of a scoop. (It is possible
     to finish direct from the bulge, via an arête to easy ground.)
3   17 m. Go up the groove and past the overhang, step left and cross
     a gully. Ascend diagonally up to the left to a junction with Route
     1.

Scout's Belt   86 m   VD   1947
A right to left traverse of mixed quality. Start as for Zero Route.
1   14 m. As for Zero Route.
2   22 m. Ascend the wall to the left of the shallow groove of Zero
     Route for a short way until a leftwards trending sequence leads
     to the arête of Route 1.
3   8 m. A descending traverse leads to a belay in the groove on Route
     2.
4   17 m. Traverse narrow ledges leftwards, crossing a groove and
     descend to a tree, which is visible from the start of the pitch.
5   14 m. Cross the juniper ledge into a corner level with an obvious
     horizontal crack. Descend steep and vegetated rock below the
     corner and traverse left using the horizontal crack to a large spike
     belay.
6   11 m. An easy traverse left into the scree gully.

About 45 metres to the right of the main crag and at a higher level,
is a rather vegetated buttress, which is steeper and smaller than the
main crag, and is of interest due to one worthwhile route.

Salmon Leap   34 m   VS   1958
The route follows the corner to the left of the overhanging nose on
the right end of the crag. It is often more suited for fish than climbers.
1   13 m. Climb steeply on good holds to a stance just below and right
     of the nose.

2   21 m (4c). Traverse left under the nose and enter a groove. Climb
    the left wall, which provides some good moves, to the overhangs,
    and pull over these to easier ground.

White Ghyll Crag   (298 071)   Alt. 400 m   West Facing

White Ghyll itself lies roughly parallel to Stickle Ghyll and about ½
kilometre to the east. It rises steeply up the fellside then the left bank
gradually steepens to culminate in a striking crag, towering above the
narrow stoney ghyll bed, and conspicuous against the skyline when
seen from the valley.

The crag is easily though steeply gained in less than half an hour from
the car park beside the Stickle Barn. Bear to the right behind the
Stickle Barn and follow a sign posted path across Stickle Ghyll at a
wooden bridge. Continue over a small slate bridge and follow the path
up to the left until a gate on the right gains a path which traverses the
hillside behind a stone wall, past the foot of a larch plantation, into
White Ghyll.

The path deteriorates into a scramble up the loose ghyll bottom until
a prominent sycamore tree standing in the centre of the ghyll,
opposite the corner of Slip Knot is reached. This is the usual base for
routes on the Lower Crag. Care should be taken when sitting here to
avoid scree disturbed by climbers descending the Ghyll above.

White Ghyll Crag forms the true left bank of the Ghyll for a
considerable distance from its summit and, for convenience of
description, can be separated into an upper and lower section, the
dividing mark being some 40 metres above the sycamore where a
grassy rake (the left-hand or upper one of a pair) slants up to the
right, drops a little to a broad grass shelf (the Great Shelf), then rises
smoothly to the top; this is Easy Rake, a convenient means of descent.

The Lower Crag begins at its right-hand lower end as a heather filled
cracked wall, it then becomes broken into a number of sharply defined
grooves which provide excellent short climbs. Left again a short steep
wall leads to the Great Shelf topped by a short secondary tier of rock.

The Upper Crag begins above and left of Easy Rake with an area of
slabs and overhangs. Left again beyond a rib and small cave, an
impressive wall is protected at half height by a formidable band of
overhangs. This central section is an incredible piece of rock
architecture providing some memorable routes and situations. On its
left the crag is split by the narrow imposing fissure of White Ghyll

Chimney. Left of the chimney is a fine sweep of slabs which gradually merge into a steep but broken hillside. This upper section of the Ghyll also provides an alternative descent from climbs on the Upper Crag.

There is little on White Ghyll Crag for the beginner and the better routes, of which there are plenty tend to be in the middle grades.

The rock is generally good and fairly clean though there are some looser sections. The crag provides an interesting variety of climbs·in impressive situations.

The climbs are described from right to left i.e. as one ascends the Ghyll.

Lower Crag

The first feature of note is a long ridge, Junction Arête, at the point where the crag turns away from the Ghyll. It can be identified by a couple of oaks in a groove to its right. Right of this groove is an area called The Sidings which offers some short pitches which cannot be recommended except to budding gardeners.

Junction Arête   46 m   S (D if first pitch is avoided)   1947
A pleasant route. Start at the foot of the ridge.
1   16 m. A short slab is followed to an awkward overhang which leads to easier climbing on the right and a stance level with the first oak.
2   30 m. Continue up the enjoyable ridge above.

Left of Junction Arête is a broad heather-clad, cracked wall. A prominent projecting nose marks the line of a rather poor route **Block and Rib** (35 m, S, 1961) which wanders its way up this wall. The groove on the left of the wall is taken by an aptly named route, **Not Much** (28 m, HS, 1979).

The next three climbs start at a large block below the second or left-hand of two grooves reached by scrambling up broken rocks a few metres left of Junction Arête.

Russet Groove   28 m   S   1949
Start at a large block at the foot of the second groove.
   An easy slab leads up to the right to a ledge in the groove. Ascend the groove for 6 metres to a ledge on the right wall, then a short steep wall on the left leads to the top. A rather heathery excursion.

★ Ethics of War   25 m   HVS   1977
An excellent, though short pitch up the undercut rib between Russet
Groove and Heather Groove. Start at the foot of the rib.
  (5a). Up rightwards to the roof and pull leftwards through it via
  an awkward move onto the slab. Climb the right side of this
  daintily, but without problems.

Heather Groove   28 m   S   1947
The steep groove above the start of Russett Groove.
  The overhanging corner above the block leads to a small ledge
  below a slab, which is climbed to a ledge on its left edge. Cross
  to the right side of the slab and follow this to the top.

The following routes are all reached by scrambling up rightwards from
the Ghyll from below the prominent groove of Laugh Not.

Not Again   25 m   S   1953
The wall right of Inferno. A start can be made up the broken rock
below if desired. Start at the foot of the groove of Inferno.
  Climb twin cracks on the right to a junction with Heather Groove
  below an overhang. Step left round the rib onto a wall above the
  overhang. Either move left into a crack, reach a narrow ledge and
  exit rightwards to the top, or traverse right out of the crack to
  finish up the airy rib.

★ Inferno   25 m   S   1949
The groove left of Heather Groove, identified by an overhang at 9
metres. The broken rocks beneath the groove can provide a start, this
is rather scrappy and usually avoided.
  Climb the groove, passing a small, square-cut overhang to a grass
  ledge on the right. Either walk off to the left or climb the short
  groove on the left.

★ Feet of Clay   25 m   E1   1978
The slim groove in the rib between the corners of Inferno and Laugh
Not marks the route. This groove is also shared by Man of Straw.
Start as for Inferno.
  (5b). A short crack on the left leads to the foot of the groove.
  Climb this to the small overhang, where a pull out to the right
  leads with difficulty onto a steep wall. Up this to a good nut belay
  on the left and immediately above the initial groove.

** **Man of Straw**   28 m   E1 ✓   1965
A delightful climb which is quite sustained but never desperate. Start
below and left of the thin groove in the arête, left of Inferno.
(5b). Climb a boot-wide crack to the foot of the groove. Climb
this almost to the roof, when a step down to the left onto a good
foothold gives access to a thin crack and the slabby wall right of
Laugh Not. Move up a little and then traverse delicately right to
follow holds on the arête which leads to the top and a good nut
belay.

Sahara   30 m   E2   1981
A good climb with a technical, but well protected crux. Start just right
of Laugh Not.
(6a). Climb rightwards to gain a small corner just left of Man of
Straw. Climb this to thin cracks (junction with Man of Straw) and
continue directly up these with difficulty to the traverse of Laugh
Not. Pull directly through the roof to finish.

Longhair   30 m   E2   1971
A difficult and sustained eliminate, whose upper section is also taken
by Sahara. Start as for Laugh Not.
(6a). Climb a short way up Laugh Not and traverse right onto the
right edge of the slab. Ascend this direct to a junction with Man
of Straw and Sahara. Finish as for Sahara, but traverse right below
the roof as for Laugh Not.

*** **Laugh Not**   35 m   HVS ✓   1953
An excellent and clean cut line which presents a fine challenge, up
the big groove left of Inferno. The corner is quite smooth but very
well protected. Start below the smooth section of the corner.
(5a). Climb the corner to the roof and traverse right past a final
delicate move to gain a ledge and good nut belay as for Man of
Straw.

* **Waste Not, Want Not**   32 m   E1   1977
Neat climbing based on an inverted, stepped fault on the wall left of
Laugh Not. Start as for Laugh Not.
(5b). Climb the corner until a traverse left can be made onto the
wall and move up to a small ledge. Climb the fault until an
awkward step left brings an easier groove into reach. Climb this
to the top.

★ **Do Not**   35 m   E1   1949
A first class route with varied climbing up the left edge of the wall
left of Laugh Not. Start at the foot of Laugh Not.
1   14 m (5b). Climb the corner until a slanting crack splits off to the
     left. Follow this past a puzzling exit to a roomy ledge and junction
     with Slip Knot.
2   21 m (5a). An excellent pitch. Climb the shallow, square-cut
     groove on the right to an overhang. Traverse steeply left across
     the wall using a flake either for the feet or hands, until a final
     awkward move round the nose leads to good holds. Easier
     climbing provides a relaxing finish.

Variation   Direct Start   25 m   E1   1960
Start below the broken looking groove in the rib between Slip Knot
and Laugh Not.
1a (5b). The groove leads to a ledge beneath the overhang. Move
     right, round the corner and follow a steep, thin crack to the stance.

★ **Antarctica**   36 m   E2   1981
An exciting eliminate climb up the wall left of Laugh Not. Start a
couple of metres below the corner of Laugh Not.
     (6a). Climb the wall to gain the thin crack on Do Not Direct Start.
     Follow this to the ledge, step right onto Waste Not, Want Not
     and follow this to the top overlap where it steps left. Climb the
     wall above direct and step right to finish up a groove.

Slip Knot Variations   41 m   E2   1971
Start below the broken looking groove in the rib left of Do Not.
1   21 m (5c). Climb the easy groove until it is possible to pull into a
     thin crack on the left wall. This leads with difficulty to a slim
     groove which in turn leads to a spacious ledge.
2   20 m (5c). Pull through the roof to reach a groove with
     considerable difficulty. Climb this directly to join the Do Not
     traverse. (Alternatively, the groove can be left low down by a bold
     traverse onto the front.)

★★ **Slip Knot**   41 m   MVS √   1947
A justifiably popular route which takes an excellent and varied line.
Pitch 2 gives an intimidating pitch and a good introduction to the Very
Severe grade. Start at the foot of the large right angled corner, topped
by a large triangular roof, above the sycamore in the Ghyll.
1   21 m (4a). Climb the corner for a couple of metres and traverse
     out onto the right wall, where excellent holds lead up to the
     spacious ledge.

2   20 m (4b). Traverse left into the corner and make a thought-provoking move across the wall to the left to gain the rib. Climb this, passing an overhang on the left and continue via good holds to the top. Belay well back. (The original start to pitch 2 descended 3 metres from the belay and traversed the wall to the rib.)

★ **The Palestinians**   37 m   E1   1981
Climbs the groove and crack line in the blunt arête between Slip Knot and Titus Groan. Start just left of Slip Knot.
> (5b). Gain a sloping ledge below a groove which leads to the first overlap. Climb up to and pull over this and continue up cracks to the larger, upper overlap. Surmount this and continue up an easier slab to finish as for Slip Knot.

★ **Moss Wall**   43 m   VS ✓   1959
An excellent route, which is considerably better than its appearance would suggest. It follows the mossy-looking right wall of the corner left of Slip Knot. Start at the foot of Slip Knot.
1   13 m. An easy pitch which leads leftwards to the foot of a shallow, square-cut groove on the left side of the mossy wall.
2   30 m (4c). Climb the groove for 3 or 4 metres and make a traverse out onto the wall on the right to good holds. Continue fairly directly up the wall to a resting place on the rib. Follow footholds leftwards into a steep groove and climb this via a small overhang to a good ledge. Continue more easily to the top.

Titus Groan   40 m   E1   1975
An oft-claimed direct version of Moss Wall up the groove left of Slip Knot. Start as for Slip Knot.
> (5b). Climb up leftwards to the foot of the groove, climb it direct moving right, then left through the overhang to rejoin Moss Wall which is followed to the top.

Shivering Timber   36 m   VS   1952
The steep groove left of Titus Groan provides the line of this climb. Start in the bed of the ghyll below the groove, 5 metres left of Slip Knot.
1   13 m. A short wall leads to a scoop. Exit left and scramble to the foot of the groove.
2   16 m (4c). Enter the V-groove from the left to overcome the initial overhang. Climb the groove and gain a resting place on the right rib. Return to the groove and climb it to a stance below a short, steep wall.
3   7 m. Finish up the short wall.

Garden Path   46 m   VD   1947
Roughly follows the line of a slanting rake left of the last route. There
is a conspicuous triangular niche in the middle of its steepest section.
The upper section is loose and good belays are a rarity. Start just left
of Shivering Timber.
1   17 m. Climb the wall to a good ledge and gain the obvious rock
    niche on the left. Good thread in the top left-hand corner.
2   14 m. Go round to the left to a small ledge, then move back right
    onto the face above the niche. Carry on to the large heather shelf.
3   15 m. Unpleasant heathery scrambling leads to a large ledge. It is
    best to traverse left into Easy Rake.

Question Not   44 m   VD   1950
An indefinite line up the right side of the large broken scoop, just left
of Garden Path. Rather dirty and vegetated. Start below a projecting
rib a couple of metres left of Garden Path.
1   16 m. Ascend the rib to a sentry box at 13 metres. Step left into
    a short V-groove and pull over a projecting block to a belay.
2   28 m. Easy slabs and then some steeper rock to the top.

Why Not   45 m   VD   1949
Climbs the large scoop left of Question Not. Although rather dirty is
still better than its easier neighbour. Start below the centre of the
scoop just left of Question Not.
1   22 m. Climb to a stance level with the holly in Hollin Groove.
2   8 m. Step right and move up to a break in the overhang. Climb
    through this to a large ledge.
3   15 m. Follow steep grass to a big pinnacle. A groove on the left
    of this leads to the top.

★ **Hollin Groove**   82 m   S   ✓   1945
A pleasant route whose main interest lies in its attractive V-groove.
Start at the foot of a short, crooked crack about 16 metres up the
ghyll from the sycamore, and below and right of the main groove line.
1   23 m. Climb the initial crack with difficulty and follow a rib on
    the left and another groove to belay at a rather battered holly.
2   24 m. Climb the fine right-angled groove to a large terrace (the
    Great Shelf) and walk 13 metres to a belay on the rib ahead.
3   12 m. The steep rib leads to a spike belay.
4   23 m. Continue up the rib to the top.

Granny Knot Direct   37 m   VS   1971
Start just left of Hollin Groove, directly beneath the holly.
1   11 m. The steep, but easy wall leads to a ledge.

2   26 m (4b). Step round the corner on the left into a shattered groove and ascend to a large overhang. Step out onto the rib on the right and continue up the splendid finishing wall and awkward bulge of Granny Knot.

Granny Knot   40 m   HS   1948
A good route which is exposed in its upper section. Most definitely better than it looks. Start 10 metres left of Hollin Groove, below and right of a large projecting rectangular overhang.
1   22 m. Climb a steep rib to a stance, below an overhang.
2   18 m. Traverse 5 metres right on comfortable holds and cross the bulge above direct, continuing up an airy ridge to reach the Great Shelf. An easier alternative is to climb direct to the overhang from the stance, when a short traverse left leads to easy ground just below the Great Shelf.

Two poor girdles of the Lower Crag have been climbed, covering very similar ground in the main: **Reckless Necklace** (75 m, HVS, 1967) starts up Question Not and finishes up Laugh Not, **Across Not** (70 m, E1 (5c), 1976) starts up Titus Groan and finishes up Laugh Not.

Upper Crag

Between the Lower and Upper Crags is the well-trodden thoroughfare of Easy Rake, which leads to the Great Shelf. The next four routes climb the right-hand side of the Upper Crag and start from the Easy Rake.

Rope Not   17 m   HVS
Above and to the left of the Great Shelf, a steep, but short slab rises from a grassy shelf. It is split by an attractive line of twin, thin converging cracks. Start by scrambling up to the foot of these cracks. Alternatively a lower pitch can be climbed up from the top of the first part of Easy Rake to the grassy shelf.
   (5a). The cracks give pleasantly sustained climbing, but protection can be difficult to arrange.

Hitcher   44 m   VS   1960
The second part of this climb takes the wall left of Rope Not. The first pitch is poor and is perhaps best avoided by a traverse in from the right. Start about 8 metres up Easy Rake, below a short, red, right-facing scoop.
1   20 m (4a). Get established in the scoop and climb the wall above to the Grass Shelf. Belay 5 metres higher at the foot of the mossy corner on the left.

2   24 m (4c). Effect a rising traverse across the slab on the right and climb the far edge to an overhang. Follow a thin crack slanting right above the overhang to the arête. Go up this for a little way and traverse back left into a short chimney-crack. Pull out right to finish.

Naztron   44 m   VS   1971
A poor route on doubtful rock. Start as for Hitcher.
1   20 m (4a). Pitch 1 of Hitcher.
2   24 m (4c). Climb the corner to the large overhang. Stride left to a resting place and finish easily leftwards.

Karma   44 m   E2   1979
The original right-hand finish to Naztron is gained by a bold exposed rib. Start as for Hitcher.
1   20 m (4a). Pitch 1 of Hitcher.
2   24 m (5c). Traverse steeply left from the foot of the corner to a rib. Climb this with interest to the ledge below the overhang. Step boldly right and climb the right wall of a shallow corner.

** **White Ghyll Wall**   68 m   VS ✓   1946
The easiest route on the central section of the crag. It avoids the main band of overhangs on the right, but offers some fine positions and a short section of technical interest. Start 12 metres above the foot of Easy Rake, just right of a small cave beneath a groove with a small ash tree.
1   25 m. Follow the rib to a ledge beneath the overhangs and traverse easily right for a few metres to a stance beneath an undercut scoop.
2   15 m (4c). Ascend the scoop, which is problematical to leave where it bulges. Step left onto a steep wall and continue directly for 6 metres until a recess on the left can be entered.
3   28 m (4b). A vague line leads delicately leftwards up the slabs to a ledge and a choice of easier finishes.

Perhaps Not   63 m   HVS   1949
An unbalanced route which is nonetheless worthwhile, if only to suffer the notorious chimney pitch! Start as for White Ghyll Wall.
1   17 m. Climb the rib to a stance beneath the overhangs.
2   16 m (4b). Climb up to the roof and traverse left beneath it to the foot of an overhung chimney.
3   9 m (5a). The chimney proves to be at the top end of its grade . (Faith in what may be above is required when the holds run out.) A step out right under the overhang eases things a little and the stance is a short way above this.
4   21 m (4b). Continue directly up the wall to finish.

Variation Short Cut   8 m   VS   1957
3a (4c). For those who find the prospect of the chimney a little too
  intimidating, the traverse can be continued to a junction with
  Gordian Knot.

Tapestry 58 m   HVS   1972
A route which passes through some impressive situations, but which
struggles to attract many suitors. Start 6 metres left of White Ghyll
Wall below a niche set in the lower band of overhangs.
1 22 m (5a). Some poor climbing leads to a move right onto a rotten
  ledge just below the niche. Pull into the niche, surmount the block
  above and make a tricky exit to the right. Traverse a short way
  to the right and take a stance on White Ghyll Wall.
2 15 m (5a). Climb through the overhang above, trending right to
  good holds on the skyline. Reach a good ledge on the slab above
  and climb to the right-hand of two breaks in the overlap. Follow
  this steeply for a few moves until it is possible to step left into the
  fault line that leads to a stance on White Ghyll Wall.
3 21 m (4b). An easier, but pleasant finish up the rib on the left.

★ **Eliminot** 65 m   E2   1957
Quite a tricky route, with some technical and strenuous moves. Start
as for Gordian Knot, at a narrow slab which runs in a single sweep
to the main roof. A large block leans against its left edge.
1 23 m (5c). Ascend the slab for 9 metres, then traverse right under
  a barrier of overhangs to a ledge beneath a break (poor peg
  runner). Pull through the break with difficulty and gain a resting
  place. Continue steeply to a stance below the chimney of Perhaps
  Not.
2 20 m (5b). Climb down to the right, reversing part of the traverse
  of Perhaps Not, until a strenuous pull round an awkward bulge
  leads onto another thin slab sandwiched between the overhangs.
  Pull through a break in the overhangs above, make a move or two
  left and pull over a small overlap. Continue to a stance (junction
  with Perhaps Not).
3 22 m (4b). Continue up the wall to finish.

★★ **The Gordian Knot** 60 m   VS ✓   1940
A great climb, following the easiest line through the bands of
overhangs. Start as for Eliminot at the foot of a narrow slab which
has a large block leaning against its left edge.
1 20 m (4b). A pleasant pitch. Ascend the slab direct, make a step
  left and continue to a stance in a recess.

2   15 m (4c). Traverse easily right for 4 metres to an exposed little
ledge below a corner. Pull through the bulge above on good holds
and move back left into a recess. Continue direct to a good stance.

3   25 m (4b). Finish up the wall above.

★★ **White Ghyll Eliminate**   59 m   E2   1971
Though the main pitch is short, it is exhilarating and strenuous and
the route as a whole provides a direct line up the crag. Start as for
The Gordian Knot.

1   20 m (4b). Climb the slab as for The Gordian Knot.

2   15 m (5c). Pull up steeply into the impressive crackline above and
follow it on an assortment of holds and jams to a stance on the
Haste Not traverse. Well protected.

3   24 m (5a). Step left to an awkward crack splitting an overhang.
Climb this and the pleasant slabs above which lead to the top.

★★ **Haste Not Direct**   48 m   E2   1971
Another direct line with some hard climbing especially on the thrilling
top crack. Start at a gloomy corner left of The Gordian Knot.

1   21 m (4c). Climb directly up the corner to the roof which caps the
corner and move right onto the rib. Move right again to belay as
for The Gordian Knot.

2   27 m (5c). A pitch of increasing difficulty which can be split just
below the final crack. Move up through the overhangs to a slim
groove which is quitted after a short way for a resting place on
the left. Steep climbing leads to the traverse of Haste Not. The
impressive crack above is both awkward and strenuous.

★★ **Haste Not**   59 m   VS   1948
Excellent climbing which features an exposed and enthralling
traverse. Start about 10 metres left of The Gordian Knot, at the foot
of a triangular overhung slab, just right of a huge block.

1   22 m (4b). Climb the slab to an inverted-V overhang and traverse
left to gain the bigger slab on the front. A shallow groove/crack
leads to a ledge and belays.

2   15 m (4c). A classic pitch. Easily rightwards until it is possible to
ascend a steep wall which gives access to a gangway running
rightwards under the big roof. Traverse this and make a hard
move across a bottomless groove. Continue across, ending with a
step down to a belay.

3   22 m (4b). Make an awkward move above the stance and continue
between two overhanging blocks to the top.

Left of Haste Not is an especially impressive area of overhangs which are breached by a number of sensational and difficult climbs. Except for The Fine Art of Surfacing the following routes all start from a ledge and block belay 15 metres up White Ghyll Chimney.

The Fine Art of Surfacing   40 m   E3   1980
Start below the impending wall left of the start of Haste Not.
1   12 m (6a). Climb up to a right-slanting diagonal break, follow it
    out to the edge and up this to a stance on the large ledge above.
2   28 m (6a). Climb Paladin for about 6 metres, to the peg runner.
    Traverse right across a steep wall to reach a triangular niche in
    the tip of the overhang. Climb the rib above to the top. A
    technical problem which might prove particularly difficult for
    those of less than average stature.

Horror   30 m   1978
Following the loss of crucial holds on the overhangs this route has not
been re-ascended. From the corner of Paladin it traversed rightwards
to a position above the traverse of Haste Not. A swing out right and
up through the overhangs to a peg runner on the left, then more
overhanging rock led to easier ground.

** **Paladin**   34 m   E3   1970
The impressive overhanging corner gives sustained, strenuous and
exposed climbing.
1   25 m (5c). Move up rightwards to the foot of the corner. Step left
    and climb a slab followed by a bulging wall until it is possible to
    move into the corner below a roof. Move right round this and
    climb steeply into a niche. Move left with difficulty into a
    subsidiary groove and follow it to a stance.
2   9 m. Easy ground to the top.

* **Warrior**   34 m   E4   1977
A fierce climb whose line, though contrived, gives sustained and
technical climbing. It takes the overhangs left of Paladin.
    (6a). Climb Paladin for a few moves, then step left onto a short
    slanting slab. Cross this and pull out leftwards. Gain the traverse
    of Chimney Variant, move left and climb through bulges to a
    groove. Climb the steep wall on the right and move slightly left
    to yet more overhangs. Move right to finish at the top of Paladin.

Variation   The Rampant Finish   E4   1972
A dirty and difficult finish to Warrior. Start from the belay at the end
of Warrior.

(6a). Traverse back left from the belay, peg runner, and pull up to reach holds above the roof. Move left, peg runner, and climb a rib and cracks to the top.

** **Chimney Variant**   36 m   E1   1966
A popular route giving some interesting climbing and excellent positions.
1   28 m (5b). Climb up to the overhang in White Ghyll Chimney. Pull over this and move right onto an obvious undercut gangway which leads to a short, but handsome groove. Climb this, quite tricky, until a step can be made out to the rib on the right. There is a small stance a little higher.
2   8 m. The easier groove above.

* **White Ghyll Chimney**   57 m   S ✓   1923
A traditional style classic up the obvious cleft which separates the central overhangs from the slabs. Start at the foot of the cleft.
1   20 m. Easily up to a terrace, then walk up to a thread belay in the Sentry Box, above which the chimney narrows to a crack.
2   25 m. Climb the cave for 3 metres and then make a difficult move to gain a sloping hold on the left. Delicately reach some small handholds and continue more easily up a steep groove, trending left to a ledge with a good belay 6 metres higher.
3   12 m. Return 3 metres from the belay and climb the wall above for 5 metres. A delicate traverse then leads back into the chimney which leads to the top.

Variation   1948
A more difficult, but often drier alternative.
2a From the Sentry Box belay, step down a short way and traverse left across the wall for 5 metres. A direct ascent on small holds avoids the chimney and leads to the steep groove on the standard pitch 2.

The sweep of slabs left of White Ghyll Chimney give some pleasant though featureless routes on the right side and a couple of good Severes to their left.

Two routes have been recorded as climbing the right-hand side of the slabs these are **Runner Wall** (38 m, VS) and **Forget-me-Not** (65 m, VS, 1963). There exact lines are rather vague and have been superseded by the following routes which take the best and most direct routes up this area.

⋆ **Dead Loss Angeles**   37 m   E2   ✓⁷   1979
Climbs the wall left of the chimney directly between two moss streaks.
Serious and scary. Start about 5 metres left of White Ghyll Chimney.
    (5b). Climb up to a break and follow a slight groove to a spike.
Cross a slight bulge and gain a ledge on White Ghyll Traverse.
Climb up to another ledge and make some hard moves up to a
good ledge at the top.

Dead Loss G.G.   40 m   E1   1980
The wall between The Slabs, Route 1 and Dead Loss Angeles. Start
below a thin crackline which sprouts from the right-hand side of an
overhang about 13 metres up.
    (5b). Gain this crack and climb it to a good spike belay just right
of pitch 2 of Route 1. Step right and climb another thin crack,
trending right to finish at the same point as Dead Loss Angeles.

⋆⋆ **The Slabs, Route 1**   69 m   S   ✓   1930
A really enjoyable excursion which has some interesting moves. Start
at the lowest point of the slabs.
1   13 m. A steady pitch following rough rock to a ledge with a belay
    at its left end.
2   15 m. Make a rising traverse across the wall on the left to a small
    ledge. The steep groove above leads to a step right onto a small
    stance and satisfying spike belay.
3   17 m. Ascend the wall 3 metres left of the belay rather awkwardly,
    and continue to the middle of three grooves. Follow this initially,
    then another which leads rightwards to the terrace which runs out
    of White Ghyll Chimney.
4   24 m. Follow the steep rib, slightly right of the belay to the top.

⋆ **The Slabs, Route 2**   36 m   S   ✓   1933
Start at the left end of the slabs, below the bounding ridge.
1   11 m. Climb a steep crack, just to the right, to a stance on Route 1.
2   14 m. Traverse left and use a good hold to pull onto the slab
    above. Climb diagonally right and ascend a crack running
    diagonally to the left. The ridge on the left leads to a stance and
    belay.
3   11 m. Follow the ridge right of a grassy scoop and then easier
    ground to the top.

Variation Start   25 m   S   1947
Start at the foot of an open chimney on the immediate left of the slabs.
    Climb the chimney until it is possible to step onto the slab on the
left. Traverse right along ledges and a delicate slab to a junction
with the parent climb, and continue up the diagonal crack of pitch
2.

White Ghyll Traverse   230 m   VS   1946

A good expedition, suitable for a quiet day. The standard is reasonably sustained and the central section quite exposed. Start at the foot of Hollin Groove.

1   33 m (4a). Pitch 1 of Hollin Groove.
2   24 m (4a). Pitch 2 of Hollin Groove, to the Great Shelf.
3   15 m. Scramble up to a block belay above the first steep section of Easy Rake.
4   22 m. Take the line of least resistance to the block belay at the foot of pitch 2 of White Ghyll Wall.
5   34 m (4b). Climb White Ghyll Wall to the ledge below the final easy section.
6   13 m (4a). Climb diagonally down to the left to the top of pitch 2 of The Gordian Knot.
7   15 m (4c). Reverse The Gordian Knot (crux) to the stance in the recess.
8   14 m (4b). Traverse left across the top of an undercut groove and gain a slab which is climbed to its top left-hand corner.
9   8 m. Continue traversing easily to a block belay just right of the chimney.
10 27 m (4c). More traversing, this time a little more difficult, firstly ascending to a shattered ledge, then descending delicately to the arête. Better holds then lead left to a spike belay.
11 14 m (4a). Traverse left to belay on The Slabs, Route 2.
12 11 m (4a). The final pitch of The Slabs, Route 2.

Variation Girdle Traverse   129 m   E1   1966

Another satisfying girdle with some exposed situations. The reversal of part of Eliminot on pitch 2 demands steadiness on the part of the last man. Start as for Hitcher.

1   27 m (4a). Pitch 1 of Hitcher, then traverse easily left to the belay below pitch 2 of White Ghyll Wall.
2   31 m (5a). Pull over the initial bulge as for White Ghyll Wall, then traverse the long, sandwiched slab on the left. Where the slab disappears, it is necessary to descend the lower overhang (part of pitch 2 of Eliminot) to gain the traverse of Perhaps Not. Follow this to the stance below the chimney.
3   15 m (4c). Step down and make an awkward traverse into The Gordian Knot. Ascend the corner and belay at the end of the Haste Not traverse.
4   17 m (4c). Reverse the traverse of Haste Not and continue into White Ghyll Chimney.
5   39 m (4a). Finish up White Ghyll Chimney.

Swine Knott   (297 070)   Alt. 330m   South and East Facing

This is the steep but rather small and vegetated outcrop which lies below and on the opposite side of the Ghyll to White Ghyll Crag. It has a number of vegetated rakes which run across it which attract more crag fast sheep than climbers.

The routes are described from left to right.

Swine Knott Chimney   33 m   VS   1958
Starts at the foot of the obvious chimney near the left side of the crag.
1   18 m. Ascend broken rock to the terrace, then climb the wall right of the chimney, gain a ledge and step left into the bottom of the chimney. Climb it to a good tree belay.
2   15 m. Climb the overhang behind the tree and follow an open groove to the top.

Slanting Grooves   37 m   S   1958
Start on a terrace, at the foot of a thin crack which slants to the right, about 6 metres right of the chimney.
1   18 m. Climb direct for 5 metres and then traverse left to a stance and flake belay.
2   19 m. Step right and move up to the foot of the right slanting crack. Follow this to a perched block, then traverse left to a short corner which leads to the top.

Porkers' Parade   42 m   MVS   1948
A worthwhile route, the main pitch is long and protection rather poor. Starts at the lowest point of the crag beneath a big blunt arête at the right-hand end.
    (4b). Climb up right to a ledge with a yew tree. Straight up above the ledge for a couple of metres then traverse left, round a bulging corner onto the front of the arête, which is followed on sloping holds to the top.

Variation   Swine Knott Buttress   VS   1958
Claimed as a separate route but with only a slight variation from Porkers' Parade.
    From the ledge with a yew tree traverse left around the corner then straight up just left of the arête to join the original route.

The Girdle Traverse   63 m   VS   1958
Start from a sloping rock ledge at the left end of the crag.
1   20 m. Traverse right below the large triangular overhangs to a terrace below a chimney. Climb the corner on the left and step

right to a ledge in the chimney, and climb it to a tree at its top.
2   28 m. Step up and traverse right then down to the tree belay on
    Swine Knott Chimney. Traverse right, round a corner and along
    small ledges to a crack (on Slanting Grooves). Traverse right to
    a small sloping ledge on the arête. Step down and round the corner
    over an open groove to a sloping ledge. Belay on the right.
3   15 m. Up, traverse a sloping ledge right then down and traverse
    right past a good hold to a small ledge on the arête. Climb this to
    the top.

Stickle Barn Crag   (294 069)   Alt. 210 m   South Facing

A small outcrop of good quality, clean and fast drying rock. This crag
has been climbed on for many years by local climbers and outdoor
centres. It lies directly up the ridge behind the New Dungeon Ghyll
Hotel. Approach by following the path to White Ghyll Crag but after
passing through the gate to contour the hillside strike directly up the
fell to the crag. The best routes lie on the Main Wall which is in fact
a huge flake with a deep chimney on each side.

A very brief description of the main lines is included. Numerous other
routes/variations are possible and have been climbed.

The routes are described from left to right.

Left Wall   12 m   VD
    Climb the wall 3 metres left of Left Chimney on good holds.

Heather Groove   12 m   S
    The heather choked groove starting just left of the chimney.

The Pillar   12 m   E2
    A protectionless eliminate up the slim pillar starting at the foot of
    Left Chimney.

Left Chimney   10 m   S
    The deep flared chimney up the left side of the Main Wall.

Main Wall Left-Hand   12 m   HVS
    Straight up the left side of the wall past a prominent spike ledge.

Main Wall Rib   12 m   VS
    Follow the slight rib near the left side of the wall.

Main Wall Crack   12 m   VS
  Direct up the centre of the wall using a thin crack at half height.

Main Wall Scoop   12 m   S
  The right-hand side of the wall is followed past a scoop at one third height.

Right-Hand Chimney   12 m   VD
  The stepped chimney at the right-hand side of the Main Wall.

Numerous opportunities exist for short routes and boulder problems on the small face below and left of the crag; on the large boulder to the right of the top of the crag and 30 metres up and left from the stone wall above the crag.

Millbeck Crag   (294 070)   Alt. 300 m   West South West Facing

A small crag which can be identified by a prominent nose at the top, and by the dark slab which leads up to the final steep headwall. A sunny situation and a lack of climbers might attract a few jaded cragsmen. The best approach is by following the White Ghyll path to where it splits to the right out of the walled lane. Continue straight up and onto the open fell. The crag can be seen up to the right. The approach is steep as well as being unpleasantly bracken-infested in summer.

The routes are described from left to right. Descend to the left.

A small oak tree growing out of the top left-hand side of the crag provides a useful landmark.

Zebedee   15 m   HS   1981
A direct line beneath the oak.
  Scramble up to a distinct groove at 6 metres. Step left at its end and follow another shallow groove to the top.

Sweep   25 m   HS   1981
Start 3 metres right of Zebedee.
  Ascend small slabs and overlaps for 9 metres and follow the smooth slab which leads into a shallow chimney behind the tree, exiting right to finish.

Sooty   30 m   VS   1981
Start a couple of metres right of Sweep at a groove system beneath the tree.
   (4c). Climb the groove and ensuing slab, stepping right to a tree. Climb the broken chimney right of the tree and the easy slabs above.

Andy Pandy   33 m   E2   1981
Start 6 metres up to the left from the lowest point of the slabs, beneath thin left to right slanting fault lines.
   (5c). Follow the fault to the top of some small ledges. Step up right and then go straight up to a small groove above the overhang. Up the groove to a ledge and climb the blank looking wall above direct. Finish up slabs to a belay.

Bill   33 m   E1   1981
Quite a good route, which finishes up the groove on the left of the prominent nose. Start at the lowest point of the slabs.
   (5b). Climb to a flat topped spike at 12 metres. Move up right to a shallow scoop, then straight up to beneath the nose and finish up the corner groove immediately to its left.

★ **Ben**   32 m   E1   1981
An interesting route with a good top section taking the line right of the nose. Start 5 metres right of Bill.
   (5b). Climb a short corner to reach a ledge level with the flat topped spike on Bill. Trend up and right to a flat topped projection and move up again to a junction with Bill under the nose. Finish up the striking corners on the right, moving rightwards round two bulges.

Variation Finish   10 m   E2 (1 pt. aid)   1981
Climbs direct over the nose.
   (5c). From beneath the last overhang on Ben move left under the nose, gain the long sling hanging from a peg and pull over to the top.

Old Man's Crack   19 m   HVS   1981
Start 5 metres right of Ben.
   (5a). Pleasant slabs lead to a good, but short jamming crack and the top.

The Girdle Traverse   39 m   HVS   1981
A line beneath the band of overhangs.

1   15 m. Any line to gain the oak tree on the left of the crag.
2   18 m (4c). Traverse beneath the overhangs to the tree below the crack of Old Man's Crack.
3   6 m (5a). Finish up the crack. The original route continued to traverse, but offered a poor finish compared with the one described.

Tarn Crag   (290 074)   Alt. 460 m   South Facing

Of similar interest to Scout Crag, Tarn Crag offers some easy climbs on clean solid rock suitable for training purposes, or as an aperitif to the more serious fare on the larger crags.

Situated on the immediate right of Stickle Ghyll about 60 metres below the level of Stickle Tarn, it is best reached by following the path up the true left side of the Ghyll, until a winding track leads off right to the foot of the crag.

A broad buttress on which the first four routes lie, is separated from the well-defined ridge on the right-hand side of the crag by a grassy amphitheatre. A tongue of vegetated rock topped by a conspicuous oak, runs up the middle of the amphitheatre to join the steeper rocks above; here lies Blandish. None of the routes are continuously steep and the sense of exposure is usually slight. Numerous other lines of similar grades exist for the adventurous to investigate.

The routes are described from left to right, descent can be made around either end of the crag.

West Buttress   38 m   D   1949
Start below the first steep wall, marked by a holly tree high on the left.
1   15 m. Climb the wall, passing just right of the holly to a ledge and up the short groove above to another ledge.
2   23 m. Traverse left for 3 metres to a rib, which is climbed for 10 metres when easy rocks lead to the top.

★ **Route 2**   38 m   D   1948
Starts at the lowest point of the buttress 6 metres right of West Buttress.
1   20 m. Steep rocks lead to a narrow ledge, step left and climb straight up on good holds to a ledge.
2   18 m. Broken rocks lead to the top.

Heather Slab   40 m   VD   1949
A smooth triangular slab lies just inside the right-hand rib of the buttress, 7 metres right of Route 2. Start below this.

1   22 m. Climb the slab and groove exiting left to a recess. Traverse
     4 metres up and left and climb a steep easy corner to a sloping
     ledge.
2   18 m. The groove on the right leads to an easy arête which is
     followed until broken rocks lead rightwards to the top.

Orchid 86 m MS   1949
A wandering route which starts below a steep crack 2 metres right of
Heather Slab.
1   16 m. Climb the crack to a ledge on the rib.
2   21 m. Up the shallow chimney ahead, past a small pinnacle, pull
     out to the left and up to a ledge.
3   15 m. Traverse easily rightwards passing a rowan in a corner and
     continue to the left end of a ledge. A short ascent leads to the
     foot of a groove.
4   10 m. Climb the groove, awkward at the top, then step right and
     continue to a ledge below a slab.
5   24 m. Up the left edge of the slab and finish up easy rock.

Blandish 54 m VD   1949
A poor, broken vegetated route. It starts behind the oak tree high up
the vegetated rock which runs up the middle of the amphitheatre,
reached by easy scrambling.
1   6 m. Climb the wall behind the tree to a ledge.
2   21 m. The steep rib above is climbed, using a thin crack on its
     left, until a traverse right leads to a corner.
3   27 m. A short wall is ascended to a ledge, then a steep groove is
     followed by easier rocks leading to the top.

Rib and Wall 38 m D   1949
Start at a subsidiary rib 3 metres left of the right-bounding ridge of
the grassy amphitheatre.
1   22 m. Straight up the rib to a ledge, belay below the wall above.
2   16 m. Climb the wall to a small ledge, traverse left to an awkward
     finish up a short steep groove.

★ **Route 1** 33 m D   1921
A well marked route up the right-bounding ridge of the grassy
amphitheatre. Start just left of the foot of the ridge.
1   15 m. A short ascent and traverse right to the nose are followed
     by easy climbing to a good stance.
2   18 m. Finish up broken rocks.

Pavey Ark (285 079)   Alt. 570 m   South East and East Facing

From the Stickle Barn, Pavey Ark is approached by ascending Stickle
Ghyll. Recent conservation work to alleviate erosion problems has
resulted in a fine new path being created for two-thirds of the climb
to Stickle Tarn. The path, which starts behind the car park beside the
Stickle Barn is obvious and well sign posted. On reaching Stickle
Tarn, the crag appears in full view. From here the drier and shorter
route is on the left of the tarn and afterwards well worn tracks lead
up the scree to the foot of the crag.

The crag in general faces south-east and enjoys rather more sun and
more varied vegetation than most of the major Lakeland crags. It is
the largest cliff in Langdale and has a fine situation above Stickle Tarn
with an outlook over the lower reaches of Langdale towards the north
end of Windermere and beyond.

It is split by gullies and ledges into several distinct buttresses. Those
to the left of Great Gully, the second and more deeply-cut gully from
the left, are very vegetated, broken and unsuitable for good climbing.
Stony Buttress comes next between Great Gully and the shallow
dirt-filled Crescent Gully, the right rib of which marks the line of
ascent of Crescent Climb. Right of Crescent Gully is the lower central
area of the crag. It is undercut at its base, with a low band of slabby
rock below its right-hand half, known as the Barrier. The left side of
this area is a sweep of smooth mossy slabs, steepening as one moves
rightwards. Towards the right-hand side is the right slanting corner of
Deception, with the impressive hanging blunt rib of Cruel Sister to
its left. Further right the rock becomes more broken and vegetated,
and easier angled.

Above and right of the lower central area, slanting down from high
on the western end of the crag to the scree at the foot of East Gully,
is a series of wide grass and scree covered ledges and short rocky
scrambles; this is Jack's Rake. The popularity of the ascent of the
Rake causes many rocks and pebbles to be knocked over the lower
crag, a point to beware of when climbing in this area.

Above Jack's Rake, the crag, bounded on the left by the upper
reaches of Great Gully, and on the right by the well defined Rake
End Chimney, is covered with much vegetation. Despite this there
are many rock walls and buttresses, which rise out from the
surrounding heather and bilberries to provide remarkably clean and
attractive pitches on very rough bubbly rock, of which Cook's Tour,
Golden Slipper and Aardvark are good examples. Beyond Rake End

Chimney, the East Buttress forms a large area of steep rock. The structure is one of smooth slabs and bulges, though still with a fair amount of vegetation and moss about. The rock is generally of good quality, and the popular routes themselves quite clean.

The right-hand end of the East Buttress bends round and becomes the East Wall, in effect a gully wall, but with the opposite side so low as to be almost non-existent. The crag here is impressively steep and of excellent rock, and standing as it does above an area of steep vegetated slabs gives one the impression that the routes are bigger and more exposed than their lengths would suggest. Several of these climbs are amongst the best in Langdale, if not the Lake District. Unfortunately for many they are also in the higher grades.

Many routes lead only to Jack's Rake which serves as an easy means of descent. From the summit a descent can be made round either extremity. It is more usual however, for parties on the East Buttress and to its left, to reverse the easy upper section of Great Gully to Jack's Rake, then down the latter. The more adventurous may decide to locate and descend either Gwynne's or Rake End Chimneys, though care is needed to avoid dislodging scree onto parties below whichever descent is chosen.

For routes on the East Wall, the most convenient way off is to descend the scree-filled East Gully. Once again, care is needed to avoid dislodging loose rock.

For ease of identification, the climbs have been divided into three sections; those below Jack's Rake, those above and on the East Buttress, and finally those on the East Wall. All are described from left to right.

Climbs below Jack's Rake.

★ **Little Gully**   106 m   M   1886
This is the most westerly gully. Start by scrambling up the gully to the fork at about 60 metres. The difficulties, such as they are, commence 16 metres up the right-hand branch.
    Climb the gully; excursions on to each wall in turn being necessary at various points.

★ **Great Gully**   100 m   D   1882
This is the right and longer one of the two deeply-marked gullies towards the western end of the crag and give one of the few good gully climbs in the district.
1   45 m. Follow easy rocks for 12 metres and then scramble to a cave beneath a large chockstone.

2   10 m. Climb the wall on the right.
3   18 m. Scramble up to a cave and climb through or over it.
4   20 m. Climb the pleasant slab.
5   7 m. Take either a very difficult scoop on the left, an easy through route, or an easy grass exit on the right. These all lead to Jack's Rake, which can be followed up or down, or the grassy gully on the right can be taken to the summit.

Stony Buttress   110 m   S   1920

The climb lies on the buttress to the right of Great Gully. A disappointing and serious climb, with some loose rock. Start by scrambling up heather for 18 metres to a ledge on the edge of Great Gully.

1   12 m. Climb diagonally to the right.
2   15 m. Continue upwards to the right until, after rounding a corner and taking a step up, a ledge is reached with a belay on the right.
3   13 m. Climb the obvious steep groove (poor rock) and break out on to steep grass ledges on the left.
4   20 m. Step right and then work back leftwards through the bilberries.
5   30 m. Follow pastures to a corner.
6   20 m. Climb onto the ledge on the right. Go up the steep little ridge to another large ledge and continue up another ridge to join Jack's Rake.

Sinistral   36 m   E1   1971

A less worthy companion to The Hobbit. Start as for The Hobbit.

(5a). Move up the rib, as for The Hobbit, to the obvious horizontal break under the first overhang. Follow this break left for 8 metres, to the foot of a short overhanging corner. Climb this and move left to a tiny ledge. Climb cracks to an overhang and traverse left to a ledge on Stony Buttress. Finish up this.

The Hobbit   58 m   E2   1969

A steep and serious climb with both dubious rock and protection, which takes an impressive line around the overhangs on the front of Stony Buttress. Start about 15 metres up the gully to the right of Stony Buttress, on the left bounding rib of the obvious wet black groove.

1   36 m (5b). Move onto the rib just above some juniper bushes, and climb this until level with the lower overhang. Move right, and climb up for 5 metres past a wedged flake. Gain the ledge on the left with difficulty; then traverse horizontally left for 3 metres until a steep crack is reached. Climb the crack to a ledge with a juniper. Move right, and climb the groove, bearing left to spike belays.
2   22 m. Climb the vegetated rocks to finish.

The Ragman's Trumpet   86 m   E2   1971
A serious route up the impressive crack in the right wall of Stony
Buttress. The wall is steep and the climbing strenuous and sustained.
Start about 15 metres up the gully right of Stony Buttress above the
start of The Hobbit, just below a tiny cave.
1   30 m (5b). Go up and across the wall on the left to gain the crack,
     just above the black groove. Follow the crack, first directly
     upwards, and then to the right as it slants across the wall, to gain
     the ledge at the top. The pull-out is best made on the right.
2   56 m. Climb the much easier ground above, or finish up Sally Free
     and Easy.

Variation   Original Start   18 m   HVS   1971
     (5a). A direct start is available up the black groove directly below
     the crack, but this is usually wet.

Sally Free and Easy   80 m   E2   1971
This is really Crescent Gully Direct, but it can be conveniently linked
with The Ragman's Trumpet, and is described that way. A serious
climb with some loose rock and poor protection.
1   30 m (5b). Pitch 1 of The Ragman's Trumpet.
2   10 m (5a). Make an awkward rising traverse to the right into the
     big corner. Peg belays.
3   40 m (5c). Follow the corner on poor rock to a niche below the
     final overhanging crack. Climb this for a couple of metres and exit
     left with difficulty onto a ledge. Ascend easily to a spike belay on
     Jack's Rake.

★ **Crescent Climb**   100 m   M   1907
The broken arête to the right of Crescent Gully, leads to an exposed
traverse across the top of Crescent Slabs. The lower section is quite
loose and requires care. Start at the foot of the gully.
1   55 m. Follow the arête to a ledge with a flake above, at the left
     end of the Crescent. Stances and doubtful belays *en route*.
2   15 m. Make a pleasant traverse to the right on large holds under
     the overhang.
3   30 m. Go up grassy slabs to join Jack's Rake.

Crescent Wall   60 m   S   1924
A rather indefinite route with a poor start but better finish on the
steep mossy slabs to the right of the first section of Crescent Climb.
Start 20 metres to the right of Crescent Climb, at the bottom of a
broken, left slanting rake.
1   10 m. Go diagonally left up the rake to a ledge.

2   30 m. Climb the steep rocks above, moving left or right, as
    difficulty indicates, until a grassy traverse leads across to a large
    sloping ledge on the right.
3   20 m. Climb the corner; then continue straight up clean slabs to
    the Crescent.

★ Black Slab   60 m   VS   1988
An enjoyable pitch following the obvious black streak up the centre
of the slabs. Start just right of Crescent Wall below the black streak.
1   24 m (5a). Climb direct up the steep pocketed slab. Belay up to
    the left below a short mossy slab. (Good nut 3 metres higher.)
2   36 m. Scramble up to the right for 12 metres to a grass ledge below
    an overhang. Pull round to its right and climb the black streaked
    slab to the right end of the Crescent.

★★ Crescent Slabs   60 m   S   1920
This very good climb follows a line roughly parallel to Crescent Wall
up the clean open slabs on the right of the moss. Start at a weakness
at the right end of the slabs; a black groove just right of some bulging
overhangs.
1   12 m. Follow a rising gangway to the left. This is usually wet.
2   12 m. Traverse obliquely right into a shallow groove. Ascend this
    for a couple of metres before working left over easier slabs to a
    spike belay.
    Alternatively, and more easily, traverse horizontally left and climb
    a slab on the left of the second small holly.
3   18 m. Go up steep slabs to a ledge and step right below a block.
    Make a difficult move up from the block into a small scoop, then,
    after a couple of metres, move left to a small ledge.
    Alternatively a rising traverse starts a couple of metres left and
    leads back rightwards to the same shelf; this is not easy either.
4   18 m. Pleasant slabs are climbed to belay at the right end of the
    Crescent traverse.

The following three routes ascend the buttress above the Crescent.
They all start from the traverse of Crescent Climb, which is easily
reached by descending from Jack's Rake or by first climbing one of
the routes up the slabs.

Crescent Superdirect   30 m   E3   †   1988
Excellent climbing up the centre of the buttress. Belay 6 metres left
of the right-hand end of the traverse. The route starts 3 metres further
left.

(5c). Pull onto the wall, move right then climb up just left of a down pointing flake until a difficult move over an overlap gives access to a square foot ledge on the lip. Continue steeply up the wall above until a slab leads to a ledge. The slab on the right leads to Jack's Rake.

Half Moon   30 m   E1   †   1988
A steep dynamic start gives access to an enjoyable curving slab that flanks the right-hand side of the buttress. Start beneath a prominent flat topped hold, 3 metres left of the right-hand end of the Crescent.
    (5c). Using a high layback hold, pull up to better holds which lead steeply up the slab above, to its right-hand end. Climb the bulging rock above to some blocks, continue up the steep wall and finishing groove to Jack's Rake.

★ **Crescent Direct**   26 m   VS   1969
The shallow groove up the right side of the buttress above the Crescent. Start from the good flake at the right end of the traverse of Crescent Climb.
1   18 m (4c). Make some awkward moves up into the groove and climb it for about 12 metres, when it is possible to traverse horizontally left onto a grass ledge on the front of the buttress.
2   8 m (4b). Climb the steep slabs starting from the left.

Alph   83 m   VS   1948
Right of Wailing Wall, the cliff steepens a little and becomes less grassy. The route avoids the main steepness by a long upward traverse to the right; then it breaks back to easier and grassier ground. A wandering sort of climb, but pleasant and open and, except for the start, without gymnastics. Start 6 metres to the left of Wailing Wall.
1   10 m (4b). Ascend the Barrier and then the overhang, where it is broken by a shallow depression (3 metres left of Wailing Wall). Traverse right to the stance at the top of pitch 1, Wailing Wall.
2   24 m (4b). Make a rising traverse to the right on rather sloping holds, to reach a small ledge with a holly.
3   20 m (4c). Step down to the left and make an awkward move out onto the left wall. Traverse delicately left for a couple of metres to a shallow groove, which is ascended to a small juniper ledge. Traverse left again to a ledge, then go up to another ledge. Climb the rib at the left end of the ledge for about 3 metres, when a horizontal traverse can be made back to the right to a good ledge.
4   29 m (4a). Traverse right for a couple of metres, then climb towards Jack's Rake via short walls and grooves, alternating with grass ledges.

Variation   Direct Start   12 m   HVS   1972

A good pitch, which is surprisingly difficult. Start below a smooth looking groove 3 metres right of the start of Wailing Wall. It is the last obvious break through the slabby Barrier on this side of the crag.

1a   (5b). Climb the groove.

Variation   30 m   VS   1971

2a   (4c). Steeper and more direct than the original pitch. Go up left for a couple of metres, as for Wailing Wall, then climb directly up, via a 'pocketed' wall, to the right end of a sloping ledge. Traverse right to reach a shallow crack line, and climb it to a small ledge. Step right to a junction with Alph, then go up left to a large ledge. Climb up again at the left end and go back to the right to the top of pitch 3 of Alph.

Wailing Wall   52 m   MVS   1939

Beyond Crescent Slabs the main, or central, buttress assumes the steepness of a wall, characterised by an obvious stratum of smooth slabby rock, the Barrier, at its foot. An obvious corner running up the left side of this steeper section marks the line. On the whole the climb is undistinguished and, though interesting in parts, is grassy and often wet. Start 12 metres to the right of Crescent Slabs below an undercut groove.

1   8 m (4c). Climb the Barrier (very low here) and then the awkward groove to a small stance.

2   12 m (4a). Traverse right into a groove and continue to a gangway running up to the left. Follow this to its left end, when a stride is made to a ledge with a large flake belay.

3   18 m (4b). Go up the corner on the right, past a smooth section, to a small stance.
     (The original line avoided the corner proper, above the smooth section, with an exposed excursion on the right wall.)

4   14 m (4b). Start just to the right of the corner, where two awkward steps bring better holds within reach. Continue up short steep walls to a ledge at about 9 metres and then traverse left into a corner. Jack's Rake can be reached by about 30 metres of scrambling.

★★ Arcturus   82 m   HVS   ✓   1962

This route, which gives fine open climbing in excellent situations takes the steep two-tier wall to the left of the big slabby corner of Deception. Start 20 metres right of Wailing Wall, near the foot of Deception and runs left up slabs, crosses the midway overhangs near its left end then makes an exhilarating traverse back right to finish.

1   35 m (5b). Climb the smooth slabby Barrier to the foot of the
    groove of Deception. Ascend the wall on the left, which guards
    access to the slab, and after about 4 metres step left to a large
    foothold. Move delicately up the slab, bearing left past a peg
    runner, to a tiny ledge, invisible from below. Avoid the smooth
    section immediately above by working left into a thin crack, which
    leads to a shallow niche and a stance on Alph at a holly, just
    above.

2   20 m (5a). Pull over the small overlap on the right and climb a
    shallow groove to a small ledge. Step back into the line of the
    groove and climb the thin crack to a narrow ledge, with a large
    ledge a little higher.

3   27 m (5a). Follow a narrow ledge along to the right beneath the
    overlap; continue the traverse across a delicate little slab
    (exposed) to a ledge. Step down and go to the right end of the
    large ledge below, where a rib leads to easier ground and a belay.
    Scramble up to Jack's Rake.

★★ Big Brother   72 m   E3   1977
An excellent though serious pitch up the wall right of Arcturus. Start
as for Arcturus.

1   30 m (5b). Pitch 1 of Cruel Sister.

2   28 m (5c). Traverse left, pull over the overhang at a thin crack
    and follow this to where it fades. Move left at a thin horizontal
    crack, then up rightwards to good holds at the base of a short
    corner. Climb this and continue in the same line to join the
    Arcturus traverse on pitch 3 which leads to a ledge.

3   14 m (5a). Finish up either Arcturus or Cruel Sister.

★★★ Cruel Sister   70 m   E3   1972
This brilliant climb, follows the superb undercut rib forming the
right-hand side of the upper Arcturus wall. Protection is adequate and
the difficulties are at the lower limit of the grade. Start as for
Arcturus.

1   30 m (5b). Follow Arcturus to a small ledge above the peg runner
    and move up rightwards to a good ledge below the obvious shallow
    groove. Climb this to the ledge under the overhang and traverse
    right to belay.

2   25 m (5c). Pull directly over the overhang and move up to a peg
    runner. Step up, traverse right to a block on the edge, and then
    go up to a good foothold. Climb the wall trending slightly left to
    a small overlap. Surmount this and gain a steep crack-line which
    leads to the good ledge at the end of the Arcturus traverse. A
    magnificent pitch.

3   15 m (5a). Move left, and crossing Arcturus; pull over the overlap on widely spaced holds. Step left and climb the obvious corner to grass ledges. Move right and back left onto the second ledge for belays.

Deception   55 m   S   1939
The route follows the grassy corner on the right of the central wall. Vegetated and often wet or greasy but with some interesting moves. Start below the Barrier, a little right of the corner.
1   6 m. Climb the Barrier to the ledge below the overhang; then walk left along the ledge to the foot of the groove.
2   35 m. Climb the groove to a good spike and step right to grassy rocks, which are ascended to a ledge in the corner. Work diagonally right over grass ledges, then go straight up to a large ledge at the foot of a slab.
3   14 m. Climb the slab at its left corner and make a delicate traverse right to a good ledge, with a good thread belay in the niche above on the left. Jack's Rake is a few metres higher on the right.

Variation Start   36 m   S   1959
A drier alternative to the usual start. Start about 10 metres right of the normal starts, where a block leans against the face of the right-hand end of the lower overhangs.
1a Follow an obvious curving line up to the belay below the final pitch.

Maggie's Farm   32 m   E3   1983
Climbs the steep wall overlooking the corner of Deception, and is unfortunately rather dirty. Start from ledges halfway up pitch 2 of Deception, level with the overhangs on Cruel Sister.
    (5c). Climb slanting cracks to gain a good ledge, from its left end pull up to another ledge. Continue straight up past a prominent spike, then the short crack on the left and more easily to a good ledge. Scramble up to Jack's Rake.

★ **The Rainmaker**   32 m   E1   1965
Except for the start which is quite awkward this route gives a fine steep pitch on splendid holds up the wall above and left of Deception. Start from the top of pitch 2 of Deception.
    (5b). Go up to the left and gain a tiny undercut glacis at the foot of the corner. Follow a small subsidiary corner on the left to a small ledge and step across to a small pinnacle on the right. Continue, more easily now, to easy ground at the top of Arcturus.

Obscured by Clouds   30 m   E4   1977

This is a steep poorly protected pitch, which takes the shallow groove
and crack in the wall right of The Rainmaker. Start at the top of pitch
2 of Deception.

(6a). Climb the obvious steep, shallow groove and pull over the
bulge with difficulty. Follow the crack above to a grass terrace.
Step immediately left, around the rib, at a loose block, and
continue up the short corner and wall above to the top.

Climbs above Jack's Rake

The following routes are above and to the right of Jack's Rake. They
can provide an excellent continuation for routes on the lower tier.
The first route starts high up at the western end of the Rake, above
and to the left of the Crescent.

Little Corner   36 m   HVS   1970

The fine long right facing corner, with a steep left wall, is
unfortunately very vegetated. Start at the foot of the steep slab below
the corner.

(5a). Go up the slab to the right one of twin grooves forming the
corner. Climb this for about 8 metres, then transfer to the left
one, which is followed until a good flake-crack on the left wall
leads to a pinnacle, and an opportunity to swing out of the corner
on to the left-hand rib. Climb up a further 6 metres to finish.

Book of Reasons   66 m   E3   1986

Ascends the wall and groove left of Roundabout Direct and gives
good climbing but is very poorly protected on the crux section. Start
3 metres right of Little Corner at a hollow sounding embedded flake.

1   10 m (4c). Climb the flake and continue rightwards up more
    flakes, onto a rib. Up this for a couple of metres and step right
    to belay in a grassy corner.
2   40 m (5c). Step back left and climb the rib to a wall with a thin
    hairline crack below a groove. Climb the wall to gain the groove
    (crux). Pull out of the groove and continue directly up the slab to
    an overhang. Pull left through this, then step back right above and
    climb the final groove to the top.
3   16 m (4c). Climb the pleasant wall on the left, just left of the arête.
    Scrambling remains.

Roundabout   52 m   S   1958

This, as its name implies, is a somewhat indirect route which almost
becomes submerged in heather towards the middle section, but later,
a delightful little airy rib gives it definition. Start 6 metres right of

Little Corner, directly below a thin leftward facing corner crack, about 18 metres up.

1   12 m. Go up and follow a slabby scoop to a large juniper below the crack.

2   14 m. Move up to the foot of the crack and traverse across the foot of the buttress on the right, on a grassy gangway. Climb a shallow square-cut chimney round the corner to a stance on the left.

3   26 m. Step off an embedded flake and climb up the left edge of the clean rib. Finish up a series of short steep walls and ledges.

★ Roundabout Direct   72 m   VS   1966

A fine strenuous route which climbs the prominent corner crack above pitch 1 of Roundabout.

1   12 m. Pitch 1 of Roundabout.

2   36 m (4c). Climb the corner until, at about 12 metres, it is possible to step left onto easier angled slabs. Go up these to a niche beneath the overhangs and pull round to the right. Move up to a ledge and continue up a couple of short walls on the left to a belay.

3   24 m. Follow ledges and walls to the top.

Digitalis   72 m   HVS   1978

A rather poor route which climbs the more broken rock left of Golden Slipper. Start at the left end of the overhangs left of Golden Slipper.

1   24 m (5a). Climb the wall below an obvious mossy groove. Step onto a downward pointing fang of rock, then up the thin groove above to a good side hold; move up and right to a small slab, then up and right again, a cleaned slab leads to a ledge. Traverse right to belay on Golden Slipper.

2   24 m (5a). Climb the slabby wall above, just left of pitch 2 of Golden Slipper.

3   24 m (5a). Move right around the rib below an overhang then up to a ledge. Climb the thin crack on the right of the smooth corner to the top.

★★ Golden Slipper   60 m   HVS   ✓   1958

This excellent open climb, ascends the slim elegant pillar which is of perfect rock, left of the obvious dark Troll's Corner. Protection is sparse though adequate on the main pitch. Start 15 metres right of Roundabout at a gangway slanting right to a line of small overhangs at 6 metres. Gwynne's Chimney is some 18 metres to the right.

1   18 m (4b). Follow the gangway, easily, to the overhang and step right onto a grassy ledge. Climb directly up the steep wall above, to another ledge and belay at the foot of the long steepening slab.

2   24 m (4c). Climb directly up the slab on superbly rough rock until
     the slab becomes a wall. Traverse across to the rib on the right
     and ascend this to a large ledge.
3   18 m (4a). Traverse left and climb a rib to the top.

★★ Poker Face   82 m   E1   1966
An excellent route which gives steep and interesting climbing up the
slim groove in the rib which seperates Golden Slipper from Troll's
Corner.
1   36 m (4b). Go up easily to a ledge on the left. Climb the slabby
     corner, past a holly, to another ledge with a large block on the
     left. Continue straight up the gangway from the block and, after
     about 5 metres traverse left to the belay of Golden Slipper.
2   28 m (5b). Go up slabby rock to the right into a thin groove on
     the edge of the buttress. Climb the groove until the crack steepens
     considerably about 3 metres below the top, where it is possible to
     make a difficult move left onto Golden Slipper. Follow this to the
     large ledge. (It is possible to continue straight up the groove,
     though this is slightly more difficult.)
3   18 m (4a). Climb the rib on the left (as for Golden Slipper).

Troll's Corner   65 m   HVS   1959
The obvious dank corner, rising from the left side of a large grassy
bay on the left of Gwynne's Chimney. The corner itself overhangs, is
often damp, and the climbing is strenuous. Start just left of Gwynne's
Chimney.
1   35 m (4c). Move up, past a small ledge with a large rowan tree to
     the big bluebell ledge above on the left. Up the corner slabs to
     below a steep wall, 5 metres higher an awkward move gains an
     obvious traverse line. Follow this to a ledge in the corner.
2   15 m (5a). Climb directly up the impending corner and, where the
     left wall drops back at 8 metres, make an awkward pull onto a
     tiny slab. Move up easily to a stance.
3   15 m (4b). Climb the steep wall and finish up a slab.

Stalag   66 m   VS   1958
This route provides an escape route from Troll's Corner and gives
interesting climbing but without much direction. Start as for Troll's
Corner.
1   35 m (4c). Pitch 1 of Troll's Corner.
2   15 m (4b). Traverse the sharp-edged flake across the steep right
     wall until a pull up can be made to a comfortable niche. Continue
     along the traverse to a small ledge, when it is possible to go up a
     short wall and slab to a stance.

3   16 m (4b). Climb the steep little slab on the left to a small exposed
    ledge; continue over a small ledge to a pile of blocks. Swing round
    the rib on the left and follow it to the top.

★ **Gwynne's Chimney**   25 m   D   1892
A pleasant little chimney. Start from Jack's Rake 12 metres right of
the rowan at the end of The Crescent.
        Climb the chimney to the Gun. Continue up the chimney using a
    thin crack in the right wall or, more pleasantly, step right from
    the Gun to the arête, then up.
        Alternatively all this may be avoided by traversing right and up –
    easier and grassier.
        The climb can be extended by following the well scratched route
    via the steep crack in the buttress above or, by traversing 6 metres
    right, and finishing up the last two pitches of Cook's Tour.

★★ **Aardvark**   55 m   E1   1972
An excellent, exposed route up the steep arête right of Gwynne's
Chimney. Start 6 metres down to the right of Gwynne's Chimney on
a small quartz glacis.
1   33 m (5c). Climb straight up to a peg runner below a small
    overhang. Move left and up, with difficulty, to reach a sloping
    ledge. Make an awkward move up rightwards across a wall to a
    small spike on the arête. Follow the arête to a ledge and spike
    belay.
2   22m. Climb a short wall on the right to meet Cook's Tour. Move
    right again and climb the obvious crack to slabs and the top.

★ **Rectangular Slab**   60 m   VS   1960
An interesting climb that ascends the large right facing slab which is
set at right-angles to the cliff above Cook's Tour. Start at a steep
shallow rightward facing corner with a juniper at its base, 30 metres
right of Gwynne's Chimney and 15 metres left of Cook's Tour.
1   15 m (4c). Climb the wall left of the corner passing several loose
    spikes until an obvious projecting block is reached at the foot of
    two grooves. Ascend the left-hand one to the big terrace moving
    out on to the steep left wall for the last couple of metres. Walk
    round to the right to belay below the Rectangular Slab (junction
    with Cook's Tour).
2   35 m (4b). Climb the corner to a holly, then a delicate traverse
    across the slab leads to its left-hand arête. Follow the thin crack
    which slants up to the right, steepening towards the finish at a
    good ledge.

3   10 m (5a). Up an easy slab to a steep little crack in the right wall. Climb this with difficulty, stepping right at the top to a good ledge.

Father of Night   70 m   E2   1984
An eliminate climb based on Rectangular Slab. Start at the steep shallow corner as for Recangular Slab.
1   34 m (5a). Climb the corner direct then up the pleasant slabs rightwards to the foot of the Rectangular Slab.
2   26 m (5b). Follow a right slanting crack across the bottom of the slab from the left-hand corner, then direct up keeping just left of the corner to a good ledge at the top.
3   10 m (5c). Climb the steep thin crack in a groove directly above the ledge.

★ **Rectangular Rib**   38 m   HVS   1974
Pleasant climbing up the left edge of the Rectangular Slab. It can be reached by following pitch 1 of Rectangular Slab, or by a long, slightly descending traverse from the top of The Rib Pitch. Start below the left edge of the slab.
1   24 m (5a). Make some thin moves up to gain the slab. Follow the left edge direct to a ledge.
2   14 m (4c). Follow short walls and slabs to the top.

Cook's Tour   88 m   VD   1943
A wandering route but it has some pleasant pitches and good belays. Start at a short easy chimney-crack, leftward facing and opposite a large rowan tree at the top of the long steep section of Jack's Rake. This is the first easy break in the rocks right of Gwynne's Chimney.
1   16 m. The open groove leads to a pinnacle platform, continue up the steep slabby corner, moving round to the right onto the top of a flake pinnacle.
2   12 m. From the corner on the left easy climbing is followed by steep bracken leading to a flake-belay at the foot of an imposing slab.
3   22 m. Move up to a large grass ledge 8 metres away on the left, walk along it for 15 metres to a flake belay below an open grassy gully.
4   11 m. Climb the gully moving right to a grass ledge. Traverse to the right round the outside of a flake, then up to a pleasant grassy corner. Ash tree belay.
5   27 m. Ascend a crack to the top of the flake, then up left to a corner, continue up the steep slab to a good ledge. Finish up the wall above, first slightly right, then straight up.

Bracken Route   112 m   S   1942

Well named! It offers only a little rock and the best of this is shared with Cook's Tour, after which it wanders off rightwards. Start as for Cook's Tour.

1   28 m. The first two pitches of Cook's Tour.
2   26 m. Climb to the right of the big slab for 6 metres, then go up to a ledge on the right. Traverse the ledge to its right-hand end, when a 5 metres descent leads to a ledge.
3   9 m. Traverse the heather to below a corner.
4   18 m. Climb the corner for 9 metres and step right onto the arête. Go up this to a good stance, jammed quartz blocks provide a thread belay.
5   9 m. Make a rising traverse right to a large pinnacle.
6   22 m. Climb the steep face behind the belay as direct as possible. Finish up the easier ground above.

Chequer Buttress   63 m   HVS   1952

This route ascends the buttress flanking Rake End Chimney on its left. It is rather dirty and with some loose rock, but has a sound crux in a good position. Start at the foot of Rake End Chimney.

1   15 m. Go up and round to the left to a steep herbaceous groove, which is ascended to a small stance.
2   21 m (5a). Traverse across the bulging wall; then climb a steep, delicate little slab on the right edge overlooking the chimney and swing back left into a shallow corner. Continue directly up to a tiny ledge, then another with a tree on the left. Belay behind the tree in a cave.
3   27 m (4c). Climb the edge of the steep slab on the right to grassy scrambling, which leads to a narrow overhanging crack. Follow this until a pull out can be made to the right, step back left and climb up to the top.

Variation Finish   38 m   VS   1970

3a   (4b). Make a rising traverse out to the rib on the right, step round the corner and join The Rib Pitch just above its crux; follow it to the top.

The Rib   65 m   E1   1977

Gives some interesting climbing in fine situations, although it is rather close to Rake End Chimney in places. Start at the foot of Rake End Chimney.

1   15 m (5c). Scramble up then traverse horizontally left from the foot of the steep part of the chimney to just below a small niche. Step up and left, and climb up with difficulty, avoiding leftward possibilities, to a hollow flake and a small stance above on the left.

2   50 m (5a). Move back right (as for Chequer Buttress) and go up
to the arête. Follow the groove, overlooking the chimney, to a
difficult pull-out onto a slab. Climb this to the superb rib (The
Rib Pitch) and finish up this. It is possible to split the pitch at a
block about 6 metres below the top.

** **Rake End Chimney**   70 m   D   1898
An excellent climb, which ascends the deep green chimney and starts
at the foot of Jake's Rake, about 50 metres up from the foot of the
crag.
1   10 m. Go up easy steps to the chimney proper.
2   20 m. Climb the chimney past two ledges and over a chockstone.
3   20 m. Walk up the gully.
4   20 m. Climb up to and through the window and then go up the
right wall to a small cave. Pass this on the left to finish easily.

Directly in front is a short wall of about 14 metres containing two
cracks. The right-hand one provides an interesting pitch of about
Severe standard.

Death Star   66 m   E3   1978
A thin and very serious pitch up the right-hand rib of Rake End
Chimney. Start below the rib.
1   36 m (5c). Climb on the right-hand side of a black mossy streak
until moves right lead to a thin vertical crack. Climb this, pulling
out right at the top. Move back left and continue up the rib to a
stance below the upper section of Rake End Chimney.
2   30 m (5a). From a chockstone where the chimney starts again,
step left onto the wall and up until moves left across a slab lead
to a junction with The Rib Pitch, near its top. Finish up this.

*** **Rake End Wall**   63 m   VS   √   1945
A steep wall climb to the right of Rake End Chimney which gives
enjoyable and sustained climbing on excellent rock. It is unfortunately
marred by its junction with Rake End Chimney at the end of pitch 3.
Start 5 metres right of the chimney.
1   21 m (4b). Climb a rib, move left and up past a wedged flake and
go up an ill-defined crack until its steepening necessitates a move
round the corner to the right. Follow a diagonal crack to the huge
block below an overhanging corner, with a stance on the right.
2   10 m (4c). Climb the imposing crack in the corner to a ledge, with
a belay 3 metres higher.

3   20 m (4c). Step round to the left from the lower end of the ledge, onto a fine slab. Ascend directly to the right of a slight overhang and make an awkward move to the arête on the left, which leads to the large terrace below the final pitch of Rake End Chimney.

4   12 m (4a). Climb the left edge of the right-bounding wall of the chimney, with a detour to the right to avoid the steepest section.

★ By-Pass Route   52 m   HVS   1958

A series of variations on Rake End Wall. The first pitch climbs the big groove below the overhanging crack of Rake End Wall. Start from a narrow ledge below the groove, 6 metres right of Rake End Chimney.

1   20 m (4c). Go up a short, very smooth wall to reach the groove. Follow the groove until it becomes steep, when it is possible to make a long step to the rib on the left, which leads to the belay on Rake End Wall below the overhanging crack.

2   10 m (5a). Move round the bulge on the right and round the corner to a shallow and very steep scoop, which leads to a ledge and junction with Rake End Wall. An exposed pitch.

3   22 m (4c). Climb directly up the wall behind the ledge, then round the rib on the left into a steep groove. Continue up this groove to the terrace in Rake End Chimney. A cleaner way is to step down to the awkward move left to the arête of pitch 3 of Rake End Wall.

Variations

Alternative Start   27 m   HVS   1980

1a (5b). Climb the short smooth wall, then climb diagonally right to the belay at the end of pitch 2 of The Bracken-clock. Traverse left and climb directly up the wall to the belay at the top of pitch 1, below the overhanging crack.

Alternative Finish   30 m   HVS   1971

3a (5a). Go up for 9 metres to a bilberry filled groove. Climb the slightly overhanging groove in the middle of the wall on the left for 10 metres, then steep scrambling leads to a belay at the top of Rake End Chimney.

★ The Rib Pitch   36 m   HVS   1958

The right wall of Rake End Chimney drops back for 6 metres or so, forming a terrace. The left-hand rib remains, standing out boldly in isolation and giving a superb pitch, steep and exposed. An excellent finish to Rake End Wall or By-Pass Route. Start from the stance at the top of pitch 3 of Rake End Wall.

(5a). Make an upward traverse left to the rib, and climb it to the top.

★ Rock Around the Clock   60 m   E3   1985

A difficult, eliminate boulder problem up the slab left of pitch 2 of The Bracken-clock, leads to an excellent sustaiend pitch up the fine wall above. Start 2 metres left of The Bracken-clock.

1   18 m (5c). Climb direct up the slabby wall and traverse a ledge left to a flake below the left-hand side of the clean cut slab.

2   15 m (6a). Climb a short corner until holds lead left to a small ledge. Step right, make a committing move to a sloping hold, then better holds above to a good ledge, shared with The Bracken-clock.

3   20 m (5c). Move right a couple of metres and pull through the bulge at an obvious crack. Continue directly up the triangular wall, until a difficult pull left can be made, where it steepens, to gain a rib. Follow this more easily to belay on the ledge above.

4   7 m (5b). Climb the centre of the tiny slab on the right, passing an overlap at its right-hand side, just below the top. Finish as for The Bracken-clock.

★★ The Bracken-clock   102 m   E2   ✓   1970

Ascends the steep, smooth walls between By-Pass Route and Stoat's Crack, avoiding the main steepness by an open groove on the right. The climbing is clean and open and although lacking any definite line it is nevertheless very good. Start 10 metres left of the foot of the buttress below a shallow groove.

1   18 m (5a). Follow the shallow groove, past a difficult bulge to the right end of a ledge. Belay at the left end.

2   14 m (5c). Climb directly up the smooth slabs with difficulty, to reach a traverse line. Step left to belay.

3   20 m (5b). Traverse to the right for about 4 metres to a tiny platform on the edge of the smooth slabs. Climb directly above this platform, over an awkward bulge, then go up to the right into an open groove overlooking Stoat's Crack. Climb this to a ledge below a smooth little scoop.

4   24 m (4a). Go up the scoop (as for Stoat's Crack) and walk to the right end of the ledge above. Follow slabs and ledges, trending right to a ledge below the final pitch of Stoat's Crack.

5   26 m. Finish up the pleasant rib about 6 metres to the left.

★ Stickle Grooves   102 m   HVS   1956

A fairly strenuous route which takes the front of the impressive East Buttress direct, crossing Stoat's Crack low down and turning the midway overhangs on the right. Start up the smooth looking wall on the left of Stoat's Crack, a couple of metres left of a shallow V-groove in the toe of the buttress and 3 metres right of The Bracken-clock.

1   20 m (5a). Climb up to the right for 6 metres to below an overhang (or climb the V-groove direct to the same point). Go left for a couple of metres, past a flake, before climbing steeply up and back right above the overhang, crux, to gain a shallow slanting groove. Follow the groove to a good ledge (junction with Stoat's Crack).

2   16 m. Go up easily to the ledge above and make an ascending traverse right to a juniper ledge.

3   24 m (4c). Traverse across the wall on the left into the bottom of a smooth, rightward-slanting groove. Move up to the left, out of the groove, into a shallow scoop and follow it, past a small ledge, to a better one below the overhangs. Peg belay.

4   42 m (4c). Climb the little slab on the right and the overhanging chimney above (very exposed), to easier ground and another smaller chimney. Go up this and the easy slabs to the top.

Andromeda   94 m   HVS   1968

This route is really a variation start to Stickle Grooves, but gains some measure of independence from the size and seriousness of its main pitch. Starts below the crack of pitch 2 of Stoat's Crack, and climbs the mossy wall to its right.

1   28 m (5a). Climb a delicate little scoop just right of the crack, pull over a bulge and gain the triangular niche above. Make a rising, rightward traverse until a short wall leads to an overhung quartz ledge. Traverse this to an uncomfortable stance on the left.

2   24 m (4c). Pitch 3 of Stickle Grooves.

3   42 m (4c). Pitch 4 of Stickle Grooves.

Variation Finish   15 m   HVS   1968

Harder and looser than the normal way.

3a   (4c). Climb the chimney/groove a couple of metres right of the overhanging chimney of Stickle Grooves.

★★ Stoat's Crack   112 m   HS   ✓   1933

This route finds the easiest way up a very big area of steep rock and gives enjoyable climbing for the mountaineer and botanist alike. The crux is quite hard, bold and with a fair amount of exposure. Start at the foot of the East Buttress where is bends round into the East Gully.

1   16 m. The grassy ledge below a prominent left slanting corner can be gained by the dirty corner on the left, the grassy wall direct or a grassy corner on the right and walking to the corner.

2   20 m. Go up the crack for about 8 metres, break out left and ascend to a stance on the corner.

3   26 m. Traverse to the groove on the left and follow this and the
    open corner above to a capacious overhung ledge.
4   24 m. Step round to the left, along the grass terrace, and climb
    an open groove, finishing to the right. Traverse left along another
    ledge to a bilberry filled groove. Climb this and grass above until
    possible to move right for 5 metres to belay below a sweep of
    slabs.
    A more difficult and direct route from the top of the open groove,
    lies up the wall to the right of the bilberry filled groove, on small
    holds.
5   26 m. Climb pleasant slabs, delicate at first, then a short wall and
    slabs lead leftwards to a huge detached block. 30 metres of
    scrambling finishes the climb.

A route has been climbed on the loose and vegetated buttress right
of Stoat's Crack and Stickle Grooves, its grade is Very Severe. The
place is not attractive and those who are interested are left to work
out their own line.

The East Wall

This is the steep and impressive east facing wall above the scree filled
gully, at the right-hand end of the crag. The start of the first six routes
can be reached by grassy scrambling from the bottom of the gully or
alternatively by climbing pitch 1 of Hobson's Choice and descending
left down a grassy ramp below the crag.

** **Brain Damage**   68 m   E3   1973
This very good and strenuous route, takes the steep groove line high
on the left-hand side of the East Wall. A tricky first pitch leads to an
exhilaratingly exposed finish up a bulging wall. Start at a large spike,
below some black streaks coming down from an overlap.
1   23 m (5c). Move up to a ledge on the left and climb the wall to
    below a downward pointing flake in the overlap. Step left under
    this, then go up with difficulty to the foot of a steep green groove,
    which leads to a ledge and peg belays.
2   45 m (5c). Gain the steep groove above and climb it to a standing
    position on a sharp flake on the right wall. Move right, round the
    rib and climb a steep wall to a peg runner below the overhang.
    Pull round the overhang and go up steep rock above to where the
    angle eases.

* **Coma**   48 m   E4   1979
Gives impressive, sustained, and very strenuous climbing up the steep

wall right of Brain Damage. Start just right of Brain Damage, and left of the dirty cleft.

1 24 m (6a). Climb straight up to the overlap, surmount this with difficulty and climb up rightwards to a horizontal break. Traverse left and belay as for Brain Damage.

2 24 m (6a). Step back right, make a difficult and bold move over the overhang and up to better holds and runners above. Traverse right into Mother Courage and climb this to its peg runner. Step down and left and climb a crack into a mossy groove which leads more easily to the top.

*** Mother Courage   43 m   E3   1976

The steep mottled wall to the right of Brain Damage gives excellent and strenuous climbing on reasonable holds. Start 8 metres right of Brain Damage, left of the obvious dirty groove.

(5c). Climb the wall to a narrow ledge just left of a holly. The wall above the short steep gangway on the left, leads strenuously to a flat hold. Continue direct to a bulge, pull over rightwards, then step immediately back left to the foot of a steep groove and peg runner. Climb the groove and pull out right to a good hold. Climb towards a juniper up on the right then boldly up a rib on the left to a bay.

* Red Groove   42 m   E1   1960

The obvious shallow red groove, right of Mother Courage, gives an enjoyable and interesting climb, gained by a traverse from the right. The start can be reached by scrambling up from the left but is most easily reached by climbing pitch 1 of Hobson's Choice and descending leftwards

1 28 m (5a). Climb easily up the wall for 5 metres to a juniper. Traverse left across the impending wall, pull up with difficulty to a higher line and step left into a niche. Climb up to the easier groove, which leads to a good ledge below the final pitch of Hobson's Choice.

2 14 m (4c). Finish up the impending V-groove to the right on superb rough rock.

Variations
Original Start   16 m   HVS   1960
A loose pitch which is better avoided, start at a dirty corner down to the left.

1a (4c). A shallow groove to a holly followed by a rightward traverse to a thread belay in a tiny corner, below the groove.

Direct Start   25 m   E1
Start directly below the main groove beside a small holly.
> (5b). Climb direct up the steep crack to the foot of the red groove and continue as for pitch 1.

★ **Kudos**   45 m   E2   1977
A pleasant eliminate route. The second pitch gives steep, bold and fingery climbing on excellent rough rock. Start as for Red Groove.
1   30 m (5b). Follow Risus for about 6 metres until a line of holds leads left onto the wall between Risus and Red Groove. Go up the groove line above, taking the left-hand branch, to reach the good ledge below the final pitch of Hobson's Choice.
2   15 m (5c). Climb the wall to the right of the final pitch of Red Groove to finish at the same point as Risus.

★ **Risus**   48 m   E2   1972
The steep first pitch is strenuous but climbed on good holds; the second pitch is however more technically demanding. Start as for Red Groove.
1   28 m (5b). Climb the first 5 metres of Red Groove to a juniper and continue up the overhanging groove, just right of a detached block at the start of the traverse of Red Groove. The groove fades out and after 6 metres a poor resting place is reached; step left and climb up to a terrace, which leads right to a stout juniper belay on Hobson's Choice.
2   20 m (5c). Climb the steep gangway, which slants right from the tree and pull over an awkward bulge to the ledge above. Go diagonally left to a small ledge at the foot of a groove. Follow this to the overhang and move left to some good holds, which lead to the top.

Solstice   48 m   E4   1977
The obvious snaking traverse line on the impending wall between Risus and Eclipse. A very strenuous pitch. Start on a ledge at the top of pitch 3 of Hobson's Choice, below the second pitch of Risus.
1   24 m (6a). Follow pitch 2 of Risus, until a crack leads up right. Climb this and traverse right to a peg runner below the 'pod'. Move down and right to a small spike, then right into the groove of Eclipse which is followed past its crux to a large ledge and belay.
2   24 m (4c). As for pitch 2 of Eclipse.

Hobson's Choice   58 m   HS   1947
Follows the easiest line up the left-hand side of the East Wall and takes the form of an ascending traverse to the left. The main interest

and difficulties are concentrated in the first two pitches. Start below and right of a sweep of slabs below the big corner of Eclipse, reached by scrambling about halfway up the left-hand branch of the easy scree gully.

1   18 m. Pull left onto the slab and follow a rising traverse leftwards, until a large flake enables a long stride to be made into a grassy groove on the left. Belay on the ledge above.

2   10 m. Climb the steep awkward little wall on the left onto a slab which leads to a stance below the impressive corner of Eclipse.

3   10 m. Take the easiest line left to the foot of a chimney crack, which leads to a good juniper ledge.

4   10 m. Climb up to a second ledge and to below a chimney at the left end.

5   10 m. Climb the awkward chimney to the top.

Stars and Bars   30 m   E5   ✝   1988
Serious, bold and strenuous climbing up the wall left of Sixpence. Start below the corner of Eclipse.
      (6a). Step left and climb up to an obvious hole. Jump up and right and continue to a poor peg runner. Traverse left to gain the crack of Solstice and follow this to where it traverses right. Finish up the hanging V-groove directly above.

★★★ **Sixpence**   33 m   E5   1981
A magnificent sustained route up the impending wall and hanging 'pod' left of the corner of Eclipse. Start from the stance at the top of pitch 2 of Hobson's Choice below the corner.
      (6b). Climb Eclipse for 6 metres to a ledge on the right. Step up into the groove above, traverse left onto the wall and climb direct to the spike on Solstice. Pull up left (peg runner), and gain the pod above. Difficult moves are made to reach a small ledge on the right, continue to a ledge and belay at the top.

★★ **Eclipse**   45 m   E4   1976
The large open corner above pitch 2 of Hobson's Choice, gives a superb, sustained pitch of increasing difficulty. Start from the stance below the corner.

1   21 m (6a). Climb the steep corner and flake crack for 6 metres to a ledge on the right. Continue up the open corner/grooves until bold and difficult moves can be made up and right to gain a good ledge.

2   24 m (4c). Climb the stepped corner above and pull out right to gain the foot of an obvious groove which leads to the top.

★★★ **Astra**   60 m   E2   ✓   1960
The superb slim groove in the rib right of Eclipse, reached by an
exposed and delicate piece of wall climbing. An excellent route. Start
from the stance at the top of pitch 2 of Hobson's Choice, below the
corner of Eclipse.

1   21 m (5c). Cross the narrow easy-angled slab at the foot of the
    impending right wall of the corner to its right side. Step round the
    rib onto a steep undercut wall and gain a prominent flake and rest
    place on the right. Climb up and left delicately to where the angle
    eases. Move up and right to a thin crack; reach hidden holds round
    the edge and swing round right to a slab and small stance.

2   34 m (4c). Climb the narrowing slab right of the groove above,
    on superb rock and continue in the same line to a ledge. The
    awkward V-groove ahead is climbed to another ledge and belay
    on the left.

3   5 m. Finish up the short crack and easy scrambling above.

★ **Supernova**   45 m   E5   1979
A bold, eliminate climb on excellent rough rock, based on the main
pitch of Astra. Start as for Astra.

1   21 m (6a). Traverse right as for Astra to a thin crack in the wall
    above the easy-angled slab. Climb this to a glacis and follow the
    slim scoop of Astra to a thin crack. Climb the steep bold slab on
    the left on small holds to the belay of Eclipse.

2   24 m (4c). As for pitch 2 of Eclipse.

Black Hole   54 m   E4   1981
A difficult and rather dirty eliminate pitch direct to the first stance of
Astra. Start from a ledge 5 metres left of Fallen Angel, below a water
worn groove.

1   15 m (6b). Climb the groove with difficulty until a lunge left can
    be made to gain the good flake hold on Astra. Step right and
    layback up the arête to the belay of Astra.

2   39 m (4c). Pitches 2 and 3 of Astra.

★★★ **Fallen Angel**   46 m   E4   1972
A superb and technically demanding climb up the impressive right
slanting pod-shaped groove. Start by traversing left from the gully
along grass ledges, above the sweep of slabs, to a good ledge below
the groove.

    (6a). Climb the wide crack leading into the pod. Up this, over a
    difficult bulge (crux) and continue until the groove opens out and
    the slab on the right can be gained. Climb this rightwards to a
    crack and good foothold (possible belay). Follow the thin crack

above for 6 metres and step right to another crack leading right
to a bollard on the arête. Move left and into a groove which is
climbed to the top.

★ **Heartsong**   46 m   E4   1978
The steep vertical finger crack in the wall right of the pod of Fallen
Angel, gives a strenuous and testing pitch. Start below the 3 metre
corner on pitch 1 of Cascade, 5 metres right of Fallen Angel, reached
by a traverse from the right.

    (6b). Gain the ledge above and follow the easy slab on the right
    as for pitch 2 of Cascade until a glacis below the crack can be
    gained. Make a difficult move left to the foot of the crack and
    climb it to the good foothold on Fallen Angel (possible belay).
    Continue up Fallen Angel to the top.

★ **Cascade**   70 m   HVS   1957
The last stretch of clean rock on the East Wall lies just left of
Bennison's Chimney and takes the line of two steepening slabs, one
above the other. An excellent climb, lacking the fierceness of its more
intimidating companions but providing a fair taste of the problems of
the East Wall. Start below the sweep of slabs, as for Hobson's Choice.
1   24 m (4c). Step across the steep wall and pull round onto the belt
    of slabs. Go up the right-hand side of the slabs, almost
    overlooking the gully, to a grass ledge at the top. Continue up a
    3 metres corner on the left to a good ledge below the first slab.
2   23 m (5a). Climb the slab just right of the corner, until steepening
    rock forces a rightward traverse for a few moves. Move up to a
    small ledge and climb a short wall to reach another ledge.
3   23 m (4b). The bulging chimney above is filled with a huge
    cigar-shaped rock. Climb the crack on either side of the cigar to
    the top.

★★ **Cascade Direct**   24 m   E2   1971
An enjoyable pitch giving fingery climbing up the fine corner left of
the final pitch of Cascade. Start below the corner, just left of the belay
below pitch 3 of Cascade.

    (5c). Gain and climb the corner past a peg runner with great
    difficulty to where the angle eases. (The original route avoided
    the steep start by stepping right up a slab then traversing left to
    the corner.) Continue up the corner and exit left at the overhang
    to a ledge and belay.

★★ **Startrek**   66 m   E2   1976
A left to right girdle of the upper section of the East Wall which covers
no new ground, but links a number of excellent pitches and gives some
magnificent situations. Start as for Eclipse.

1   18 m (5c). Climb the corner of Eclipse for 6 metres to a ledge on
    the right. Move right into Astra and cross the wall past the thin
    crack, to reach the fine little stance at the top of Astra's first pitch.
2   33 m (5b). Climb the slab above the stance to a good spike and
    traverse right to the arête. Step right and go down a groove, until
    a couple of awkward moves lead onto the slab of Fallen Angel
    which is followed to a good foothold (possible stance). Follow the
    thin crack above for 6 metres and step right to where another
    crack leads diagonally right to a bollard on the arête, which gives
    a good belay without a stance.
3   15 m (4c). Swing down into Cascade Direct and traverse right to
    finish up the bulging chimney of Cascade.

Bennison's Chimney and Gibson's Chimney   1910
The two final weaknesses of the East Wall, starting high up the scree
gully. The former will be enjoyed only by the nerveless devotee of
vertical grass climbing; the latter is less frightening but offers only 15
metres of climbing.

Girdle Traverse   220 m   HVS   1950
A rather poor and arduous route, which takes a slightly descending
traverse line across the crag from right to left. Steep rock pitches are
interspersed with much vegetation, the crag not lending itself
particularly well to this type of route. A brief description is included
to point the ardent explorer in the right direction. Start as for
Hobson's Choice.
    Follow pitch 1 of Hobson's Choice then left along an obvious
break, passing the holly on Mother Courage, and on past the belay
of Brain Damage. Continue over vegetation and rock to the large
ledge in Rake End Chimney. Descend a short way then traverse
left, then down to Jack's Rake. Reverse Deception and traverse
left, below the overhang of Cruel Sister. Continue, rising slightly
to a junction with Crescent Climb. Finish up or down this.

East Buttress Girdle   170 m   HVS   1969
A slight improvement on the origional girdle traversing from left to
right across the Eastern side of the crag. Still not a very worthwhile
route. Start as for Rake End Chimney.
    Climb the right rib, move right into Rake End Wall and follow
this to a stance at the top of the rib. Move right and down into

Stoat's Crack. Follow this then traverse right and continue past the belay of Brain Damage and the holly on Mother Courage. Easy ledges then lead right to a finish up Cascade.

Harrison Stickle   (282 073)   Alt. 630 m   West Facing

The summit crags of Harrison Stickle, are impressive from a distance but prove disappointingly broken on closer inspection. Several routes have, however been recorded on the west face but none seems to merit description except those given below. Innumerable variations are possible. Happy gardening.

Harristickorner   26 m   VD   1921
Lies up the corner where the north and west faces meet. Start at a well-scratched corner.
   Climb the corner to a ledge at 5 metres. Climb the wall to the right to a small stance. Traverse horizontally right for 3 metres then climb up to a mossy groove and the top.

Porphyry Slab   73 m   VD   1942
Starts in a grassy bay about 60 metres to the right of Harristickorner, below a broad mossy slab.
1   30 m. Scramble up heathery ribs on the right to a triangular grass ledge at the foot of a crack.
2   18 m. Climb the wall on the left to a ledge. The pleasant slab is climbed direct, moving left at the top to a good ledge.
3   21 m. From the right-hand end of the ledge climb diagonally right to another ledge. Climb the wall easily to a ledge below a short wall.
4   4 m. Climb the wall with difficulty.

Waller's Crack   12 m   VS
   A steep, obvious crack round to the left from Harristickorner.

Raven Crag

Raven Crag is the line of buttresses and outcrops stretched across the hillside above the Old Dungeon Ghyll Hotel. Middlefell Buttress and Raven Crag Buttress are situated side by side directly above the Old Dungeon Ghyll Hotel; West Raven Crag immediately to their left; Far West Raven Crag some 500 metres to the west; East Raven Crag, Far East Raven Crag and Far Far East Raven Crag are the line of outcrops starting about 100 metres east of Raven Crag Buttress and slanting down towards the Stickle Barn.

The crags can all be reached by following the well marked path which starts at the rear of the Old Dungeon Ghyll Hotel and leads up to the foot of Raven Crag Buttress. The East Raven group can also be reached by following the Gimmer Crag path from the Stickle Barn, which leads up the ridge above the crags then descending at the east side of Far East Raven Crag and following the path along their base.

Far West Raven Crag   (280 063)   Alt. 220 m   South and East Facing

This crag is situated about 500 metres west of and at about the same altitude as Raven Crag Buttress. It can be reached in about 10 minutes by following the Raven Crag path from the Old Dungeon Ghyll Hotel, then taking the left-hand branch towards Gimmer Crag until above the first stone wall. This is then followed across the hillside to below the Lower Crag. The routes are short but the rock is steep and clean, and quick to dry.

Lower Crag

Two small buttresses split by an easy angled arête, situated immediatley above the stone wall. Descend down the right-hand side. From left to right the routes are:

Annie's Song   13 m   VS   1986
Start at a large flake at the foot of the left-hand buttress.
    (4c). Climb direct up the slab to a left slanting corner. Climb round the overhang on the right and follow a crack and easier slab to the top.

Before the Storm   13 m   HVS   1986
Start as for Annie's Song.
    (5a). Up the rightward slanting slab to a ledge, then good holds up the steep wall above.

Baldy's Wall   13 m   E3   1986
Start 4 metres right of Annie's Song.
    (6b). Long reaches up the centre of the lower wall, then pull round right to a slab. Direct up the steep wall above passing a peg runner near the top. (The peg can be pre-clipped by climbing up to the left on large holds.)

Bumble Arête   23 m   D   1986
The easy angled arête between the two steep buttresses. Start below
its slabby left side.
    Climb the slab to gain the arête and follow it on good holds to
the top.

Flower Pot Man   13 m   HVS   1986
Right of Bumble Arête a dirty V-groove starts at 3 metres. Start at a
left slanting ramp 2 metres right of this.
    (5b). Climb the ramp with difficulty and the short wall above to
gain and finish up the right arête of the dirty V-groove.

Slaphead's Groove   13 m   E2   1986
Start just right of Flower Pot Man, at the right-hand side of the
buttress.
    (5c). Bridge the slabby corner until it is possible to gain the steep
shallow groove on the left. Up this to good spikes on the left then
move left onto a small slab. Step left and finish direct up the wall.

Variation
    (5c). From the small slab climb up rightwards past a small niche.

Upper Crag

30 metres up and right of the Lower Crag is a short steep clean cut
wall with a holly tree high on its left-hand side.

Sport For All   10 m   VS   1986
Start at a shallow niche below the holly tree.
    (4c). Climb the left side of the niche and groove above finishing
left of the holly.

I Crashed a Vulcan Bomber   30 m   VS   1986
Start just right of Sport For All.
1   22 m (5a). Climb over a block above the niche to gain a square
    cut niche at 4 metres. Continue past the tree and up an easy ridge
    to a grassy ledge.
2   8 m (4b). Finish up the centre of the small buttress above.

Marilyn 60 Today   28 m   E2   1986
Start below the steep clean cut wall.
1   20 m (6a). Climb the middle of the wall with difficult moves past
    a peg runner to gain a sloping shelf. Continue up the steep crack
    above to a sloping ledge.

2   8 m (5c). The slim leaning groove in the small buttress above leads
    to the top.

★ **Hogweed Direct**   27 m   E1   1986
Start at a steep groove at the right-hand side of the wall.
1   17 m (5c). Climb the steep, awkward corner, then move left and
    climb the steep, thin, vertical crack to a sloping ledge and large
    block belay.
2   10 m (5b). Climb the stepped corner above the block, then move
    right to the overhanging corner crack which is short but strenuous.

★ **Blade Runner**   27 m   E1   1986
Start as for Hogweed Direct.
1   17 m (5c). Climb the awkward corner and continue direct up the
    problematic groove above past a peg runner to a sloping ledge
    and large block belay.
2   10 m (5b). Pitch 2 of Hogweed Direct.

Return of the Giant Hogweed   28 m   HVS   1986
Start below an easy groove immediately right of Hogweed Direct.
1   18 m (4c). Up the easy groove for 3 metres then traverse left along
    a ledge for 5 metres to the second, and more prominent crack
    line. Climb this to a small ledge then up right to a sloping ledge
    and large block belay.
2   10 m (5a). Climb the steep layback crack/flake and short corner
    above.

Far from the Stickle Barn   28 m   S   1986
Start as Return of the Giant Hogweed.
    The easy groove leads to a gangway. Move 2 metres left, around
    the corner then up the groove on the right and finish right of the
    nose above.

Higher Upper Crag

50 metres up the hillside is a rather dirty slab just right of a gully with
a holly tree near its top.

Langdale Ferrets   25 m   VS   1986
    (4c). Climb the slab to a small overhang then continue up the left
    slanting crack.

Variation   Direct Finish   E1   1986
    (5b). Continue direct up the slab above the overhang to the top.

West Raven Crag (284 063)   Alt. 180 m   South Facing

This is the area of broken rocks which lie between Middlefell Buttress and a small stream running down to the rear of the Old Dungeon Ghyll Hotel. Overlooking this steam is a small buttress with a prominent clean rib.

Sun Street   26 m   HS   †   1986
Start left of the tree below the centre of the crag.
    Climb the broad rib to the top passing an overlap at two-thirds height on its left.

Don't Look Back!   26 m   E2   1989
Start at the lowest point of the buttress at a short wall split by an obvious thin crack.
    (5c). Climb the wall left of the crack to gain a wide broken crack. Step left to a steep jamming crack which leads to a ledge. Step left and make an awkward move up to a niche. Bold moves left and up gain the edge of a prominent prow. Finish straight up.

Middlefell Buttress (284 064)   Alt. 200 m   South Facing

Middlefell Buttress is situated behind the Old Dungeon Ghyll Hotel and is separated from Raven Crag Buttress by a broad tree filled gully (Raven Crag Gully).

The buttress is divided by a large terrace at two thirds height and the most obvious feature is the rounded left rib which the popular Middlefell Buttress climbs. Just right of this route and about 50 metres higher is the long blank looking wall of Mendes. Hidden in the left bounding gully (Middlefell Gully) is a steep "armour-plated" wall which is taken by Armalite.

Descent is to the left where a good path leads down a broad shoulder before entering the gully near the bottom. An alternative is to follow the gully bed but this is much steeper.

The first five routes all start from the bed of Middlefell Gully and climb the right wall.

They are described from top to bottom.

White Rabbit   43 m   HS   1986
About 30 metres above an embedded boulder at the top of the descent route is an area of broken rock to the right of the gully. Start 6 metres left of a small tree at the foot of a short rib.

1   13 m. Climb the rib to gain a grass ledge with a perched oblong block.
2   30 m. Move up blocks on the left, than make a difficult move up the short wall (crux). Traverse left to a ledge and holly bush then continue up a corner to a heather ledge. Gain the slabs on the right and finish pleasantly in an exposed position.

D.G. Corner   22 m   HVS   1979
The obvious deep corner situated about two thirds up the gully.
(5b). Climb the corner and make an awkward exit where it steepens at the top.

★ **Walk Tall**   22 m   E2   1979
The right rib of D.G. Corner gives a serious route.
(5c). Climb the rib passing two overhangs. Poorly protected.

Trambiolina   22 m   VS   1986
Takes the slab and wall about 15 metres right of Walk Tall. Start below a crack in the slab.
(4c). Climb the crackline up the centre of the slab and wall above, moving left at the top on widely spaced holds.

★ **Armalite**   30 m   E4   1979
An absorbing pitch with poor protection up the impressive armour-plated wall at the bottom of the gully. The rock requires care. Start from a sloping block beneath a vague crack in the centre of the wall.
(5c). Climb the crack for 4 metres to a peg runner, step down and move left to gain a long, narrow foothold. From the left end of the foothold move up leftwards on tiny incuts to a large hidden pocket (peg runner). Pull up to reach the rock shield above (small wires). From the base of the shield make a move up and right to a good flat hold at the base of a short groove. Climb the groove to easier ground above which leads to the top.

Perfect Head   30 m   E4   1988
A worthwhile variation on Armalite which takes the shield direct. Start as for Armalite.
(5c). Climb the crack for 4 metres to a peg runner, step down and move left to gain a long, narrow foothold. From the left end of the foothold move up leftwards on tiny incuts to a large hidden pocket (peg). Pull up to reach the rock shield (small wires). Follow the shield up and leftwards to a shallow scoop. Step left and climb a thin crack to the top.

★★★ Middlefell Buttress   75 m   D   1911
   A popular route which can be climbed (and is) in all conditions. Takes
   a line up the longest part of the buttress. Pitch 1 is Severe but can be
   avoided. Start at the lowest point of the crag.
   1   15 m. Climb the highly polished and strenuous crack to a large
       stance. The crack can be avoided by an easier alternative to the
       left.
   2   45 m. Follow the left side of the buttress easily to another large
       stance.
   3   15 m. Start the wall above by traversing from either left or right,
       then up a fairly steep section to the finishing balcony.

Variation   Castration Crack   15 m   S
1a The crack to the right of pitch 1 can be climbed. This is much
    harder than the rest of the route.

Variation   Curtain Wall   20 m   D
    An additional pitch can be obtained by climbing a short, steep
    slab higher up on the right.

The next 7 routes climb the Mendes Wall which is about 50 metres
up and to the right of Middlefell Buttress. At the foot of the wall is
a long overhang (Power of Imagination) and at the left end above a
tree is a pinnacle.

Bradley's Damnation   42 m   HVS   1952
Climbs a short hanging groove on the wall directly above the pinnacle.
A good route on steep rock. Start at the foot of the pinnacle.
1   33 m (5b). Climb the pinnacle easily to a small ledge below the
    steep groove. Move up the groove until a huge jug enables the rib
    on the left to be gained. The angle soon eases and grassy slabs
    lead to a terrace.
2   9 m. At the back of the terrace is a short steep wall. Climb it to
    the top.

★★ Mendes   47 m   VS   1953
A good route with some excellent positions up the centre of the wall.
Start at some slabs at the left end of the overhang.
1   12 m. Climb up easily leftwards passing the overhang to gain a
    shallow groove. Follow this to a stance on the right.
2   26 m (4c). Traverse right for a couple of metres and climb up on
    good holds until a pull up left gives access to easier angled rock.
    Continue up to a good ledge.
3   9 m (4a). Climb the short steep wall to the top.

Shower of Vegetation   24 m   E1   1984
Takes the left end of the overhang just right of Mendes. Start as for
that route.
> (5b). Climb up to the roof and pull over to reach a slim groove
> above. Move up this to join the traverse of Mendes. Finish as for
> that route.

The Power of Imagination   30 m   E4   1983
A good 'little' roof problem through the largest part of the overhang.
Start below a short crack in the roof.
> (6b). Gain the crack and a good hold over the roof. Pull up and
> climb straight up the steep wall bearing right until below the final
> headwall. Hand traverse left to join Mendes. Go up this then pull
> back right to continue up broken rock to a tree belay.

The Gamekeeper   38 m   HVS   1967
An excellent pitch up the centre of the wall. Start at a vague crack
about 2 metres right of the short hanging corner at the right end of
the overhang.
1   30 m (5b). Climb the vague crack line until an awkward move
    right can be made into a shallow scoop at about 15 metres. Move
    up to gain the left end of a grassy bay.
2   8 m. Climb the groove to the top.

Variation
> Move left at 10 metres to join Mendes. This was originally the
> direct start to that route.

★ **Bryson's Flange**   21 m   E2   1983
Steep climbing up the right side of the wall. Start just left of the holly
tree at the right end of the crag, where a thin crack leads out left onto
the wall.
> (5c). Climb the crack leftwards and then continue straight up the
> steep wall on good, well spaced holds.

Mendes Traverse   45 m   HVS   1960
A right to left traverse of the Mendes wall. Start at the holly tree at
the right end of the crag.
1   36 m (5a). Climb up through the holly to an overhang. Traverse
    out left to a small ledge. Move down until hands are level with
    the ledge. Make a strenuous move on a doubtful flake to gain
    better holds out left. Keep traversing until Mendes is reached.
    Finish as for Mendes to reach the large ledge.
2   9 m. Climb the short steep wall to the top.

Raven Crag Buttress (285 064)   Alt. 200 m   South Facing

Raven Crag Buttress is the large dome-shaped buttress directly behind the Old Dungeon Ghyll Hotel. In the centre of the crag is the strikingly smooth wall of Centrefold which is capped by a curving band of overhangs and undercut at its base by a diagonal overlap which is followed by Pluto. To the left of the wall is the superb overhung corner of Trilogy and just left again is the fine groove line of Holly Tree Direct, an area of easier slabby routes then lead left towards Raven Crag Gully. Round to the right of the smooth wall, the right-hand face of the crag is more broken and leads up to the slanting Oak Tree Terrace. Above this are a number of short pitches whilst to the right and split by Bluebell Gully is the Amphitheatre which has some good though shorter routes.

Raven Crag has some excellent climbs throughout the full range of grades. The crag generally has a sunny disposition and good quality rock which is mainly clean.

Descent is easiest by a large grass shelf (Oak Tree Terrace) to the right of the crag which gives access to the Amphitheatre. The terrace is reached from the top by a short descent over some large split blocks behind an oak tree. A steep descent can also be made down Raven Crag Gully.

The routes are described from left to right.

The Patella Pinch   42 m   E1   1988
An eliminate line left of Evening Wall. Start below the blunt rib at the foot of Raven Crag Gully.
1   20 m (5a). Climb the rib to a downward pointing spike. Pull up over the small overhang and follow the rib to a small diagonal overhang. Climb this then traverse right and upwards for 8 metres to belay below a heather filled chimney/crack.
2   22 m (5b). Step back left 2 metres and climb a small slab leftwards to reach an overhanging niche. Pull boldly into this on good holds and climb the rib more easily to the top.

Evening Oak Variations   42 m   VS   1955
A good climb up the left edge of the crag. Start below a shattered groove at a point where Raven Crag Gully begins to narrow.
1   21 m (4c). Climb slabs leftwards to the groove. Move up this with increasing difficulty to the overhang. Step left and pull up to easier ground which leads, still steeply, to a ledge.

2   21 m (4b). Move right and climb a shallow chimney through the
    overhangs to easier rocks, which lead to the top.

★ **Evening Wall**   47 m   S   1947
Start from Raven Crag Gully, about 6 metres to the left of the large
pinnacle on Oak Tree Wall.
1   11 m. Climb up for 4 metres until the wall steepens, make a
    traverse right into a shallow corner. Step right, and move up to a
    small stance and belay on Pitch 2 of Oak Tree Wall.
2   15 m. Climb up to a ledge then traverse left and go straight up to
    a bulge. Step up and traverse left again to a good ledge.
3   21 m. Move right onto the exposed arête which leads to the top
    on good holds.

★ **Holly Tree Traverse**   46 m   VD   1949
An interesting left to right traverse with some fine positions across
the easiest section of the buttress. Start by scrambling up to the
pinnacle on Oak Tree Wall from the foot of Raven Crag Gully.
1   23 m. Climb the groove behind the pinnacle for 3 metres until it
    is possible to make an awkward traverse right to a sentry box on
    the Original Route (possible belay). Continue traversing up and
    rightwards to an obvious tree in the groove of Holly Tree Direct.
2   14 m. Climb the rib to the right of the groove and traverse right
    to a ledge below a small right-angle corner.
3   9 m. The corner is climbed on good holds to the top.

Variation Finish   22 m
2a Climb the groove, move left on to the rib and finish up this,
    working slightly leftwards towards the top.

Oak Tree Wall   45 m   MS   1947
Start about 12 metres left of the toe of the buttress below a prominent
oak.
1   14 m. Climb a short crack to the roots of the oak, move out right
    onto the wall and go up to a large ledge with a pinnacle at its left
    end.
2   17 m. Move up the rib behind the pinnacle to a small ledge below
    a bulging wall, where an overhung gangway leads up right to a
    small exposed stance.
3   14 m. Climb up and slightly right to a ledge below a bulge. Then
    up to the bulge which is turned on its left by a shallow scoop.

Nadir   47 m   VS

Pleasant enough, with one or two interesting moves. Start below a small rib just to the right of Oak Tree Wall.

1   12 m (4b). Climb the rib delicately to a good ledge.
2   35 m (4c). Move rightwards along the ledge until it is possible to pull awkwardly to a flake. Step right into a steep flake crack, then climb steeply up to Holly Tree Traverse and continue directly to the top.

** **The Original Route**   61 m   MS   1930

An excellent route which starts at the lowest point of the buttress at a large holly tree.

1   12 m. Climb up just right of the holly tree and pull into an awkward crack which is followed to a good ledge below a fine narrow pillar.
2   15 m. Climb the pillar on good holds to a ledge which leads left to a large pinnacle.
3   14 m. Step back right from the pinnacle and climb the steep wall above, trending slightly right to a group of ledges.
4   20 m. Go straight up for 4 metres, then move left to a ledge under a bulge. Step left along the ledge and climb a steep section which gives access to easier ground and the top.

* **Holly Tree Direct**   70 m   VS   1952

A good route with a steep delicate section up the long groove in the centre of the buttress. Start at the toe of the crag at a clean wall between a holly and oak tree.

1   12 m (4c). Climb the wall, starting from the right, on good holds to a ledge below an obvious corner.
2   14 m. Climb the corner to a large ledge below the steep upper section of the groove.
3   21 m (4c). Climb up onto a white coloured slab to the left of the groove, then gain the recess in the groove above by a short delicate traverse across the smooth rib. Pull out to the right and climb up to a resting place. Continue up the groove, steep and delicate at first, then easing, to reach a tree.
4   23 m (4c). Step out left from a couple of metres above the tree and follow the left rib of the groove.

Variation   18 m   HVS   1963
2a   (5b). Climb directly up to the groove, steep and poorly protected.

The Watch   81 m   E5   1980
A contrived traverse of the central wall which packs some impressive climbing. Start as for Holly Tree Direct.
1   26 m (4c). Pitches 1 and 2 of Holly Tree Direct.
2   9 m (5c). Climb up 4 metres to a glacis and traverse right around the rib into the corner of Trilogy (at half height).
3   24 m (6a). Traverse right and down slightly to join R'n'S Special and follow this to Fine Time.
4   18 m (5b). As for Fine Time. Climb up to the roof, turn this on the left and finish up slabs to the top.

The next two routes start up the steep narrow wall 5 metres right of Holly Tree Direct and directly below the corner of Trilogy.

Kalashnikov   56 m   E4   †   1980
An eliminate up the left rib of Trilogy, sustained and poorly protected. Start just left of the bottom crack of Pluto, at a steep, narrow wall.
1   20 m (5c). Climb the middle of the wall following a thin crack to reach the ledge below Trilogy.
2   36 m (6a). Climb the wall above a short slab just left of the rib (unprotected), to a junction with Holly Tree Direct. Move across the wall on the right and climb up to poor undercuts and a large pinch-hold. Climb directly up the steep wall passing an old peg on the left. Easier climbing then leads to the top.

★★ Pluto   73 m   HVS   1958
A contrived route which nevertheless gives some interesting climbing in good positions. Start at a steep crack at the foot of the crag in line with the corner of Trilogy.
1   20 m (4c). Climb the crack to a good ledge and block belay below the corner.
2   27 m (4b). Traverse rightwards below the overlap until an awkward move across a groove leads to a good ledge on Bilberry Buttress.
3   26 m (5a). Step down onto the rib on the left and climb this on small holds until it is possible to move right and up to a traverse line (Bilberry Buttress). Traverse left and finish on good holds.

★ Variation   Green Groove Finish   27 m   E2   1972
A good alternative to the last pitch of Pluto, which climbs the obvious groove to its left. Start from a ledge on Pitch 3 of Pluto.
3a (5b). Step down left into the obvious groove. Climb this with a move to the left to avoid a bulge at 8 metres. Exposed.

The next three routes start from the large ledge below the central overhanging corner of Trilogy. The ledge is easily reached by scrambling in from the left.

★★★ Trilogy 31 m E5   1979
A magnificent pitch up the great overhung corner which bounds the left side of the central wall. The route has an abundance of old pegs in place, though is quite bold in its lower section.

> (6a). Climb the corner to a resting place below the large upper overhang. Pull through this to a tiny ledge on the left, step back right and continue directly to the top up a short steep groove.

★★ Centrefold 31 m E6   1984
The much fancied line up the blank looking wall above R'n'S Special gives a superlative route. Start below the corner of Trilogy.

> (6b). Traverse rightwards under the overlap until it is possible to pull through the roof to enter a shallow scoop (as for R 'n' S Special). Climb straight up the wall past 2 peg runners, then traverse right for 3 metres to finish up the obvious hanging flake on the skyline.

★★ R'n'S Special 40 m E5   1977
A heart-stopping trip across the bottom of the wall right of Trilogy. Sustained, delicate climbing with the minimum of protection. Start below the corner of Trilogy.

> (6a). Traverse rightwards under the overlap as for Pluto, until it is possible to pull through the roof to enter a shallow scoop. Climb the wall to a peg runner on the right. Step down and traverse right to a good hold and climb directly to some sloping footholds. Reach blindly right round the rib then move up and right to better holds leading to the final roof (junction with Fine Time). (Alternatively climb straight up to the roof and move right on underclings to gain Fine Time). Pull leftwards through the overhang on good holds to easy slabs which lead to the top

The next route starts at the foot of the crag below a large ivy patch.

★ Fine Time 46 m E4   1972
The fierce crack above the right end of the central overlap. Very strenuous and with a desparate clip. Scramble up to the foot of a rib below and left of the crack and a mass of ivy.

> (6b). Climb the rib to a ledge below the roof. Step right to the crack which is followed with difficulty past a peg runner to reach

another slanting crack. Climb this then continue more easily to the top overhang which is turned on the left to reach the finishing slabs.

★★ Bilberry Buttress   76 m   VS   1941
A classic climb with plenty of interest and a fine airy finish. Start at the lowest point of the right side of the crag below a curving crack.
1   20 m (4b). Scramble up to the foot of the crack and follow it to a ledge.
2   15 m (4c). Climb the thin crack in the steep left wall past a bulge to a magnificent finishing hold. Follow the ridge to a large sloping ledge.
3   41 m (4b). Traverse the ledge rightwards to a shallow crack. Climb this for a couple of metres and make a short traverse left beneath a large detached block to a scoop. Continue traversing across a green groove to an easy finish.

★ Savarnake   77 m   MS   1943
A wandering route up the right side of the crag. Start at the lowest point of the crag just right of Bilberry Buttress.
1   26 m. Scramble up to a large V-crack which is followed to a good ledge.
2   21 m. Walk down left, and then go up broken rocks in the corner which gradually steepens to a fine exposed finish at the top of pitch 2 of Bilberry Buttress.
3   15 m. Traverse the sloping ledge to its right end and climb a broken corner for 2 metres until a step left can be made into a dirty scoop. Continue up over a detached block to reach a ledge and oak belay on Oak Tree Terrace.
4   15 m. Walk to the right and finish over large blocks.

Nutcracker Cleft   79 m   HVS   1952
A good, strenuous route up the big overhanging cleft at the bottom right side of the buttress. Start below the cleft.
1   24 m (5a). Traverse left to the holly tree then follow the overhang to pull out onto a slab on the right. Climb the short steep crack in the corner and continue to a small slab where the difficulties ease. Move right and climb easier angled rock to a ledge.
2   20 m (4b). Climb up easily, then more steeply to a ledge; move right to belay below a bulging chimney-crack.
3   23 m (4b). Enter the chimney by a short traverse from the left and continue to reach the split blocks.

Photo – Golden Slipper, Pavey Ark

4   12 m. Climb the steep red wall just left of the overhanging V-chimney (Kneewrecker Chimney) on good holds.

★ **Revelation**   50 m   S   1948
A good route on clean rock up the prominent buttress on the right-hand face of the crag. Start at the foot of the buttress.
1   12 m. Climb the buttress on small holds to a good ledge below an overhanging wall.
2   15 m. Climb the short strenuous crack in the wall; continue past a small ledge and over a projecting nose to a sloping stance just left of Kneewrecker Chimney.
3   23 m. Continue straight up over bulging rocks to Oak Tree Terrace. Either walk off right, or finish up the blocks behind the tree, as for Savernake.

Kneewrecker Chimney   38 m   HVS   1949
An interesting route with a strenuous top pitch. Start just left of two oaks around the rib right of Revelation.
1   12 m (4b). Climb the wall on the left until an open scoop can be gained. Follow the scoop to a sloping ledge.
2   15 m (4b). Step back to the right and climb a strenuous crack to Oak Tree Terrace.
3   11 m (5a). Attack the overhanging V-chimney behind the oak to reach a tiny ledge. Step up, and move left round the corner on good holds. Climb more easily to the top.

Raven Girdle   97 m   S   1948
A left to right traverse which gives good climbing and airy situations. Start from Raven Crag Gully, about 6 metres to the left of the large pinnacle on Oak Tree Wall.
1   11m. Climb up for 4 metres until the wall steepens, make a traverse right into a shallow corner. Step right, and move up to a small stance and belay. (Pitch 1, Evening Wall).
2   14 m. Follow the overhung gangway of Oak Tree Wall rightwards to a small stance.
3   24 m. Traverse right making for the prominent ledge on the skyline. From the ledge, descend to a gnarled tree and cross the wall on the right to a ledge below a small right-angled corner (Holly Tree Traverse).
4   10 m. Climb down past two large blocks to a delightfully exposed slab and traverse rightwards across it to a ledge.

Photo – Fine Time, Raven Crag Buttress

5   23 m. Descend a little and traverse right, to an incipient gully; move down again and continue the traverse up to the right to a ledge. Follow the ledge to its end, and step down to belay behind a pinnacle.

6   9 m. Climb a little slab and continue the traverse to Oak Tree Terrace.

7   6 m. Finish behind the split blocks as for Savernake.

The next three routes climb the steep wall above Oak Tree Terrace and left of the Amphitheatre. Two obvious cracks split the wall. The routes are easily reached from the right end of the descent route.

★ **Muscle Crack**   18 m   E1
The thin ragged left-hand crack gives a brilliant pitch, reminiscent of a gritstone route.
   (5c). From the foot of the crack climb it to the top. An easier start can be made by traversing from the right.

Muscle Wall   18 m   E3   1983
An open route up the centre of the wall right of Muscle Crack. Start below a large pinnacle in the centre of the wall.
   (6a). Climb the pinnacle then move up left to a small spike. From the spike move up and slightly right to reach a short thin crack at the top.

Campaign Crack   24 m   E1   1983
A good route up the wider right-hand crack.
   (5b). Follow the crack direct to the top.

The Amphitheatre

Right of the descent route is the Amphitheatre, high up on the right of the main crag. It is split in its centre by the steep grassy Bluebell Gully.

● **Jaundice**   56 m   S   1953
   Climb the overgrown rock to the left of Bluebell Gully, starting at a short chimney just left of the gully. Not recommended.

Bluebell Gully   45 m   S   1948
Start at the foot of the gully.
1   15 m. Climb the gully to a grassy corner.

2   30 m. Continue up the gully for a couple of metres until an awkward traverse leads out onto the right wall. Climb up to a ledge. Continue above the ledge until it is possible to step into the gully on the left which leads to the top.

Bluebell Arête   43 m S   1948
Follows the steep arête just right of Bluebell Gully. Start about 3 metres right of that route.
1   15 m. Climb into a groove on the right and follow it until it is possible to climb the steep right wall to the level of a rowan. Traverse left to the arête and continue up this to a small stance.
2   28 m. Continue up the steep edge of the arête to the ledge on the final pitch of Bluebell Gully. Finish up this.

Centipede Direct   31 m E2   1980
A combination of the Direct Start and Variation Finish. Start at the thin hairline crack just left of the start of Centipede.
1   11 m (6a). Climb the desperate crack past a peg runner to belay below the overhang.
2   20 m (5c). Step right below the overhang and pull up past a peg runner to a small ledge. Continue up the arête to a ledge.

** **Centipede**   90 m S   1948
A gem of a route up the fine pinnacle of rock which forms the right side of the Amphitheatre. Start below a wide hanging crack just right of the base of the pinnacle.
1   18 m. Climb the steep rib on good holds to reach the upper part of the crack. Follow this to a good ledge.
2   15 m. Climb the steep slabs and turn the overhang on the left. Go up to a stance below a crack.
3   15 m. Step down and traverse across the wall on the right to join the arête at a small ledge immediately above the overhang. Follow the arête to a good ledge.
4   42 m. Continue up the ridge by a series of steps, some of which are rather awkward. This pitch can be easily split.

Right of Centipede there is a large grassy terrace. **Confidence** (47m, S) takes a blunt arête above this terrace and starts by climbing any one of three obvious short ribs below the terrace.

About 100 metres right of the Amphitheatre is a small, broken buttress. The next five routes start from a terrace below the overhanging left wall of this crag which is easily reached by scrambling.

Potluck   13 m   E2   1986
At the left end of the crag is a hanging slab above a holly tree. Start
below the holly.
> (5c). Scramble up to the holly then climb an overhanging crack to
> gain the hanging slab. Follow the slab then climb directly to the
> top.

★ **Mythical M.M.**   20 m   E3   1986
A good route up the overhanging wall just left of Sexpot. Start behind
the large pinnacle at the base of the wall.
> (6a). Climb up leftwards on big holds to a ledge. Climb up directly
> to a peg runner and then up rightwards past a peg runner and two
> in situ nuts to the top.

Sexpot   19 m   E2   1983
A steep route with some loose rock up the overhung crack above the
pinnacle. Start at the pinnacle.
> (5c). From behind the pinnacle climb up left to gain a scoop at 3
> metres. Traverse right to the foot of the crack and climb this to
> the top using holds mainly on the right.

Marilyn Monroe Please   19 m   E2   1983
The overhanging groove about 3 metres right of the pinnacle. Start
at a thin crack at the toe of the rib to the right.
> (6a). Climb the thin crack to reach the ground again. Continue
> up the overhung groove with the crux moving past a peg runner.

Hotpot   22 m   VS
A good route up the fine rib that runs down the centre of the crag.
Start just left of the toe of the buttress.
> (4c). Traverse right to gain the arête and move up to a narrow
> ledge. Climb up steeply until a swing left can be made round the
> corner to reach a scoop above; continue straight up to the top.

Stewpot   32 m   S   1949
Start at the lowest point of the buttress, about 12 metres below the
terrace.
1   12 m. Climb up broken rocks to a large detached block. Move
>   over the block and continue up a slab to a ledge with another
>   detached rock. (This is where the other routes start).
2   10 m. Climb a small slab and then broken rocks to another ledge
>   with a large pinnacle on the left.
3   10 m. Climb onto the pinnacle and finish up the wall to the right.
>   (The finish is much harder than the rest).

Variation Start   10 m   1957
Start at the left-hand side of the large detached flake.
1a Climb the chimney between the block and wall to the narrow ledge
    at the top of the block, then the crack trending right to the top of
    pitch 1.

Variation Finish   12 m
3a Climb a short crack down to the right near the arête; slightly
    harder than the normal way.

Potty   19 m   E1   1983
Start at the pinnacle below the arête of Stewpot.
    (5c). Climb the crack just right of the corner, then straight up the
    arête.

Crackpot   20 m   HVS   1983
Start 3 metres right of Potty below a crack.
    (5a). Climb up easily to a tree, then climb the overhanging crack
    above.

East Raven Crag   (287 065)   Alt. 220 m   South Facing

Some 100 metres to the right of Raven Crag Buttress is the start of
the buttresses of East Raven Crag. They are generally smooth with
few features, with the exception of a deeply cut right-angled gully,
containing a large holly, about halfway along, and a big unpleasant-
looking overhanging cleft at about the three quarter mark; these
break the crag up and serve as convenient markers.

The rock is generally sound and quite compact, though rather dirty
and vegetated in parts. Descent can be made down either end of the
crag. The climbs are described left to right.

★ **Mamba**   18 m   MS   1950
A steep and pleasant wall. Start at a rib about 5 metres from the left
end of the crag.
    Up to a ledge at half-height, then up slightly leftwards to the top.

★ **Jingo**   18 m   MVS
Another pleasant wall climb. Start at the same point as Speckled
Band.
    (4b). Climb directly up the wall, pulling up leftwards from a small
    pinnacle at half-height.

★ Speckled Band   20 m   VD   1950
The obvious right slanting line starting 6 metres right of Mamba.
  Follow the gangway rightward, then finish straight up the wall on
  good holds.

Variation Start   VD
The short gangway groove 6 metres right is climbed to join the main
route.

Variation Direct Start   VD
The crack in the steep wall 10 metres right of the origional then the
short wall to the top.

Jungle Wall   25 m   HS   1950
A poor vegetated climb up the corner containing a large oak growing
on a ledge 10 metres up. Start where a fence meets the crag below
the tree.
1   15 m. Climb up and right to a large sloping ledge and tree belay.
2   10 m. The wide crack on the right leads to the top of a rickety
    pinnacle; step left and finish up the gully.

Festerday   36 m   HVS
The steep crack in the wall left of Rowan-tree Groove. Start 8 metres
right of the fence.
  (5b). Climb directly up the wall to a slab. The steep crack above
  eases after the first 10 metres and slabs lead to the top.

★ Rowan Tree Groove   36 m   VS   1957
A good climb up the groove which starts halfway up the crag with a
small rowan and an overhang at the top. Start 5 metres left of the
V-groove of Casket.
  (4b). Climb the steep wall to a blunt pinnacle; step up and then
  left to gain the slab below the groove. Enter the groove with
  difficulty and climb it to the overhangs. Traverse right to the rib
  and follow it to the top.

Ramrod   30 m   VS   1966
A clean and direct line up the slim groove right of Rowan Tree
Groove. Start 2 metres left of Casket.
  (4c). Climb up left to a blunt pinnacle and continue up the
  left-hand rib of a smooth little V-groove to a ledge below the
  overhangs. Pull directly over and climb the slim groove above to
  the top.

Men at Work   30 m   E1   1984
An eliminate line between Ramrod and Casket. Start as for Ramrod.
   (5b). Climb straight up to an overhang at 5 metres. Over this and
up a crack to a ledge. Follow the awkward groove above moving
leftwards to finish.

Casket   30 m   HVS
The obvious steep V-groove 8 metres left of the deep right-angled
holly-filled gully.
   (5a). Climb the groove, past a tree on a ledge, to easy ground.

★ **The Chopper**   30 m   HVS
The steep, clean wall right of Casket gives a rather contrived climb.
Start below the middle of the wall.
   (5a). Climb the wall; the crux being a rising traverse leftwards to
gain the tree on Casket. Finish up this.

Variation   Bryson's Finish   HVS   1983
   (5a). From the start of the leftward traverse, follow thin cracks
up the wall above to a ledge and the slim pillar above to the top.

★ **Baskerville**   30 m   VS   1949
The steep rib immediately left of the deep right-angled gully gives a
pleasant pitch.
   (4c). Either climb a groove in the rib or traverse right from the
foot of Casket to gain a ledge at 5 metres. Follow the rib, over
an awkward bulge at 10 metres, then easier ground to the top.

Barman's Saunter   25 m   E1   1981
A poor climb up the dirty left wall of the gully, just right of
Baskerville.
   (5c). Move up to a bulge at 3 metres; pass this on the right and
continue passing a small niche to easy broken rock above.

Ornithology   25 m   S
Climb the right wall of the right-angled gully. Start at the rib on the
right.
   Climb the rib to the right end of a grassy ledge, then the centre
of the wall above, which eases towards the top.

Shizen Groove   30 m   VS   1959
The heather chocked groove system in the steep wall right of
Ornithology. Start 5 metres right of Ornithology.
   (4b). Climb the groove system trending rightwards to finish.

Jocker's Slab   32 m   E1   1973
Fine open climbing right of Shizen Groove. Start as Shizen Groove.
    (5b). Climb up to below the overhangs at 8 metres, move right
into another groove then up rightwards over two bulges, and
follow a traverse line leading right. Move up and right then back
left to finish.

Brown Trousers   30 m   HVS
Quite a good route up the clean rib above the left end of the
overhangs, which lie right of the overhanging cleft. Start 6 metres
right of a tree below the cleft.
    (5a). Climb a slab to the left end of the overhangs. Pull up, and
traverse right above the overhangs to a blunt rib, which leads to
the top.

Variation   Pink Panties   10 m   E3   1986
    (5c). From the wedged block at the top of the slab below the
overhang, pull up steeply to gain the rib of Brown Trousers and
follow this to the top.

Finger Swing   28 m   E3   1981
Strenuous moves up the thin crack in the overhang just left of Sign
of Four.
    (6b). Climb the slab to the left side of a holly below the overhang,
old peg runner above. Pull over the overhang using the thin crack,
then easier rock to the top.

⋆ **Sign of Four**   28 m   VS
Start at a corner below the right-hand end of the band of overhangs,
right of the overhanging cleft.
    (4c). Climb the corner to a holly below the overhang. Traverse
awkwardly right onto the foot of the buttress; after a delicate step,
climb directly to the top.

⋆ **Watson Wall**   30 m   HS   1949
Climbs the blunt rib right of Sign of Four.
    Up the rib, over a bulge, then left to a shallow niche (or gain this
direct over the overhang (5c)). Ascend diagonally right to a small
ledge on the rib, which is then followed, trending left to the top.

Subsidiary Ridge   28 m   VD
Climbs the rather broken subsidiary buttress 12 metres right of
Watson Wall. Start 2 metres left of the lowest point of the buttress.

Ascend to a ledge, step up and left and climb to the top, keeping left of the crest all the way.

Two very poor routes climb rocks about 10 metres right of Subsidiory Ridge, they arc **Sherlock** (26m, MS, 1966) and **Eighty Foot Slab** (25m, VS).

Far East Raven Crag   (288 065)   Alt. 200 m   South Facing

Some hundred metres nearer to Stickle Barn, and lower down the fellside, is another short, steep buttress known as Far East Raven Crag. The rock is similar to East Raven Crag, though the central rib is more broken and scarred following a recent rockfall. The area to its right, below the large capping overhangs is very vegetated.

Descent can be made down either end off the crag. From left to right the routes are:-

Pianissimo   18 m   S   1984
The arête at the extreme left end of the crag. Start behind a holly bush.
   Climb to a ledge, gain the arête and follow it to the top.

Pianola   20 m   E2   1988
The right facing groove immediately right of Pianissimo.
   (5b). Climb the groove past an overhang to gain a heather choked ledge and old peg runner. Continue up the groove, finishing rightwards over more broken rock to the top.

The Shroud   22 m   HVS   1967
Start 8 metres right of Pianissimo below a wide, shallow groove which slants to the right.
   (5a). Follow the groove up rightwards, below a line of overhangs, step up right then trend left to a dirty finish near Pianissimo.

★ **Frankie Goes to Kendal**   30 m   E1   1984
Start about 12 metres from the left end of the crag at a short, mossy, rightward-slanting glacis.
   (5b). Climb the glacis to a ledge; then the short steep crack above its left end to another ledge. Climb the wall above for 3 metres, trend leftwards then pull up into a shallow scoop. Ascend the flake on the right and hand traverse up rightwards to finish up a dirty groove.

A recent rockfall from below the overhangs on the right has removed part of the top pitch of **Jericho Wall** (HVS (5b), 35m, 1953) and left a lot of unstable blocks. This route is now best avoided.

The next route has also suffered somewhat from the rockfall and extra care is necessary with some loose rock.

Babylon   30 m   E1   1951
A difficult second pitch through the break in the summit overhangs gives an unusual atmosphere of seriousness for such a small crag. Start 10 metres right of Frankie Goes to Kendal at a broken rib below an old oak tree, just left of the large vegetated corner.
1   16 m (4a). Climb straight up through the tree and groove above
    until possible to step right round a corner to a belay.
2   14 m (5b). Climb the rib on the left then follow the curving break
    above through the overhangs with sustained interest.

Right of Babylon is a large corner and a stretch of steep, rubbishy, vegetated rock topped by a large overhang which is taken by the following route.

Warlock   30 m   E5   †   1981
A free version of an old aid route through the intimidating overhangs. Care is required with the rock.
1   15 m. Any of several easy ways up to a holly tree belay below the
    roof.
2   15 m (6b). Traverse right and climb up to the roof, which is then
    taken direct, just left of the old in situ pegs. A long reach is useful.

Caustic   40 m   HVS   1959
A rather poor, dirty and wandering route. Start 8 metres right of the corner.
1   22 m (4b). Straight up the left side of a rib; a short wall then gains
    a slab below the roof which is followed leftward to a large holly
    and yew tree belay.
2   18 m (5b). A leftward rising traverse and tree climbing gains the
    final pitch of Babylon which is followed rightwards to the top.

Nineveh   28 m   VS   1951
Start 10 metres right of the corner below a groove system.
    (4b). Climb the grooves and pull up right to a slab. Climb the rib
    on the left of a shallow groove and the slab above slanting right
    to the top.

★ Nazareth   32 m   HVS   1983
A pleasant route on solid rock. Start 2 metres right of Nineveh, just
left of a short groove.
1   10 m (5a). Climb slightly rightwards up the wall to a small
    overhang. Pull over this and up to a ledge and holly belay on
    Samarkand.
2   22 m (5a). From the block behind the holly climb the steep groove
    for 2 metres until possible to pull left onto the nose. Climb straight
    up to a corner, just left of the top overhangs, bridge up this to
    the top.

Samarkand   34 m   HVS
A route with both steep and delicate climbing. Start 15 metres right
of the corner below a holly on a ledge.
1   12 m (4b). Climb the wall to the holly.
2   22 m (5b). Ascend the right side of the steep shallow groove to a
    peg runner and make a difficult exit left. Continue delicately
    leftwards then move up to a small ledge. Step back right above
    the overhangs and finish up the wall above.

Jerusalem   30 m   E2
Ascends the steep groove system in the wall right of Samarkand. Start
just right of Samarkand.
    (5c). Climb the slab and green wall right of a holly to the steep
    grooves. Climb the central groove line through a notch in the top
    overhangs.

★ Damascus   42 m   VS
The line of square-cut grooves gives enjoyable climbing on sound
rock. Start 5 metres left of the lowest point of the buttress.
1   18 m (4c). Scramble to an oak tree, climb the first groove to a
    stance below the next.
2   24 m (4b). Climb the groove and pull out right onto a slab. Step
    round a rib on the left and follow the last and smallest groove to
    an exit on the left, and on easy finish.

Peascod's Route   40 m   MVS   1945
Start 8 metres right of the lowest point of the crag at an easy angled
rib.
1   26 m (4a). Go up to the higher of two ledge below a bulge, work
    right and pull up to a sloping ledge, then scramble up to below
    the steep right angled corner.
2   14 m (4b). Up the corner to the overhang, step left under it and
    finish up a small slab.

Variation   22 m   HS
1a. Scramble to the first groove of Damascus, move right to a steep
   gangway and follow it to the ledge below the right-angled corner.

Right of Peascod's Route   26 m   S   1959
Start about 10 metres right of Peascod's Route below a pinnacle at
the top of the crag.
   Climb up left to a grass ledge, then up the rib on the right to a
   small ledge below the final steep wall which is climbed on good
   holds to the top.

Variation   1983
   The heather covered slab 4 metres left of the start can be climbed
   to the grass ledge.

Girdle Traverse   90 m   VS   1952
An enjoyable expedition, sustained at Severe level with one or two
short sections a little harder. Start at the left end of the crag as for
Pianissimo.
1   12 m. Climb through the tree, gain the arête on the right and belay
     a couple of metres higher.
2   20 m (4c). Follow the obvious line right, move down a little and
     make a long stride across an open groove to good holds which
     lead to a holly belay.
3   18 m (4b). Move round the corner, step down behind a large holly
     and cross the slab below the large overhangs to a tree belay at its
     right end.
4   10 m (4a). Descend the rib and traverse right to a ledge and holly
     belay.
5   10 m (4a). Traverse across then up right to a ledge below the
     second groove of Damascus.
6   20 m (4b). Climb the groove, until a short slab leads right to the
     right-angled corner on Peascod's Route. Ascend this to the
     overhang and traverse right to an awkward finish.

Far Far East Raven Crag   (289 065)   Alt. 180 m   South Facing

Sixty metres right of Far East Raven Crag a stone wall abuts the third,
and by far the smallest of the trio of East Raven Crags, which contains
a couple of extended boulder problems.

Deadly Dave's Demon Rib   14 m   S   1983
Start below the rib 2 metres left of the stone wall.
   Climb the rib on its left side direct to the top.

Deadly Dave's Demonic Groove   14 m   HVS   1983
The open groove directly above the stone wall.
(5a). Climb the groove, step left to the rib using handholds above the overlap, then up the wall above to the top.

Gimmer Crag (277 070)   Alt. 525 m   North West to South East Facing

This huge, barrel shaped sweep of grey rock, with its contrasting characters and fine situation is one of the most popular crags in Lakeland. It lies high above Mickleden, between and lower than the summits of Harrison Stickle and Pike O'Stickle, topping a steep and uncompromising section of fellside. Though its profile can be seen from the Old Dungeon Ghyll area, it is best viewed from the Mickleden side of The Band, when its scale and position can be best appreciated.

There are a number of approaches starting from the Old Dungeon Ghyll car park. The first, and probably hardest, is to walk along Mickleden until the twin gates are passed, at which point an open area is reached. A steep and unforgiving path leads up through the bracken to join a path which traverses in from the right, meeting the crag below South-East Gully. It is also possible to gain the left-hand side of the crag from this approach, by following a path which cuts under a short, steep crag and then leads steeply up to the foot of North-West Gully.

The second way is to walk up the path towards Raven Crag until just over a stone slab bridge, a left fork leads across to a stile and behind a wall to a steep section, up which the path zig-zags. Keep following this until a welcome waterfall is passed, after which the crag is soon reached.

A third way is to start by climbing Middlefell Buttress. From its top continue up a short pitch up to the right (Curtain Wall), and continue scrambling up little outcrops until a level section of path is reached. Follow this leftwards, then up a steeper and often wet section until it levels off and trends left. A small path leads off to the left again just before the final steepening and leads gently round to the crag. This is a satisfying method of ascent as it involves least walking. The path reached on this route can be gained by starting behind the Stickle Barn and following the path which leads up towards the Langdale Pikes, on the left side of Dungeon Ghyll. When a flat section is reached, continue as for the Middlefell Buttress ascent.

Timewise, there is little to choose between the approaches, 45 minutes being a reasonable time for any of them.

Seen from the valley, the crag presents a clean and smooth looking face, which needs to be examined more closely if its different facets are to be revealed. The main buttress is in fact barrel shaped, and is bounded on the right by South-East Gully. The pleasant Main Wall lies right of this gully and the prominent feature of Gimmer Chimney splits the wall to its left, which is known as the South-East Face. The lower section of the Mickleden Face of the crag consists of a series of broken walls, separated by heather and bilberry ledges. These gradually steepen to form the smooth West Face. The crag steepens on its left-hand side and veers round to eventually join Junipall Gully. This area is known as the North-West Face. The Crack, an immaculate line up the centre of this wall is a good landmark. The North-West Face has a lower section extending rightwards from the foot of The Crack up which a number of short pitches lead to ledges on the West Face. Junipall Gully runs down steeply and at right angles into North-West Gully. Much of North-West Gully is loose and eroded, so care is required in places. The wall above and left of Junipall Gully is known as Pallid Buttress.

The best descents are via South-East Gully for routes on that side of the crag, and via a heathery spur left of the North-West Face for routes in that vicinity.

The climbing on Gimmer Crag is open and exposed. The rock is immaculate; quick drying, rough, clean and generally solid. Its aspect means that it is usually possible to find one part of the crag which is attracting some sun, or shade during those hot summer days!

The climbs are described from right to left.

Main Wall

The first routes lie on the wall which bounds the right-hand side of the lower part of South-East Gully. Though this wall can be climbed by a number of variations, the routes described offer the best climbing.

★ **Main Wall Climb**   49 m   VD

An excellent route on good rock. Start 6 metres below and right of a large detached flake, at an embedded flake at the foot of the wall.

1   18 m. Pleasant, direct climbing on satisfying holds, leads to a ledge and small belays.

2 18 m. Move diagonally left to a ledge, then step right and continue
   directly up again to a good belay.
3 13 m. Start the pitch on the left and continue up to a finish left
   of a block, or by a scoop on its right.

Grondle Grooves   49 m   HS   1957
Dirtier and less frequented than the last route, but still worthwhile.
Start at the foot of the large detached flake.
1 11 m. The thin crack on the right of the flake, or the easy
   chimney/crack on the left.
2 18 m. Climb the wall for a couple of metres and then follow a
   rather dirty crack which trends up to the left. This ends in a pale
   groove, the stance is just above this.
3 20 m. Climb to another ledge 6 metres higher and traverse left
   round a blunt rib. Continue up and leftwards to a short steep wall
   which ends the climb.

Variation   Direct Finish   30 m   MVS
   (4b). From the belay on the first pitch, climb direct up a series of
   walls.

A route has been climbed which starts midway between Grondle
Grooves and Main Wall at a whitish scoop, and rejoins the former to
finish via the Direct Finish. It is called **Centrepiece** (VS, 4c, 1979).

South-East Face

South-East Gully
An easy scramble which provides a useful descent from the crag top
to the routes starting on this side of the crag. The descent follows the
gully bed at first and then moves onto its left side (looking down).

The first three routes start in the gully proper, opposite Main Wall.

Gimmer Gorilla   15 m   E1   1983
The gloomy crack splitting the overhanging left wall of South-East
Gully (looking up), provides a thrutchy climb. Start 8 metres right of
Bachelor Crack.
   (5b). Climb the strenuous crack and easy rib above.

Bachelor Crack   54 m   HS   1941
The route generally follows the right edge of the face which overlooks
South-East Gully. Start at a corner crack in a sloping recess, at the
highest accessible point on the left wall of the gully.

1   18 m. Climb the corner to a small ledge (junction with Chimney Buttress, which goes up to the left). Overcome the bulge and traverse delicately to the rib on the right, belay a short way higher up at a small ledge.

2   36 m. An easier pitch which ascends the walls and slabs above, over several vegetated ledges.

Chimney Buttress   64 m   S   1923
A long second pitch provides the meat of the route. Start in South-East Gully, 2 metres beneath the start of Bachelor Crack.

1   13 m. Climb a short crack and scramble up and leftwards to a spacious ledge just right of Gimmer Chimney.

2   27 m. Climb diagonally rightwards to a big block near the edge of South-East Gully (junction with Bachelor Crack). Ascend the steep wall above, past the 'piano pitch' until slabs lead to a good ledge.

3   24 m. The slabs above lead pleasantly to the top.

** **Gimmer Chimney**   80 m   VD   ✓   1902
This striking feature which is obvious from some distance provides a classic route. Start at a broken rib under the main line, about 15 metres up from the gearing up point and 10 metres up and right of Bracket and Slab Climb.

1   32 m. Climb the rib and ensuing easy chimney to a steep section, which proves awkward. Easy climbing then leads to a good stance on the right.

2   17 m. Traverse left for 3 metres into a tricky groove, which leads into a sentry box. Good holds on the right rib of the crack facilitate progress up to a stance at the right end of the Gangway, and beneath the twin chimneys which are so obvious from below.

3   11 m. The left-hand chimney is part of Bracket and Slab Climb, and should only be undertaken by those who desire a genuine struggle at Hard Severe standard. Most will traverse right into the easier chimney, which leads to a belay in the open gully above.

4   20 m. Start by climbing the gully bed, then the rib on the right to the top.

** **Bracket and Slab Climb**   97 m   S   ✓   1923
An excellent and varied route, which is slightly harder if the strenuous chimney is included. Start at a pointed flake which leans against the wall 15 metres left of and 7 metres up from the gearing up point.

1   11 m. Climb over the tip of the flake to a ledge and then past an awkward slab to another ledge.

2   20 m. Move right to a rib, which is followed for 10 metres to a grassy bank. Follow this to a belay in the rocky corner at the top.
3   12 m. The Bracket. Climb up a little and make a devious traverse right for 6 metres, past and over blocks, until a groove leads up to a stance.
4   20 m. Traverse right over easy ground, past Amen Corner, to reach the start of the Neat Bit. Follow the ledge running left for 5 metres and then climb a crack which leads to the Gangway.
5   6 m. Easily rightwards to the foot of the chimneys.
6   9 m. The left-hand chimney is best suited to thin people. Stouter individuals or the faint-hearted may prefer the easier chimney on the right.
7   19 m. Climb out of the gully leftwards to a ledge. Work back right to a point overlooking the chimney and continue up the pleasant slabs above.

Variation Start
A clean slab, split by a prominent crack 5 metres right of the normal first pitch is a worthwhile but harder start.
1a   (4b). Climb the crack in the slab, passing an overlap at 9 metres. This leads to the grassy bank.

Absence of Malice   83 m   E2   1983
A poor series of variations with one short difficult section. Start as for the variation to the first pitch of Bracket and Slab Climb.
1   16 m (4b). The variation start to Bracket and Slab Climb, then the arête above to below a loose flake.
2   34 m (5a). Climb up, then step left to a groove. Move up again and step left to Bracket and Slab Climb (direct is harder). Follow Bracket and Slab Climb to a belay below the chimney.
3   13 m (5c). 5 metres left is a thin crack in a bulging wall. Gain it via a short flake and follow it; quite strenuous.
4   20 m (4a). Trend left up easier walls to the top.

South-East Lower Traverse   29 m   D   1902
A short cut from South-East Gully to the West Face. Start at a little cave about 15 metres above the foot of the gully.
1   17 m. From the small cave, follow a fault running up to the left to a small sentry box.
2   12 m. Climb out over the left wall and traverse left to the foot of Amen Corner.

A higher and easier traverse leads from the start of Chimney Buttress across Gimmer Chimney, then via slabs to the Gangway at the top of Amen Corner.

The West Face

Prelude   75 m   D   1940

An uninspiring route up the broken slabs below Ash Tree Ledge.
Start at the lowest point of the buttress by an ash tree below a sweep
of slabs.

1   14 m. The slab leads to a grassy corner and spike belay.
2   20 m. Climb a groove round to the left and easy rocks above it to
    the foot of a rib.
3   17 m. Scramble up the rib to a large flake.
4   24 m. Climb a short slab, traverse left and climb another slab to
    easy ground beneath the main face.

The following batch of routes are reached from Ash Tree Ledge which
lies below the main upper wall of the West Face. There are two easy
ways of reaching this. Either climb the first pitch of Bracket and Slab
Climb – the ledge lies leftwards from the belay. Alternatively from
the gearing up point at the foot of South-East Gully, a couple of small
trees can be seen horizontally left on the skyline of the crag, (one of
which might not last much longer). Just above them, a short scramble
over well worn rock, leads onto a grassy terrace on the front of the
crag. Follow this for 20 metres and then move up past some large
blocks. Go right past these, then back up left to reach Ash Tree
Ledge.

★ **Crow's Nest Direct**   65 m   VS   1940

Good climbing, if a little contrived. Start at the lower right-hand end
of Ash Tree Ledge, below a large and obvious niche. The Bracket on
Bracket and Slab Climb, is just above on the right.

1   14 m (4c). Climb an easy crack to the foot of the open groove in
    the left wall of the corner. Gain the groove with some difficulty
    and climb it to a ledge.
2   17 m (4b). From the small pedestal at the rear of the ledge, climb
    the bulging wall to a narrow layback crack which is 5 metres left
    of Amen Corner. This leads to the Gangway, which is followed
    leftwards to a belay beneath a small overhang.
3   18 m (4c). A sensational rising hand traverse across the
    overhanging wall on the right leads to an exit onto a small ledge
    above the overhang. Climb leftwards to the arête on the right of
    Green Chimney, which is followed to the Crow's Nest. Altern-
    atively climb a steep thin crack above the start of the hand traverse
    to the arête.
4   16 m. Step left into a corner and follow this and the slabs above
    to the summit.

Variation Start   Green Gambit   14 m   VS   1946
An easier, but still interesting alternative to pitch 1. Start 8 metres
left of the normal start.
1a (4b). Easy rock leads to the green overhanging groove, which is
    climbed to a difficult exit.

★★ 'B' Route   62 m   S   ✓   1907
An entertaining and popular climb. Towards the right end of Ash
Tree Ledge, where it slopes down to the right, a large platform can
be seen up on the right, guarded by a short wall with the letters ABCE
scratched on it. Start at this wall.
1   10 m. Scramble up to the platform up on the right.
2   11 m. A short crack on the right leads to Thompson's Ledge.
    Easily right for 6 metres to the foot of the impending corner.
3   5 m. Amen Corner. The overhanging and leaning corner is
    awkward though succumbs to a positive approach. Belay on the
    Gangway.
4   9 m. Ascend the Gangway to the left to a good ledge.
5   12 m. Climb the chimney – Green Chimney, which is immediately
    above, until a short traverse right leads round the corner into the
    Crow's Nest.
6   15 m. Step right and follow pleasant slabs to the top.

★ 'C' Route   62 m   S   ✓   1918
A classic route giving some fine climbing in good positions, following
a fairly direct line. Start as for 'B' Route.
1   10 m. Scramble up to the large platform up on the right and belay
    well to the right.
2   22 m. 3 metres left of the belay a short but steep wall leads into
    a steep recess, which is climbed with difficulty to Thompson's
    Ledge. Move right to a flake at the foot of a groove. Get into this
    via the right side of the flake and follow it until a step right leads
    to a belay at the foot of Green Chimney.
3   30 m. Traverse left and then climb diagonally left (across Lyon's
    Crawl), to a ledge below a prominent square-cut overhang. This
    point can also be reached by climbing the left edge of Green
    Chimney, until a traverse left leads to beneath the overhang.
    Climb through the overhang to the left and reach a ledge. Step
    back into the groove and climb it direct, in an exposed position
    to the finishing balcony.

★ 'A' Route   67 m   MS   1903
A great climb on excellent rock, so typical of this part of the crag. It
takes a series of steps rising to the left from Thompson's Ledge. Start
as for 'B' Route.

1   10 m. Scramble up to the platform up on the right.
2   5 m. Climb the initial crack of 'B' Route, to belay on Thompson's Ledge.
3   9 m. Traverse left along Thompson's Ledge to the foot of the Forty Foot Corner.
4   18 m. Climb the delightful corner to a good spike and traverse left and slightly up to a ledge and belay at the foot of an open groove, traditionally known as Lichen Chimney.
5   11 m. Climb Lichen Chimney. A good flake belay exists on the wall 2 metres above the finish.
6   14 m. The rock staircase on the left leads across to a steep finishing crack.

Diphthong   53 m   HS   1926

A direct, but artificial line, originally climbed as a direct start to the upper part of 'E' Route. Start as for 'B' Route.
1   10 m. Scramble up to the large platform up on the right.
2   20 m. Climb the wall about 3 metres left of 'C' Route, direct to the foot of the Forty Foot Corner. Follow the right edge of the corner and belay across to the right at the foot of Green Chimney.
3   23 m. Step back left and go straight up to the right of 'C' Route's overhang, towards the upper part of Green Chimney. Finish off with a vague arête just right of 'C' Route.

'E' Route   66 m   HS   1924

A delicate and somewhat exposed route, originally a direct start to 'A' Route, but now with it's own finish. Start as for 'B' Route.
1   12 m. Climb up then the little overhanging corner on the left leads to easy rocks and a stance.
2   17 m. Traverse diagonally left across the flakey wall for 12 metres and continue across to belay on the right rib of a crack.
3   10 m. Climb the crack for 5 metres and traverse delicately right to the foot of Lichen Chimney.
4   27 m. Continue traversing up to the right, crossing the blunt arête to reach a small ledge. Go back round to the left for a short way to a groove and climb up to a ledge which runs from 'C' Route to the top of Lichen Chimney. Continue up the steep wall to finish left of 'C' Route.

Lichen Groove   49 m   HS   1949

One of the most direct lines on this part of the crag, following a groove which becomes most pronounced as Lichen Chimney. Start on Ash Tree Ledge, just left of 'B' Route at a slight nose.

1   9 m. Up the nose by way of a thin crack on its right edge to join
     'E' Route.
2   18 m. Move up diagonally to the right for about 1 metre and climb
     the awkward wall which gives access to a shallow groove. Follow
     this up to the left on small holds, taking a belay at the foot of
     Lichen Chimney.
3   22 m. Either climb Lichen Chimney or, as on the first ascent, the
     ill-defined groove to the right and finish up the final corner on
     good holds.

★★ **Oliverson's Variation and Lyon's Crawl**   56 m   VD   1907
Although this is the easiest climb on this part of the crag, it is
nonetheless varied and interesting. Start from Ash Tree Ledge, 5
metres left of the start of 'B' Route.
1   10 m. Climb up easily to a good belay on a narrow ledge.
2   16 m. Traverse horizontally right on good holds for 5 metres to
     the left edge of the Forty Foot Corner. Climb this to its end. Belay
     low down.
3   15 m. Lyon's Crawl. Traverse upwards and to the right using an
     obvious crack for the hands, to a large ledge. Continue up
     rightwards into Green Chimney and then across the right wall into
     the Crow's Nest.
4   15 m. Step right and follow pleasant slabs to the top (as for 'B'
     Route).

★ **'D' Route**   31 m   S   1919
A brilliant pitch, which follows a fine crack line, the initial section of
which is quite delicate. Start 12 metres above Ash Tree Ledge at some
terraces with small blocky belays, below a triangular recess. This is
just right of a very smooth sweep of slabs which are topped by a
square cut roof. It is reached by scrambling up from a point 6 metres
left of Oliverson's Variation.
     Climb up easily into the recess and make a dainty traverse out left
to gain the right slanting groove and crack line. Follow this,
passing the Forked Lightning Crack just below the final
steepening which is overcome via holds on the right wall.

Musgrave's Traverse   43 m   HS   1929
The best of a number of possible traverses across the right-hand
section of the West Face linking the end of South-East Lower
Traverse with 'D' Route. Start from Thompson's Ledge at a crack a
short way left of Amen Corner. (This is the crack on pitch 2 of Crow's
Nest Direct.)

1   17 m. Layback the crack to a sloping ledge on the right. A slim
    ledge now leads up to the left for 6 metres to an airy right-angled
    corner, from which a delicate descending traverse can be made
    into 'C' Route. Up this to the foot of Green Chimney.
2   13 m. Traverse delicately left again, past the top of the Forty Foot
    Corner and move up a little to the foot of Lichen Chimney.
3   13 m. Continue leftwards to join 'D' Route. Finish up this, or
    perhaps more fittingly descend Hyphen.

** **Spring Bank**   43 m   E1   ✓   1979
A direct eliminate with some pleasing wall climbing and a testing roof
in a fine position. Start just left of 'D' Route.
    (5c). Follow the rib just left of 'D' Route then thin cracks in the
    slab to the roof. Pull over this on small holds and continue more
    easily up the slab.

* **Whit's End Direct**   43 m   E1   1972
An enjoyable route with a particularly fine section through the roof.
Start as for Whit's End at a thin slanting crack.
    (5b). Ascend the crack and continue direct up a line of slim cracks
    to a stepped section in the left end of the overhangs. Make an
    exhilarating move rightwards onto the slab and finish more easily
    on small, but positive holds.

* **Whit's End**   50 m   VS   1947
A continuously sustained climb whose variety and difficulty make up
for a rather hybrid line. Start a couple of metres left of 'D' Route at
a thin crack.
1   14 m (4c). Climb the thin left slanting crack and continue
    diagonally left via a good flake to a small stance beneath the
    overhang.
2   16 m (4c). Follow the corner above ('F' Route) for 5 metres until
    a traverse across the steep slab on the right is possible. Continue
    the traverse to the right edge of the slab on small ledges, rising
    slightly towards the end. Step down awkwardly into 'D' Route and
    take a belay, which is actually half way up Forked Lightning
    Crack.
3   20 m (4c). A short distance above, a very thin horizontal crack
    leads out to the left. Traverse this and pull up into a scoop. From
    the top of the scoop, step across its left wall and make an
    intimidating move onto the front, where difficulties ease and
    enjoyable climbing on good holds in a fine position leads to the
    top.

★★★ **'F' Route**   40 m   VS   ✓   1941

The last of the alphabet routes provides a classic crack climb with a well positioned crux. It takes the corner which separates the bulging front face from the slabby Whit's End/Spring Bank Area. Start just left of Whit's End below easy ledges.

(4c). Scramble up easy ledges to a junction with Hyphen and follow this across to the right to a small ledge above the thin crack of Whit's End. Follow the good flake from here to a small ledge beneath the overhangs. Move up right into the corner proper and follow it to a fine and bold finish.

★★ **Poacher**   38 m   HVS   1963

The slim groove left of the upper part of 'F' Route provides the meat of this exposed climb. Start as for 'F' Route.

1   26 m (5a). Follow 'F' Route to a niche at the foot of the corner proper. Climb up to the small roof and swing boldly left onto the face. Step up and make a series of moves diagonally leftwards to a spike at the foot of the slim groove. Climb this to an outstanding stance.

2   12 m (4c). Finish up the groove directly above the ledge.

Poacher Right-Hand   38 m   E2   1979

Interesting but artificial climbing up the rib between Poacher and 'F' Route.

(5b). Follow 'F' Route to the niche of Poacher. Pull straight over the roof and make some thrilling moves up the rib to the right end of the Poacher belay ledge. Climb the wall above with difficulty.

Enormous Room   37 m   E3   1977

A rising traverse across the bulging wall left of 'F' Route provides some exposed climbing with a few very hard moves. Start as for 'F' Route and Poacher.

(6a). Follow Poacher to the good spike. Move down and make a long stretch across leftwards into Eastern Hammer. Continue leftwards to join Kipling Groove and cross this to finish up another groove to the left.

Hyphen   28 m   S   1938

A pleasant traverse, connecting the top of Asterisk with 'D' Route. Start from Ash Tree Ledge at the top of Asterisk, 15 metres below the large overhangs on 'F' Route.

Climb direct to a small ledge beneath the overhang and traverse diagonally up to the right to a narrow ledge which leads into a bulging corner. A delicate two-step move leads round into 'D' Route and a belay just above, below the Forked Lightning Crack.

★★ Eastern Hammer   38 m   E3   1974

Excellent, fingery climbing up the bulging wall left of Poacher. Start by scrambling up to the ledge below the overhangs left of 'F' Route.
(6a). Pull over the overhang onto the steep wall and climb to a peg runner. Follow the crack to a good hold beneath the final bulges. Step up, move to the left end of the bulge and pull across it rightwards to a small ledge. Finish more easily up the final cracks of Kipling Groove.

★★★ Equus   43 m   E2   1976

An excellent and sustained pitch involving some difficult bridging up the slim groove between Eastern Hammer and Kipling Groove. Start by scrambling up to the ledge as for Eastern Hammer.
(5c). Move up leftwards to the centre of the roof which forms the Kipling Groove undercling. Pull over this and continue up the groove on small holds until forced left to a junction with Kipling Groove. Up this a short way to a resting place beneath a bulge and swing left to a small ledge. Climb the groove and exposed wall on the right to gain a horizontal crack, which is followed leftwards to finish.

Variation   Original Finish   1976

From the junction with Kipling Groove, climb the bulge directly above the peg runner moving slightly right to better holds. Up the wall above to finish immediately left of a large block overhang.

★★★ Kipling Groove   52 m   HVS ✓   1948

A magnificent and popular classic route taking an impressive line up the steep front face of the buttress. Start from the left end of Ash Tree Ledge as for Hyphen.
1   10 m. Scramble up easily to a ledge below the overhangs.
2   11 m (4c). The much photographed undercling pitch. Move up to and traverse left beneath the roof to a crack which leads to an overhung recess.
3   31 m (5a). Climb the right wall of the recess past a dubious block to the overhang, step right onto the edge and follow a crack to a resting place beneath the bulge. Pull across strenuously to a diagonal crack and peg runner (crux), and continue to a horizontal crack. Traverse right to a small ledge and ascend a crack to easier ground and the top. A first class pitch.

Photo – North West Arête, Gimmer Crag

Variation   Direct Finish   10 m   HVS   1959
    (5a). After the diagonal crack, move left and go up to a narrow
    ledge at the foot of a smooth little groove. Either climb this
    awkwardly or step round the corner to the left and climb the wall.
    Both options are harder than the normal finish.

Barry's Traverse   23 m   MVS   1936
A direct link between Ash Tree Ledge and The Crack and Hiatus,
useful as a continuation of the various West Face traverses. Start at
the extreme left-hand end of Ash Tree Ledge.
1   12 m (4b). Climb leftwards over easy ground until a short, steep
     descent to the left leads to a ledge on the right wall of the
     'unclimbed section' of The Crack.
2   11 m (4c). Make a delicate descending traverse into the corner,
     from where a strenuous pull up leads to a ledge on the left wall,
     which can be followed to the pedestal belay of The Crack. Hiatus
     is just to the left.

North-West Face (Lower Section)

These routes can be reached most easily from the gearing up point
under South-East Gully by descending beneath the crag and ascending
a well worn path which leads up through North-West Gully to a huge
chocked boulder and an eroded area up near the start of The Crack.
They can also be reached by crossing a terrace beneath Ash Tree
Ledge to a point where a 12 metre descent, (Herdwick Buttress pitch
1), leads to the Ash Tree Slabs area. This last descent is tricky and
most climbers would want to use a rope.

Interlude   27 m   VD   1940
Starts about 15 metres below a large detached flake standing in the
lower part of the gully, just below a smaller flake, and takes the line
of an arête.
    Climb the wall on the right of the arête until a tricky move left
    leads to the arête proper. Several metres of easier slabs lead to a
    belay, but it is just as well to continue up the easier ground above.

Cartwheel   21 m   VD   1947
A parallel line to Interlude, following grooves on the left side of the
arête. Start at a small flake about 10 metres below the large detached
flake.
    An initial bulge leads to a right angled corner. Cross a bulge in
    the groove above and continue without difficulty.

Photo – The Crack, Gimmer Crag

Herdwick Buttress   27 m   VD   1925
Start just to the right of the foot of Ash Tree Slabs.
1   12 m. Ascend the open chimney on the right to a good ledge. (The
    descent of this pitch is the easiest way down from Ash Tree Ledge
    and the terrace which gives access to this face from the South-East
    side of the crag.)
2   15 m. Climb up between two large flakes to beneath twin cracks
    which lead to the terrace below 'D' Route.

Introduction   22 m   HS   1948
Follows the left edge of the steep slab left of Herdwick Buttress. Start
at a small grassy bay beneath Ash Tree Slabs.
    Easy ground leads across to the slab, which is climbed as near to
its left side as possible. Surmounting a bulge well up the route is
the crux.

Crystal   38 m   E1   1981
The steep wall overlooking Ash Tree Slabs. Start as for Ash Tree
Corner.
    (5a). Scramble up to the right for a short way from the foot of the
corner to below the wall. Climb up and slightly left, then direct
alongside a slim groove to easier ground.

★ **Ash Tree Corner**   48 m   VS   1981
The fine corner on the right of Ash Tree Slabs.
    (4c). Gain and climb the corner from the grassy bay at its foot.

★★ **Ash Tree Slabs**   48 m   VD   ✓   1920
A great little climb up the handsome sweep of slabs 25 metres up the
gully from the large detached flake. Start at a small bay at the foot
of the slabs.
1   16 m. Climb 3 metres up the corner and traverse diagonally left
    on good holds to the edge of the slab and follow this to a ledge.
2   32 m. Climb 3 metres up to the left to a platform from which a
    groove leads up to the right. Follow this until it eases and continue
    up slabs to finish on a ledge midway between Ash Tree Ledge and
    'D' Route.

★ **Joas**   47 m   VS   1928
Quite strenuous and taking a contrived line, the route is not
particularly popular, but is nonetheless worth doing. Start from a
platform 8 metres left of Ash Tree Slabs, at a left to right slanting
groove.

1   9 m (4c). The overhanging groove leads up to the right to a broken terrace.
2   13 m (4c). Climb a crack on the right of an overhanging block to a small recess. Move left on a good flake and make a long reach for a good hold which enables a small ledge to be reached above the overhang. Continue slightly left until a long step across to the right gives access to a thin crack. Ascend this with difficulty to the platform on pitch 2 of Ash Tree Slabs.
3   25 m (4c). The narrow slab on the left leads to a corner and a finish up the arête on the right.

★★ Intern   48 m   HVS   *E1*   1963
A really worthwhile route which is sustained and varied. It provides a fitting start to Kipling Groove, when the resulting combination provides one of the best outings of this grade in the valley. Start as for Joas.
1   18 m (5b). Follow Joas for about 3 metres and cross the narrowing, left-slanting slab to its left edge which overlooks the gully. Pull up into a short groove and climb this to the foot of a left-slanting gangway. A technical and sustained pitch.
2   30 m (5a). Climb the gangway for a short distance before moving back right to climb the wall above the belay. Crossing a bulge necessitates some bold moves which lead into a steep groove. Follow this to a rib, which leads to the final steep crack of North-West Arête.

Langdale Cowboys   44 m   E3   1981
Starts about 5 metres left of Intern at a steep crack, slanting to the left. This route avoids the continuation of the crack by stepping right into Intern.
1   21 m (5c). The steep, diagonal crack is strenuous and awkward, but well protected. Over the bulge the crack forms a slot, pull out right into Intern and move right again into a parallel groove. Climb this to Intern's stance.
2   23 m (5b). Gain a thin flake system on the wall above and climb to a standing position on a spike at its top. Pull up the arête to a junction with Joas near the top.

Variation   Langdale Cowboys Continuation   19 m   E4   1984
A direct version of the first pitch of Langdale Cowboys gives a hard technical problem.
    (6b). Climb the steep, diagonal crack as for Langdale Cowboys, but continue directly up it past the slot to join North-West Arête.

★★ North-West Arête   42 m   MVS   ✓   1940

An exposed route on good rock and generally excellent holds. Start below an overhang to the left of the arête and a couple of metres right of Asterisk.

(4b). Climb the wall and traverse right to gain the foot of a groove which cuts through the left side of the overhang. Climb this and move right immediately above the overhang to gain the arête, which can be climbed more or less directly to a final thin flake crack which needs to be treated with care.

★★ Asterisk   38 m   HS   ✓   1928

A really excellent climb, mostly on jugs, up the steep wall left of North-West Arête. Start opposite a large jammed boulder in the gully bed.

Climb the left side of the wall on good holds for about 18 metres until a rightwards traverse on good footholds leads to the arête. Climb up leftwards to a thin crack which provides a worrying finish. It is also possible to finish up the wall on the left of the crack, or to traverse right, avoiding the final section, but this also avoids the issue.

Samaritan Corner   38 m   HS   1948

A slightly easier companion to Asterisk up the obvious corner to its left. Start at the foot of the corner.

Follow the corner fairly directly for 20 metres and finish up the right wall.

Girdle Traverse of Lower North-West Face   56 m   VS   1956

Start as for Ash Tree Slabs.

1   16 m. Pitch 1 of Ash Tree Slabs.
2   30 m (4c). Step left and down from the belay and climb the small slab to the top. Make a difficult swing round the corner to a narrow slab which is climbed to where it narrows. Swing round left on to a steep wall which is crossed to belay on North-West Arête.
3   10 m. Traverse left into the corner to finish.

North-West Face (Upper Section)

★★ Midnight Movie   77 m   E4   1982

An excellent, direct though eliminate line providing a fine way up the crag and which deserves to become popular. Start as for The Crack.

1   25 m (5b). Climb The Crack for 12 metres to a ledge. Climb up twin cracks in the impending wall above past a hanging niche to belay on a grass ledge.

2   16 m (6b). The thin crack in the wall above is well protected apart from the final section, and gives some hard climbing leading to the Kipling Groove undercling. Take a belay down to the right.

3   36 m (6a). Pull through the middle of the roof as for Equus and follow this for 6 metres. Pull right into a groove/crack line which proves technical and strenuous. This leads to the crux of Kipling Groove, up which it finishes.

★ **Breaking Point**   74 m   E2   1976
Undoubtedly an eliminate climb but nevertheless worthwhile. Start at the foot of The Crack.

1   25 m (5a). Climb the slab on the right until the wall steepens. Step up to the left, then climb rightwards to gain a crack. This leads to easier territory on the right and a belay 6 metres beneath the unmistakable wide crack of Gimmer String.

2   25 m (5c). Climb to the foot of the wide crack and step down left onto a large spike. A long stretch then enables a bold pull over the roof to be made. Climb strenuously left to a groove and follow it to a good ledge in The Crack (The Bower).

3   24 m (5c). Climb the wall above and step right to a junction with Gimmer String. Go up the steep groove where Gimmer String escapes left to the rib, and move right to finish up another steep groove.

★★ **Gimmer String**   77 m   E1   ✓   1963
A fine combination of pitches, strung together to provide enjoyable climbing in exposed situations. Many people miss out the first two pitches as described, and approach the route via the Kipling Groove undercling. Start as for The Crack.

1   25 m (4b). The first pitch of The Crack.

2   25 m (4c). Traverse right to the top of a pinnacle beneath a roof (Breaking Point breaches this). Step right into the wide crack and climb it to the stance on Kipling Groove.

3   27 m (5b). Climb straight up for a short way to some dubious blocks, then traverse left to a small ledge on the rib which is both undercut and overhung. Climb a thin crack on the right of the rib for about 5 metres, until a difficult pull leads round to the other side of the rib overlooking The Crack. Climb the arête from here, trending left up a thin crack, to a final difficult short wall which leads to an abrupt finish.

Variation   Direct Start   47 m   HVS   1976
Start as for The Crack.

1a   25 m (5b). Climb the slab on the right until the wall steepens. Step up left, then right to gain a crack which is followed to easier ground. Continue for 8 metres to a belay at the foot of steep slabs on the left.

2a   22 m (5a). Traverse left to the edge and aim for a junction with Gimmer String at the wide crack and follow this to the stance. Not a very satisfying excursion.

***The Crack**   74 m   VS   ✓   1928

The obvious great corner cleaving the crag from top to bottom. A combination of a fine line, exposed and sustained climbing and excellent rock make this one of Lakeland's finest crack climbs, undoubtedly deserving its classic status. Start at the foot of an easy angled corner, which leads up to the foot of the crack proper.

1   26 m (4b). Scramble into the corner and climb the crack until a delicate traverse left leads to the foot of a short groove. Climb this to a ledge and pedestal belay. (An infrequently taken and strenuous alternative to the traverse is to continue up the crack for 3 metres before traversing left to the belay.)

2   26 m (4c). Climb some thin cracks above the belay, moving left and up to a large ledge at 8 metres. A hard pull up on the steep ridge leads to better holds and then an easy traverse back right into the crack. This is the Sentry Box. A strenuous pull out of this leads to a good ledge up on the right – The Bower.

3   22 m (4c). A sustained pitch directly up the crack.

Gimmer High Girdle   58 m   E1   1976

A high level, exposed and enjoyable traverse from The Crack to Whit's End. Start from The Bower, at the end of pitch 2 of The Crack.

1   34 m (5a). Climb the wall above The Bower and step right to a junction with Gimmer String. Follow this up the thin crack and the arête until it is possible to swing right to a small ledge. Swing right in a very exposed position and move down to the good resting place below the crux of Kipling Groove. Pull strenuously across to the diagonal crack (crux of Kipling Groove) and continue right along a break until it is possible to step down onto the stance of Poacher.

2   24 m (5b). Traverse right and swing round into 'F' Route. Move right to join Whit's End Direct and follow this through the steps in the roof, continue traversing along the lip of the roof to join Whit's End. Finish up this.

Dight   71 m   E1   1953

Interesting and quite technical climbing up the wall left of The Crack. Start as for The Crack.

1   21 m (5b). Climb The Crack to a crack which bends left to the foot of two grooves. Climb the right-hand one, which has a series of slanting steps. This leads to the first belay of The Crack.

2   34 m (5a). Follow The Crack to the top of a rib. Trend easily rightwards to a ledge below the overlaps. Pull over the left side of the overhang with difficulty into the thin crack above. Follow this past a second and smaller overhang and climb more easily to a sentry box on the left. Ascend the crack on the left to some more small overhangs, and move right to a small stance.

3   16 m (5a). Climb the corner above the stance for a couple of metres before pulling up strenuously, round a small rib, into the groove on the right. Ascend this to easier ground and the top.

Variation Start   21 m   VS   1979
1a (4c). The groove left of the stepped groove of pitch 1.

Variation   Outside Tokyo   67 m   E2   1979
An inferior series of variations on Dight, linked to give a route of dubious merit and origins.
2a 31 m (5c). An artificial variation which leaves The Crack earlier and follows a thin crack taking a more direct line to the stance.
3a 15 m (5b). Step out right onto the wall and go direct to the top.

Dancin' Barefoot   87 m   HVS   1979
Another series of eliminate type variations. Start as for The Crack.
1   20 m (4b). The wall to the left of the grassy crack and a groove above it to the pedestal belay on The Crack.
2   13 m (5b). The crack above to a small juniper. Move up and left to a belay above the midway point of the second pitch of The Crack.
3   32 m (5a). Up the arête on the left until, it is possible to move left into a groove (Inertia). Up the crack above until a step down right leads to the edge, and cracks left of Inertia. Up these to overhangs and traverse right to belay.
4   22 m (5a). Follow Inertia to the corner, then climb the rib on the left.

★ Hiatus   100 m   VS   1927
A route which climbs rather scrappily up to the big overhangs left of The Crack and then makes up for it by way of a fine exposed traverse beneath them. Start 2 metres left of the foot of The Crack.
1   32 m. Up the steep wall to a terrace, easily up left to a corner then a scoop on the right followed by a ridge and slabs to a ledge in the corner on the right below a grassy gully.

2   32 m. Climb the gully for 9 metres until it is possible to move left
     along a ledge and then return to the gully via another ledge. A
     little higher in the gully, a traverse leads left across a mossy wall
     to some ledges.
3   21 m (4b). Go up into the corner under the overhang. Step across
     a large block and follow a rising traverse left, below the
     overhangs, to a steep corner. Climb this for 3 metres and step left,
     first up and then down, and continue the traverse under an
     overhanging rib to a second rib. Climb this to a good niche.
4   15 m (4b). Climb the slab on the left and then a short, awkward
     scoop, which leads to easier climbing.

Variation   Bridge's Variation   33 m   VS   1931
3a   21 m (4c). From the steep corner, climb up and over the rib to
     the same niche.
4a   12 m (4c). Climb the steep, black looking chimney above.

Grooves Traverse   34 m   HVS   1936
A harder finish to Hiatus, turning the overhangs by a long traverse
to the right. Start from the stance at the end of pitch 2 of Hiatus.
1   17 m (4c). Follow pitch 3 of Hiatus until level with the large block.
     Make a strenuous traverse right from here across the steep wall
     and into a groove which leads to a small stance below a scoop.
2   17 m (5a). Climb the scoop for 3 metres and make a very dainty
     traverse right beneath a small overhang. Continue rightwards up
     a slanting groove which leads to the top.

★ **Grooves Superdirect**   40 m   HVS   1949
An exposed route with some technical and inspiring climbing. Start
from a ledge on pitch 2 of Hiatus about 27 metres above the stance
and below and to the left of an obvious overhang.
1   23 m (5a). Go up to the overhang (above and to the left of the
     groove on Inertia) and stride across under it until some strenuous
     pulls lead to the edge of the slab overlooking Dight. Work up to
     the left to the stance on Grooves Traverse.
2   17 m (5b). Climb the scoop direct on small holds to a small flake
     at 6 metres. A hard move leads from here into a shallow groove
     on the left. Move left again and ascend back right on improving
     holds to rejoin the main groove, which is followed more easily to
     the top.

Variation   16 m   HVS   1976
2a   (5b). Climb the groove direct.

** **Inertia**   51 m   HVS   ✓   1959

The slabs left of Dight are approached via a steep groove in the bounding rib of Hiatus. Start from a ledge on pitch 2 of Hiatus, below the groove.

1   27 m (5a). Climb the groove to the top of a small pedestal in the corner and pull round the overhang into the groove on the right. Ascend this for a short way and traverse out to the rib on the right. Make a difficult move up this and go up and across to the Dight sentry box. Climb the crack on the left until stopped by the overhang and step right to a small stance.

2   24 m (5a). Above on the left, a long narrow slab slanting up to the left finishes against a line of small, square cut overhangs. Climb the slab, then the corner crack where it steepens to the end of these overhangs. Climb up to the right to finish.

Carpetbagger   75 m   VS   1968

A slightly more difficult companion to Hiatus. Start at a little slab below the right-hand rib of Godiva Groove.

1   27 m (4b). Climb the short slab to a ledge at 6 metres. Climb the shallow groove above and continue on the right of the rib for 10 metres to another ledge. Traverse horizontally right beneath a dubious flake, to a stance below a large overhang.

2   27 m (4b). Move out left and make a long ascending traverse to the left below some overhangs. Just before the rib of Godiva Groove, pull up onto a little slab and climb an awkward groove above directly to a stance on pitch 3 of Hiatus.

3   21 m (4b). From a standing position on the belay, make a short semi-hand traverse to the right, pull up and continue more easily to the top.

The Dream Merchants   61 m   VS   1979

A direct line up the slabs left of Carpetbagger. Start below a corner, halfway between Godiva Groove and Hiatus.

1   22 m (4c). Climb a thin crack on the left wall and step right to a ledge. Climb the wall above, with an awkward entry to the groove on the right rib of Godiva Groove. Climb this and exit right to a small stance by a juniper.

2   27 m (4c). Follow the crack above, past an overlap, to a steep groove leading to the niche of Hiatus.

3   12 m (4c). The steep groove above the variation finish to Hiatus.

Godiva Groove   57 m   MVS   1950

A fairly direct, natural line up the conspicuous V-groove left of Hiatus. Start by scrambling out of North-West Gully to a ledge beneath the left bounding rib of the groove.

1   9 m. Make a rising traverse to the right into the groove which leads to a stance.
2   23 m (4b). Climb the groove for 5 metres, then move left to a ledge on the edge. Follow the rib, then the groove again to a stance and belay just above the junction with Juniper Buttress.
3   25 m (4b). Climb the groove for a short way and move onto the left wall, which leads to the overhang. This is overcome by moving left into another mossy groove. A steep, broken wall leads to the top. (An alternative finish is to climb the clean rib on the right of the belay, moving right past a ledge to a belay below the last pitch of Hiatus.)

Juniper Buttress   58 m   MS   1922
A rather infrequented, but quite pleasant climb on the right-bounding wall of Junipall Gully. Start by scrambling out to the right just above the bottom of the gully to a ledge just below and to the right of a small ash.
1   14 m. Climb the rib immediately to the right of the ash, to a large flake belay in a gully on the left.
2   16 m. Traverse right for 9 metres to a corner beneath a nose. Climb over this nose into a V-groove and follow this past good holds on the rib to a small stance.
3   17 m. Continue in the line of the rib and then make a traverse left, initially across a gully, then across ledges and a slab. Climb up a little, then step across a troublesome corner and round a rib to an adequate recess.
4   11 m. The steep rib on the right leads to easy ground.

Junipall Gully (1907) separates the North-West Face from the buttress to the left, Pallid Buttress. It can be descended, but most people prefer the path which leads down the spur to the left.

Pallid Buttress

Nocturne   58 m   MVS   1945
Another unpopular route which deserves more traffic. Start in Junipall Gully, on its left side, a short way above the foot of the buttress and below a prominent line of overhangs.
1   18 m (4b). Traverse leftwards across a narrow slab towards a rib, to a point at which the overhangs have virtually disappeared. Pull over at a mossy crack and trend right to a good ledge.
2   27 m (4b). Climb directly to another overhang and avoid it by a short traverse to the right. Ascend a shallow crack and when it gets hard, traverse back left and go up to a recess and belay.

3   13 m (4b). Climb diagonally leftwards to a small ledge on the arête. A further corner and a thin crack lead to an easier finish.

Variations   1946
1a 13 m. Start higher in the gully, a few metres below its first short chimney pitch and follow a zig-zag crack to the same stance.
1b 33 m. Climb a groove just right of the zig-zag crack until a step left leads to a junction with pitch 2.

★ **Pallid Slabs**   57 m   S   1926
Delicate and very enjoyable climbing. Start a short way to the left of Nocturne, from the top of a large boulder.
1   19 m. Step from the boulder onto the slabs and make a long, rising traverse to the right, under a series of small overhangs to a good ledge and a junction with Nocturne.
2   16 m. The wall on the left is climbed to a ledge on the left, the gaining of which is a delicate manoeuvre.
3   22 m. From the left end of the ledge, step round into a groove and climb up past a tiny cave, some heather ledges and a corner, to finish up a short, steep crack.

Paleface   48 m   S   1940
An increasingly interesting route, with a good finish. Start below a shallow chimney, 6 metres left of the start to Pallid Slabs.
1   23 m. Climb mossy rocks, passing a conspicuous spike at 16 metres to a steep and mossy wall which leads to a ledge.
2   25 m. Climb directly to the overhang and circumvent it by means of an impressive traverse to the right which leads up to a flat ledge. Traverse easily back left and climb a 5 metre wall on sloping holds to an abrupt finish.

Wall End   38 m   MS   1940
The easiest route on the buttress though not the best. Start at the foot of a rib forming the left end of the main Pallid Buttress. A steep, shallow gully on the left separates the climb from the last, poor looking area of the wall.
1   29 m. Climb the rib until forced right. Continue traversing right for about 5 metres to a narrow ledge at the foot of a vertical V-groove, which leads to a niche. Climb diagonally left and gain a sloping ledge with some difficulty. A short, steep wall leads to an accommodating ledge.
2   9 m. Easy slabs above or the more difficult groove on the right.

Ashen Traverse   63 m   MVS   1946
A right to left girdle of Pallid Buttress, ending with the ascent of a
smooth slab on the section of crag left of Wall End. Start from a ledge
in Junipall Gully at the top of its first chimney pitch.

1   22 m (4c). A 5 metre traverse to the left gains a large flake, just
     right of a streak of black moss. Step awkwardly across the moss
     (especially if wet) to the shallow crack on pitch 2 of Nocturne.
     Follow this for a couple of metres until a traverse left, round a
     corner and across a slab leads to a heathery ledge at the top of
     pitch 2 of Pallid Slabs.
2   9 m. From the left end of the ledge, continue the traverse across
     a chimney and follow a rounded ledge which leads to a belay in
     a nook.
3   13 m. Step round the corner and follow a ledge downwards to the
     left, past a groove, until a long stride leads round into a large
     recess below an imposing crack.
4   19 m (4c). The Crimson Crack. Follow the crack direct, or perhaps
     better, leave it after 5 metres and climb diagonally left across the
     wall for a short way, then climb direct to the top.

** **The Girdle Traverse**   201 m   HVS   1949
A long and sustained expedition which offers some exposed and
interesting climbing, especially across the North-West Face. Highly
recommended, but not on Bank Holiday weekends. The route may
be extended by following Ashen Traverse across Pallid Buttress. Start
in South-East Gully at the foot of Bachelor Crack.

1   34 m (4b). Climb the corner on Bachelor Crack and surmount the
     bulging wall above. A horizontal traverse leftwards leads to a
     belay above the twin chimneys of Bracket and Slab Climb and
     Gimmer Chimney. Continue round the corner and over easier
     ground to a belay overlooking the Gangway.
2   13 m (4c). Step down a couple of metres and cross the impending
     wall to the Gangway by a descending traverse (part of pitch 3
     Crow's Nest Direct, reversed). Continue up the Gangway to the
     foot of Green Chimney.
3   29 m. Follow the easiest line leftwards to the foot of Lichen
     Chimney and follow Musgrave's Traverse across the steep wall to
     'D' Route, and a belay below the Forked Lightning Crack.
4   16 m. Step down and traverse diagonally left to reach the stance
     at the start of Kipling Groove. (Hyphen, reversed.)
5   18 m (5a). Traverse left beneath the overhang to the crack, as for
     Kipling Groove, and continue the traverse into another groove on
     the left, which is ascended problematically to gain The Bower.

6   3? m (4c). Climb The Crack for a short way and traverse left across
some mossy, but pleasant slabs to the sentry box on Dight. Pull
into the crack on the left and follow it to some overhangs.
Traverse left beneath these and make a long stride to a good hold.
A short groove above leads to the stance on Grooves Traverse.

7   12 m (4c). Traverse down to the left to the large detached block
on Hiatus. (Pitch 1 Grooves Traverse reversed.)

8   16 m (4b). Continue the traverse of Hiatus pitch 3 to the fine
niche.

9   32 m (4b). Move round the corner to the left and pull across an
open chimney to a traverse which leads to a junction with Juniper
Buttress. Continue leftwards to the edge and either finish up the
rib of Juniper Buttress or via Ashen Traverse, which lies across
the gully from the traverse before the final rib.

Variation

6a   26 m (5a). Climb The Crack past the overhang to a small ledge.
A short distance past here traverse horizontally left for 3 metres
to a steep corner, bounded on the left by an overhung groove.
Climb the corner until it is possible to trend diagonally left to a
stance in a broken groove. (The final groove of Grooves
Traverse.)

7a   11 m (5a). Step down and make a delicate traverse below a small
overhang into a scoop, which leads down to a small stance. (Part
of pitch 2 Grooves Traverse, reversed.)

Pike O'Stickle   (273 073)   Alt. 670 m   South West Facing

A large sweep of rock just below the summit and facing Bowfell is
impressive to look at but disappointing on close inspection. A small
buttress on the right side of the gully, on the immediate right of the
Stickle offers the only route worth describing.

Merlin Slab   85 m   D   1954

Opposite the man made cave in the gully is a huge white scoop. A
slab slants up from the right into the scoop. Start at the foot of the
slab.

1   15 m. Follow the slab leftwards, then climb up into the big scoop.

2   24 m. Traverse across the foot of the slab on the right and climb
the outside edge to a large grass ledge.

3   10 m. Climb the crack to the big terrace above.

4   36 m. Follow the line of the blunt arête to the top.

Other routes which have been recorded include **Chip Groove** (D, 1954) which start 45 metres up the gully from Merlin Slab on a small ledge, starting up a shallow groove. **Cave Buttress** (VD, 1954) which starts left of a cave at the foot of a large buttress on the main sweep of rock near the summit of Pike O'Stickle. **Stickle Slab** (VD, 1956) starts in the central gully at its steepest section, up the mossy slab.

It is possible to climb virtually anywhere at Very Difficult to Severe standard. Care is required to avoid the large number of perched blocks.

Bowfell

The main climbing on Bowfell is on four separate crags which lie in a rough semi-circle high on the eastern side of the mountain. The easiest approach is from the Old Dungeon Ghyll car park. Follow the road to Stool End Farm (no parking allowed here), then up the long ridge of The Band between Oxendale and Hell Ghyll. After the steep preliminary section the path levels out, passing above Neckband Crag which lies on the Mickleden side. When the ridge on the right running up to Bowfell is reached, the main track, which now turns left and ascends to Three Tarns is quitted and the path up the ridge followed. After a steep scree covered section turn right and follow the undulating Climbers Traverse path below a line of outcrops to the foot of Flat Crags. Cambridge Crag, North Buttress and Bowfell Buttress lie a short distance up to the right. This approach takes about 1½ hours. An alternative approach is to follow the Mickleden path from the Old Dungeon Ghyll Hotel until a left branch leads up Rossett Gill before striking up leftwards for Bowfell Buttress and the north end of the Climbers Traverse. This takes about 2 hours.

Flat Crags   (249 064)   Alt. 750 m   North East Facing

Flat Crags lies beyond the top of The Band, a rocky bastion guarding the sweeping expanse of The Great Slab on the east side of Bowfell.

The crag is very solid and most of the routes are steeper than they look from below. The rock is of a peculiar formation, very solid and compact and many of the holds sloping. It does however give excellent climbing. In the centre of the crag is a large bay with a striking clean cut right wall (Flat Iron Wall) which can be clearly seen on the approach walk up The Band, and catches the morning sun.

A rocky sloping terrace runs up leftwards under the crag, from which most of the routes start. The routes are described from left to right. Descents can easily be made at either end of the crag.

Mary Ann   42 m   VD   1971
Quite a good route on excellent rock. Start just right of a large flake about 6 metres right of a mossy cave near the top of the terrace.
1   22 m. Climb a short crack, step right to another crack which is followed to a line of overhangs. Traverse left below these and go up into a slabby bay. Huge flake belay up on the right.
2   20 m. A short crack on the left gives access to a rising traverse leftwards across the slabby wall. Finish steeply on good holds.

★ **Sunshine Crack**   25 m   E2   1988
Climbs the centre of the short steep wall about 10 metres right of Mary Ann. Start below the thin central crack. An interesting pitch.
     (5c). Climb the crack line and pull up right on layaways to a good foothold. Follow the crack above then pull right to a good hold below the top overhang; move left and gain the ledge above. Continue up the easy leftward slanting faultline above.

Moon Shadow   35 m   E1   1988
Start in the overhung corner above the rock step on the sloping gangway, 5 metres right of Sunshine Crack.
     (5b). Climb a crack in the edge of the right wall to the roof. Pull round to gain a groove line above and follow the left side of this to a ledge. Continue directly up the centre of the bubbly slab and short wall above to the top.

Edge of Darkness   35 m   E3   1988
A bold route up the steep wall left of Slowburn and the easier slabs above. Start from a slanting gangway 3 metres left of the arête.
     (6a). Climb up right to a ledge and good runner in a slanting slot on the right. Gain a good handhold up left then straight up to a sloping ledge and pull up right to the arête (junction with Slowburn). Step left and climb a steep little groove to a ledge. The groove on the righthand side of the slabs above is followed to the top.

In the centre of the crag is a large bay with the striking right wall taken by Flat Iron Wall. The next three routes start at the foot of the broad slab that runs down leftwards from the centre of the bay.

★ **Slowburn**   33 m   E2   1979
A good route, steeper than it looks which follows the left bounding
wall of the bay on sloping holds! Start just below the toe of the slab
at a short corner.
  (5b). Climb up easily to an obvious small pocket in the left wall.
  Pull out left to a loose spike. Follow a ramp that leads rightwards,
  to its top. Traverse delicately up and leftwards to a ledge on the
  arête. Pull up and follow the edge of the wall up and right in an
  exposed position until a steep move gives access to easy slabs
  leading to the top.

Solaris   36 m   E3   1978
Takes the obvious steep right facing groove in the left wall of the bay.
A very good though rather dirty route with some committing moves.
Start directly below the groove, on the slab.
  (6a). Move up the groove and climb it until a large ledge can be
  gained on the right. Make a committing swing down and across
  left to climb the very steep left arête of the groove to easy slabs.

Flat Crag Corner   42 m   VS   1960
Climbs the large corner in the middle of the bay. Start at the toe of
the slab, at a short corner.
1   24 m. Climb the corner and follow the easy slab rightwards until
    the steep corner is reached.
2   18 m (4c). Climb the corner, past a ledge to a short, steep finishing
    chimney with a doubtful chockstone.

★ **B.B. Corner**   38 m   HVS   1969
Takes the mossy corner just right of Flat Crag Corner. Start directly
below the corner.
1   23 m (5a). Climb the corner direct to a good ledge.
2   15 m (5a). Follow the corner past a difficult bulge to the top.

★ **Flat Iron Wall**   42 m   E1   1971
An excellent bold route up the wrinkled wall right of B. B. Corner.
Start as for that climb.
1   19 m (5a). Make a rising traverse rightwards to gain a small ledge
    above the overhangs. Step right and climb directly up the wall to
    a ledge on the right arête. Move up to a stance on the larger ledge
    above.
2   13 m (5a). Climb three, successive, little corners on the left to
    finish.

★ **Afterburner**   36 m   E4   1988
A bold, serious eliminate up the narrow steepening slab between B.B.
Corner and the crack of Fastburn. Start at the steep blunt arête
midway between these routes.
    (6a). Straight up to a good hold, then left and up on good slots
to gain a slab. Up this to a tiny ledge below the thin crack (the
top section of which is taken by Fastburn). Climb the crack for 5
metres and step left below a small overlap. Straight up the wall
above to an overlap and pull up left onto a good ledge. Continue
more easily to finish up a short steep groove.

★★ **Fastburn**   36 m   E2   1979
A superb pitch which goes directly up Flat Iron Wall. Start at a
hanging crack about 5 metres down and to the right of B. B. Corner.
    (5b). Climb the crack and hollow flake above to a good ledge.
(Junction with Flat Iron Wall). Continue delicately up the wall,
trending left to join the obvious thin slanting crack. Follow the
crack, moving out right at the top to a good ledge. Move
immediately back left and climb the awkward wall to easier
ground above.

1984   43 m   E5   1975
The huge bottomless groove right of Flat Iron Wall. An amazingly
contorted start gives access to the easier groove above. Start from the
hanging 'bog' below the groove, 5 metres right of Fastburn.
1   23 m (6b). Climb the grey slab and make a hard move, from an
    undercut to reach the hanging crack. Thrutch upwards to squat
    on the massive 'chicken head.' Struggle right to enter the hanging
    groove and follow it easily to a belay 5 metres below some perched
    blocks.
2   20 m (5a). Climb up and right to a groove, up this and the crack
    above to the top.

★★ **Ataxia**   46 m   E5   1979
An incredibly sustained pitch up the vague crack/groove line at the
right end of the crag. Start about 5 metres left from the foot of the
sloping terrace, below an audacious looking roof crack.
1   23 m (6b). Attack the roof via an offwidth crack to gain a ledge
    on the right. Step back left and follow the steepening crack to a
    narrow ledge below a short groove. Pull into the groove and make
    some hard moves to reach good holds at its top. Move up to a
    small ledge and belay.
2   23 m (4c). The slabs above trending leftwards.

★ Exposure   33 m   E4   1980
A good sustained route up the groove line below the prominent
curving overhang at the right end of the crag. Start directly below a
green streak under the overhang.
>   (6a). Climb the short wall to a slab, step left and gain a slim groove
>   leading to the lower overhang. Step right and gain the groove,
>   then up to the top overhang passing a peg runner with difficulty.
>   Move right on small holds to a ledge, then gain the slabs above
>   which lead more easily to a broken rake.

La Wally   40 m   E3   1988
Steeper than it looks with a bold finish. Start at the very base of the
terrace, 2 metres right of an obvious straight crack line.
>   (6a). Climb the wall to gain a faint crack which leads rightwards
>   to a niche. Pull up and right to a small sloping ledge. Climb the
>   very faint crack above to a bulge. Move boldly over this and up
>   the short steep wall above to a ledge. Climb the slab direct to a
>   block belay well back.

Hanging Corner   40 m   HVS   1988
A short route with the crux in the first three metres. Start from the
top of the massive detached block at the right end of the crag, below
a short hanging corner.
1   30 m (5a). Climb the corner by a long reach to a good crack in
     the slab above. Follow the crack to its top; then climb directly to
     a large grass ledge.
2   10 m. Follow the pleasant ramp leftwards to the top.

Flat Crags Climb   40 m   S
A poor route up the slabs at the right end of the crag. Easily
escapeable from any stance. Start just right of a large flake that leans
against the crag.
1   30 m. Climb the slab, step left to a recess at 5 metres. Traverse
     right slightly and make an awkward move to gain the grassy
     terrace above. Move up to the next terrace and traverse left 10
     metres to a spike belay below a crack.
2   10 m. Climb the crack pleasantly to the top.

Cambridge Crag   (246 066)   Alt. 775 m   North East Facing

Cambridge Crag is just above and to the right of Flat Crags,
overlooking the Great Slab of Bowfell. The crag is a mass of jumbled
pinnacles, short walls and ribs. Two routes from the 1920's have been

climbed here. There is an obvious waterspout at the toe of the crag. Descent is down the left side of the crag.

Borstal Buttress   70 m   S   1928
Start about 40 metres above and to the left of the waterspout, at a large corner with a steep right wall. After a good first pitch the climbing becomes broken and pitches can be avoided.
1   22 m. Traverse right across the wall, to a crack. Follow this to a steep V-chimney which is loose at the top.
2   13 m. Climb the rib on the right and cross a slab rightwards to a crevasse and large boulders.
3   20 m. Steep grass leads to the left by several small chimneys, the last one may be avoided on the right.
4   8 m. Cross the rib on the right and descend into a V-corner. Belay on the right wall.
5   7 m. Climb a thin groove on the left and scramble to the top.

The Cambridge Climb   76 m   VD   1922
A very good climb, with some excellent positions. Interesting in the wet! Starts about 10 metres left of the waterspout at the foot of a broad slab sloping upwards to the right.
1   10 m. Climb the slab to a corner.
2   8 m. Step round the rib on the right and climb up to a good ledge with an overhanging block belay.
3   14 m. Traverse left to the second of two grass niches, climb past a sharp jutting flake above to another grassy corner.
4   15 m. Climb the pleasant chimney to a ledge on the right.
5   11 m. Step back left into the chimney and climb to a large terrace.
6   18 m. A giant's three-step staircase leads up and rightwards (the middle step is awkward) to an exit on the ridge. Easy scrambling leads to the main ridge.

North Buttress   (246 066)   Alt. 785 m   North East Facing

North Buttress is just above and to the right of Cambridge Buttress and almost opposite Bowfell Buttress. It is a large and broken crag at its left end with many short ribs and smooth walls. The right-hand side is more continuous and contains three obvious fine grooves which are climbed by (from left to right) Gnomon, Mindbender and Sword of Damocles. Despite its appearance the crag has some excellent climbs on some of the roughest rock in the Lakes. Because of its isolation a team could well have the crag to themselves even on a busy summers day.

Descent is best made down the scree shute at the extreme right end of the crag. The routes are described from left to right.

★ Riboletto   43 m   E3   1988
A brilliant pitch up the fine rib that lies at the top of the broad grassy gully about 20 metres right of the waterspout. Scramble up the gully and belay at a groove just right of the truncated rib.
1   33 m (6a). Climb the groove for 5 metres, then make a delicate move left to gain a narrow hanging slab below the rib. Move left again to a thin groove and crack; continue up this (crux) using a hidden hold on the right wall to reach a good ledge. Follow the rib past another small ledge to below a short wall.
2   10 m (4c). Easily up the wall.

Siamese Chimneys   82 m   S   1952
A scrappy, disjointed route that climbs two chimneys which are separated by acres of grass. Start at the obvious chimney in a steep tower below and left of Gnomon.
1   18 m. Steep but easy rocks lead into the chimney which is climbed to a large overhang. Step right onto a slab and climb up to a sloping grass ledge.
2   26 m. Move round to the right into a triangular corner which is climbed and left by a narrow crack on the left. Continue rightwards up easy rocks to belay below a large chimney just left of the corner.
3   20 m. Climb the chimney (taking care with detached blocks near the top). Easy climbing leads up and rightwards to a final buttress.
3   18 m. Climb the buttress moving right to a ledge. Move up directly to a small crack which is followed to the top.

The Gnomon   63 m   HVS   1960
A good pitch up the left of the three big grooves. From the ledge of Sword of Damocles scramble down and left to belay below the groove at a spike belay.
1   40 m (5b). Climb the crack in the corner to a niche. Step left and climb a short wall to a larger niche. Move left to a small ledge on the left rib, swing back right and climb past an ancient peg with difficulty to a good ledge. Follow the steep groove above to more broken rock. Scramble up to belay below a tower.
2   23 m (4b). From the centre of the tower move up and then follow a line of holds rightwards to the edge. Climb directly to the top.

★ Mindbender   28 m   E2   1979

A fantastic pitch up the central groove. Start from the ledge directly below the groove.

   (5b). Climb the groove, past a difficult bulge to a steep, airy finish. Scramble to the top.

The Gibli   56 m   HVS   1963

A contrived route that gives some interesting climbing. Start from the ledge below Sword of Damocles.

1   6 m (4c). From the small pinnacle at the left end of the ledge, pull into a short steep crack and climb it to a stance behind a huge pinnacle.

2   9 m (5b). Climb the left-hand V-groove. Belay up on the right, as for Sword of Damocles.

3   26 m. Follow the cracked wall, pleasantly to a ledge on the arête and continue easily up the grassy gully to below a steep crack in the nose on the right.

4   15 m (4c). Climb the overhanging crack, then move rightwards to the top.

★★ Sword of Damocles   56 m   E1   1952

A classic route from the '50's, which climbs the right-hand and largest of the three grooves. The 'Sword' a wedged rock spike which gave the route its name has long gone. Start from the ledge, below and just left of the groove, at a prominent curved crack.

1   23 m (4b). Climb the crack to enter the groove on the right. Move up easily to the foot of a groove behind a huge pinnacle. Go up the groove until a long stride right can be made to gain a ledge on the edge of the buttress; move up a little until a semi-hand traverse can be made across the groove to a stance on the left wall.

2   15 m (5b). Climb the groove (where the 'Sword' was), past an awkward bulge. Move right above this to a small stance.

3   18 m (5a). Climb the steep, impressive flake-crack to a resting place; continue up the crack, until a move right leads to easier climbing and the top.

★ Mindprobe   56 m   E3   1973

A bold impressive route up the slim grooves in the arête to the right of Sword of Damocles. Start from the same ledge as for Sword of Damocles.

1   16 m (5b). Climb a slabby groove to below two steep grooves. Move up the left groove and make an awkward move into the right groove to finish on good holds.

2   12 m (5c). Move left and climb the green, open groove to a peg
    runner; continue with difficulty to better holds and swing up right
    to a ledge.
3   28 m (5b). Go across left to the foot of an overhanging corner.
    Jam the corner to reach a pinnacle. Move up right to the arête
    and finish up this.

The Scabbard   46 m   VS   1960
Quite a good route with some nice positions, although spoiled
somewhat by the grassy band in the middle. It climbs the wall around
to the right of Sword of Damocles. Start below a thin crack about 12
metres right of the ledge of Sword of Damocles.
1   7 m (4c). Climb the thin crack to a grass ledge. Scramble up to a
    belay about 20 metres above.
2   13 m (4c). Above the belay on the left, and curving down towards
    the left, is a shallow scoop a couple of metres from the edge of
    the rib. Climb steeply for a couple of metres, then make an
    awkward move to gain this scoop. Follow it to a stance and high
    thread belay.
3   26 m (4b). Climb the widening crack above to finish up broken
    grooves.

Swastika   119 m   HVS   1963
A right to left girdle of North Buttress; rather contrived but
enjoyable, clean and interesting, with a superb third pitch. Start as
for Sword of Damocles.
1   10 m (4c). Follow the upward-curving crack into the groove on
    the right; climb this for a couple of metres and then go back left
    behind an enormous pinnacle.
2   30 m (4c). Move left, and drop down to a large sloping ledge below
    a smooth-looking groove. Swing down round the far edge and pull
    up into a niche. Traverse delicately left and go down and round
    to the left, to a grassy niche. Step down and continue to a large
    grass ledge.
3   24 m (5a). Move up and round the rib to reach a big white scoop,
    move across to the corner on the far side. Step up across the
    corner and gain the front of the impressive pillar on the left. Step
    delicately to reach a steep, sharply undercut crack and follow it
    to some ledges.
4   30 m. Climb up easily to the foot of a cracked wall.
5   25 m (4c). Start at the left end of the wall and climb up to a
    pinnacle on the ridge at about 7 metres. Step right into a line of
    cracks which are followed to the top.

Bowfell Buttress   (246 067)   Alt. 750 m

North East to East
Facing

Bowfell Buttress is the last of the crags which lie in a rough semi-circle towards the north-east side of Bowfell. It is the most obvious of the three, and can be seen as a fine nose of rock from the valley. The crag appears from below to lie against the fell side. In fact it is cut off from behind by a cleft, which runs south, over broken rock and scree, into the fan-shaped scree shute from the main ridge, and north to join North Gully, which bounds the buttress on its right-hand side. High in the centre of the crag is a fine white wall which is climbed by Bowfell Buttress Eliminate. Most of the routes climb solid rock.

The routes are described from left to right. Descent is by the scree shute to the left of the crag.

The Plaque Route   85 m   D   1931
Originally climbed the left edge of the buttress, starting from a large boulder where scree and a grass terrace meet at the foot of the crag. Pitches 5 and 6 of this route now lie somewhere in the valley bottom, the victims of a massive rockfall. The lower pitches can still be climbed but an area of loose rock has to be negotiated to reach the top. This route is not recommended.

Sinister Slabs   100 m   HS   1932
A broken route near the left edge of the crag. Start about 6 metres left of the base of the crag, below a rib.
1   32 m. Climb the rib for about 9 metres until a move right can be made over a block. Move back left for 12 metres then climb straight up to a grassy shelf. Climb the slanting grassy chimney on the left to a belay below an overhanging corner.
2   28 m. Ascend a narrowing slab, slanting left; continue over some doubtful blocks and, after a couple of metres, go up a rib on the right. Make a move or two up the rib and traverse right into a groove until an awkward step leads right to a good ledge.
3   23 m. Climb first a chimney, then a grassy gully, followed by a rib.
4   17 m. Follow easy rock and then a crack in the steep rough slab to a flat ledge. Finish up the little wall above.

★★ **Bowfell Buttress**   106 m   VD   1902
A classic mountain route which takes the easiest way up the buttress. Start below a ridge, slightly left of the lowest point of the crag.
1   14 m. Climb the ridge to a good belay.
2   9 m. Climb the short chimney on the right and go up easy ground to a terrace.

3   12 m. Climb the steep wall above, moving diagonally left to a sentry box in a chimney.

4   18 m. Follow the chimney for about 12 metres and continue up easy ledges to a terrace sloping down to the right; walk along it for 7 metres to a crack on the right.

5   17 m. Climb the awkward crack to its top, then go up leftwards to slabby rocks leading to a pinnacle belay.

6   18 m. Move left and ascend a groove leading into a chimney. Go up to a slab and continue up the wall above until a long stride left leads up to a platform and large belay.

7   18 m. Step back to the right and follow a groove and its left branch to the finish.

★ **The Central Route**   76 m   HS   1931
An interesting route with some good climbing. Start about 3 metres right of Bowfell Buttress. The route keeps to the left of Bowfell Buttress after the first pitch.

1   13 m. Climb the broken groove to a stance at the top of the initial rib of Bowfell Buttress.

2   16 m. Climb the overhanging chimney and its easier continuation to block belays.

3   20 m. Step left from the belay and follow the easiest line up to a stance below a large block.

4   27 m. Step onto the block and climb a thin groove, with increasing difficulty, to an awkward finish into a recess. Climb the steep rib on the right; then follow a slanting slab on the left and finish by scrambling.

Rubicon Groove   100 m   E1   1951
A line of grooves, more or less directly up the centre of the crag. The crux involves some committing moves in an exposed position. Start as for The Central Route.

1   15 m. Climb the shallow groove, step left and ascend to a stance below the overhang.

2   20 m (5b). Above on the left is a steep, deeply cut groove which is undercut at its base. Climb diagonally left under the overhang into a corner, which runs parallel to the groove. Climb the corner for 4 metres until a traverse can be made across the right wall to a good hold on the rib. Keep moving right until the bed of the groove is reached. Continue up the groove more easily to a good belay.

Photo – 1984, Flat Crags

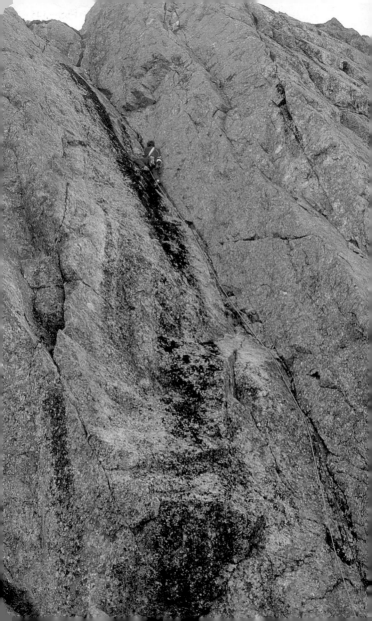

3   35 m (4c). Step back left across the groove and climb diagonally left up steep slabs to the foot of two twin cracks. Climb these, and the chimney formed by their union to a good ledge.

4   30 m (4c). Follow the easy ridge to below the steep rough slab of Sinister Slabs. Move right and climb an awkward niche in the wall to the top.

★ **Bowfell Buttress Eliminate**   108 m   E1   1964
A good route which takes the white wall high on the right edge of the crag. Start at a slanting crack in the steep wall at the toe of the buttress.

1   25 m (5b). Climb the crack which is awkward to start. Step right and continue more easily to a grassy ledge just left of a long slim groove.

2   25 m (4c). Climb the groove direct to a belay below the polished crack on Bowfell Buttress.

3   23 m (4b). Step down right and climb the deep V-groove to a ledge below a steep wall. Climb the corner on the left for 3 metres before swinging back right onto the steep wall above. Go up easier rock to a small niche on the left. (The corner can be avoided by climbing a good crack direct.

4   12 m (5b). Boldly climb the smooth white wall to a short, thin crack which leads to a fine narrow ledge.

5   23 m (5b). Step right, and make some awkward moves right to the edge of the buttress. Climb a steep crack on the right to easier ground and the top.

Variation   Direct Finish   15 m   E1   1975
5a (5b). Climb the obvious break through the overhangs to the summit.

Ledge and Groove   102 m   S   1945
A rambling route on the edge of the crag overlooking North Gully. The route can be quitted from several points by easy scrambling to the right. Start about 30 metres right of the base of the crag and about 4 metres left of the gully.

1   17 m. Climb a short wall and groove to a large ledge, continue up a rib to another ledge and follow it to its right end.

2   21 m. Go up a short wall, followed by a staircase to the right leading to a ledge below a small overhang. Move left on good holds for 4 metres and then go back right to a stance which overlooks the gully.

Photo – Mithrander, Neckband Crag

3   12 m. Step up, traverse right to a groove and go up it to a sloping ledge. Follow this leftwards to the ridge which leads to a stance.
4   15 m. Crux. Make a delicate traverse right and continue rightwards to a chimney; go up this to a ledge.
5   20 m. Climb the groove on the right to a ledge and traverse left to the foot of a steep crack. Go up this for 2 metres and make an awkward move onto a small ledge on the left, followed by some awkward moves past a projecting block to a large grassy terrace.
6   17 m. Climb diagonally left to a crack, climb this and the short wall above to finish.

★ Right-Hand Wall   58 m   VS   1924
An interesting route up the steep left bounding wall of North Gully, pleasant and exposed in its middle section. Start just above the steep chockstone pitch in the gully, at the foot of a conspicuous corner.
1   20 m. Climb the corner to a ledge.
2   20 m (4c). Traverse left across the wall on good flakes to a short crack. Climb the crack to a ledge. Move diagonally leftwards delicately to another small ledge. Climb the thin groove with difficulty until good holds lead to a grass ledge.
3   18 m (4b). Start a couple of metres to the right and follow a crack to a grassy terrace. Another short crack leads to the top of the Low Man.

Right-Hand Wall Traverse   42 m   VD   1924
Traverse the left-bounding wall of North Gully from right to left. The major part of the climb is incorporated in Ledge and Groove. Start about two thirds up the gully below a series of grass ledges.
1   13 m. Follow the broken and grassy rock slanting up leftwards to a large grass ledge.
2   6 m. Scramble left to the foot of a steep crack.
3   6 m. Climb the crack and make an awkward move onto a small ledge on the left, followed by more awkward moves past a projecting block to a large grassy terrace.
4   17 m. Climb diagonally left to a crack, climb this and the short wall above to finish.

Right Wall Eliminate   63 m   HVS   1975
A good route on clean rock up the left wall of North Gully. Start about 5 metres up the gully bed above the steep chockstone pitch.
1   33 m (5b). Climb a short corner and continue straight up to a quartz band. Traverse right to a ledge. Move up the crack at the right-hand end of the ledge to a bottomless groove. Make a hard move to reach the ledge above.

2   30 m (5b). From the block at the right-hand end of the ledge climb
the crack until a step right can be made into a short steep corner.
Climb this and make an awkward move to gain the top of a large
spike. Step right and finish up a smooth groove.

Grey Corner   40 m   S   1949
Climbs the long corner about two thirds the way up North Gully. Start
at the foot of the corner.
1   28 m. Climb the corner and move out right to a ledge on the rib.
Follow a series of large holds, slanting left awkwardly then go
right to belay.
2   12 m. Straight up the line of the corner to the top.

Grey Rib   47 m   S   1949
The right-hand rib of Grey Corner is clean and attractive but in its
upper half the difficulties are avoidable on the right.
1   20 m. Follow the rib, more or less direct to a good ledge.
2   27 m. Continue up the rib which is awkward at first to the top.

Bowfell Buttress Girdle   150 m   MVS   1942
A wandering route, much of it rather indefinite, but with a fine finish
across the big right wall of the buttress. Start from a large boulder at
the point where scree and grass meet at the foot of the left end of the
crag. As for Plaque Route.
1   24 m. Go straight up to a crack, followed by easy rocks to a rib
which leads to a small ledge.
2   10 m. Climb the mossy groove above and belay at the bottom of
a grassy terrace which slopes up to the left.
3   12 m. Traverse right, moving down slightly to gain an obvious
crevass-like crack. Move up slightly and make an awkward step
round a small rib. (Junction with Sinister Slabs).
4   20 m. About 6 metres right is a huge wedged block. Traverse right
to this and continue delicately to a stance and embedded boulder.
5   15 m. The short wall above is climbed diagonally from left to right
to a junction with Bowfell Buttress.
6   11 m. Move left and climb a groove leading into a chimney,
continue up to a slab and flake belay.
7   20 m. Descend slightly to the right to the foot of a chimney groove.
Make a difficult step round the corner on to a steep slab. Work
delicately across until a final awkward move enables a descending
line of large holds to be reached. Follow them across to a grass
ledge on the corner of the buttress.

8   20 m. Reverse the last few steps of the last pitch until a line of
    holds leads back right onto the corner of the buttress. Climb it for
    about 3 metres until a scoop can be reached on Right-Hand Wall.
    Up this to a ledge.
9   18 m. Start a couple of metres right of the belay and follow cracks
    to the top. (As for Right-Hand Wall.)

Variation   The Soft Option   18 m
8a. Step round the corner and climb the wall moving rightwards to a
    grassy ledge. Walk off right into the gully.

North Gully   S   1882
The large gully to the right of the buttress contains two short
chockstone pitches. The second pitch is about Severe with an
awkward landing onto loose scree above.

Hanging Knotts   (243 073)   Alt. 650 m   North West Facing

A scrappy crag high on the north-east side of Bowfell overlooking
Angle Tarn. When viewed from the Tarn an 'X' formation can be
seen, the upper 'V' consists of rock bounded by two gullies, the lower
'V' of rock strewn grass. **Dons' Delight** (46 m, D, 1949) climbs the
rock in the upper 'V'.

Bowfell Links   (246 063)   Alt. 800 m   South Facing

The links lie on the Eskdale side of Bowfell just above Three Tarns.
There are twelve short chimneys or gullies mostly of the chockstone
variety, but the rock is poor, uninteresting and liberally provided with
scree. Grades for the routes range from Moderate to Severe.

Neckband Crag   (256 062)   Alt. 550 m   North East Facing

This superb little crag lies about two thirds of the way up and on the
north east side of The Band. It is best approached from the Old
Dungeon Ghyll car park via Stool End Farm then following the broad
footpath up The Band until a flat section is reached. This is where
the footpath separates, the main path heading for Three Tarns and
the smaller path up the ridge on the right leading to Bowfell and the
Climbers Traverse to Flat Crags. From here descend steeply a gully
on the right to the crag. An alternative approach is to follow the
Mickleden path for 2 kilometres from the Old Dungeon Ghyll, then

climb the well named Grunting Ghyll direct to the crag. Either way takes approximately 1¼ hours.

The crag is compact with an outcrop type atmosphere and abounds in many fine cracks and grooves. Some areas are mossy and because of its aspect it needs about ten days of good weather at the start of the season to dry out. It is a cool haven in hot summers! Descents can be made at either end of the crag.

Three fine corners are the most obvious features – Mithrandir, Efrafa and Virgo take these lines. The routes are described from left to right, with particular reference to these corners.

★ **Wilkinson Sword** 27 m E5   1979
A tremendous route, serious and sustained, which climbs the left bounding wall of the crag. Start directly below the wall at a short corner.
    (6b). Climb the corner, then step right and follow a thin crack to its top; then make some hard moves left to a steep, shallow groove. Move up this to a ledge on the right. Step back left and climb the desperate thin finger crack to the top. Very strenuous.

★ **Cravat** 35 m MVS   1950
Good, exposed climbing, on excellent rock. Start as for Wilkinson Sword.
    (4b). Climb the corner to a ledge. From the right end climb a short crack until a line of holds lead rightwards to a scoop in the arête. Move up this to a grassy ledge. Go around the rib on the right and climb diagonally rightwards to reach a good crack 2 metres left of the corner. Follow the crack to the top.

Jagged Edge 30 m E4 †   1987
A technical route up the blunt arête, left of Mithrandir. Serious. Start below the left side of the arête at a flake.
    (6b). Pull off the flake into a small scoop. Follow a short crack rightwards to a long flat hold. Make a hard move into the groove above. Climb to the top of the groove then step right and follow the right side of the arête delicately to the top.

The next two routes climb the left wall of Mithrandir.

★★ **Sweeney Todd** 35 m E2   1983
A brilliant eliminate squeezed between Aragorn and Gandalf's Groove. Start 3 metres left of the corner, below a short overhanging flake crack above some large blocks.

(5c). Climb the crack and wall above to a small niche; pull onto the steep slab above to a crack. Follow the crack strenuously to the top.

⋆ **Aragorn**   40 m   E2   1971
Interesting climbing with excellent positions and an exciting finish. Start as for Mithrandir.
   (5c). Follow the corner for about 4 metres, then traverse an undercut slab left to a spike on the arête. Move into a niche above and follow this until some awkward moves left lead to a groove. Climb the groove and attack the desperate finishing crack above.

⋆⋆ **Mithrandir**   32 m   HVS   1972
A classic line up the large left corner of the crag.
   (5a). Climb the corner direct to a steep finish. Brilliant.

⋆ **Gandalf's Groove**   36 m   E1   1964
The original route which avoided part of the corner of Mithrandir by a detour onto the left wall. It is a great route giving delicate climbing on superb rock. Start as for Mithrandir.
   (5b). Ascend the corner for about 16 metres, until a descending traverse leads easily out left to the rib and crack. Climb the crack (crux) until an obvious traverse leads back right to the corner. Finish up this.

Variation   36 m   E2   1983
An alternative airy finish to Gandalf's Groove.
   (5b). Follow Gandalf's Groove to the crack on the left rib at the end of the traverse. Climb the right side of the rib delicately and boldly to the top.

⋆⋆ **Cut-throat**   30 m   E3   1978
A fantastic pitch. A vicious start leads to a fine groove and crack. Start below the thin overhanging crack 3 metres right of Mithrandir.
   (6a). Climb the crack to a slim groove; step right to a larger groove (junction with Gillette). Pull rightwards into a small niche in the rib and make an awkward move into the crack above, which is followed to the top.

⋆⋆⋆ **Gillette Direct**   30 m   E2   1968
A brilliant, well protected climb up the narrow hanging grooves right of Mithrandir. The route starts at a ragged crack below a line of overhangs.

(5c). Climb the crack to the overhang. Traverse left on undercuts and enter a slabby groove with difficulty. Follow this delicately to a small ledge. Move up to a better ledge and climb the steepening groove above to a superb finishing crack. Belay. Traverse off left.

Variation Gillette 30 m E1   1968
The original easier finish.
    (5a). From the small ledge below the top steep groove, traverse right to a rib. Move up and awkwardly enter the crack above. Follow this to the top.

** **Razor Crack** 72 m HVS   1966
A strenuous route up the superb crack that splits the slabby left wall of the central corner of Efrafa. Start at a ragged crack to the left as for Gillette Direct.
1   35 m (5a). Follow the crack to an overhang at 3 metres; pull over this moving right and climb a wider crack above over several overlaps to a good ledge.
2   37 m (4c). Climb a wide crack on the right. Step back left across a steep slab. Follow easier angled rock to finish just inside the left-hand skyline.

* **Close Shave** 34 m E3   1980
Takes the delicate slabby wall right of Razor Crack. Well protected by small wires.
    (6a). Follow Razor Crack until just above the first overhang. Traverse delicately right for about 3 metres, then climb directly up to the next line of overhangs. Climb mossy flakes rightwards to a thin crack which leads to a good ledge.

Efrafa 50 m E2   1974
The fine large central corner, which has become overgrown!
1   35 m (5c). Climb the corner for 20 metres until a traverse left leads to a shallow groove. Follow this past a bulge, then move back right to a ledge.
2   15 m. Step back left and continue up the line of the corner to the top.

To the right of the central corner of Efrafa is a long large overhang at about 4 metres split by two inverted grooves and a broken crack at its right end; the next three routes climb through this overhang at these faults.

Tonsor   30 m   E3   1980

An interesting, well protected roof problem. Start directly below the left inverted groove.

(6b). Climb a thin awkward crack in the wall to the overhang. Pull over this to some welcome jugs and a small ledge. Move left to a crack, then follow the slab, stepping back right near the top to a good ledge. Belay. Continue to the top via easy slabs.

Tonsure   30 m   E3   1987

Takes the right inverted groove, by some painful jamming.

(6a). Climb the wall to the groove. Jam the wide crack through the overhang to a small ledge. Follow a good crack pleasantly past three small overhangs to a good ledge and belay. Climb the corner and continue to the top via easy slabs.

Adam's Apple   47 m   HVS   1974

A very good crack climb. Start at a large pinnacle below the right end of the overhang at a steep chockstone filled crack.

1   27 m (5a). Follow a short corner to below the flaked crack. Climb the strenuous crack above to easier angled rock; continue in the same line to join the left end of the large overhang above. Step delicately left and climb up to a corner and good ledge.

2   20 m (4c). Move back left for 2 metres and climb the short wall past a loose block on small holds to a groove on the right. Step right and continue up the slab to a large block belay.

The Gizzard   53 m   VS   1949

Takes the fist wide tufted crack in the left wall of Virgo. Start below the crack at a pile of blocks.

1   33 m (4c). Follow the crack to a narrow sentry box; continue to the large overhang above. Traverse left to the far end of the roof. Step delicately left and climb up to a corner and good ledge.

2   20 m (4c). As for pitch 2 of Adam's Apple.

Virgo   60 m   HVS   1959

A good first pitch up the right corner of the crag. Not very well protected. Start at the foot of the corner.

1   24 m (5a). Climb the corner to an overhang at 10 metres. Pull awkwardly round to enter a groove on the right. Follow the groove until a traverse right to the rib can be made. Ascend the rib more easily to a good ledge.

2   36 m. Traverse left for 4 metres and climb a rib to a ledge. Continue up the short slab on the left; then a thin crack and easier climbing to the top.

The next two routes climb the wall and arête to the right of Virgo, the large corner near the right-hand end of the crag.

Razor's Edge   30 m   E5   †   1987
Fingery and serious climbing up the fine right wall of Virgo. Start at a pinnacle block below the middle of the wall.
    (6b). Climb the wall past a peg runner; then move up to a flake and poor nut runner. Make increasingly difficult and committing moves up and rightwards to the arête. Follow its left side more easily to a ledge and belay. Traverse off rightwards.

★ **Flying Blind**   30 m   E4   1978
Steep, bold, technical climbing up the blunt right arête of Virgo. A brilliant little pitch. Start from a pinnacle block to the left of the arête.
    (6a). Move up rightwards to gain the arête. Follow this to a flat topped spike. Pull up right to reach a steep crack in the overhanging wall, and make a hard move to gain a jammed block below the next overhanging crack. Move immediately left to regain the arête, which is followed easily to a good ledge. Traverse off rightwards.

Variation   1987
An easier finish avoiding the difficult step back to the arête.
    From the jammed block below the top overhanging crack climb directly to the top.

Nectar   55 m   MVS   1949
A disappointing route after a good first pitch. Start directly below the arête of Flying Blind.
1   19 m (4b). Climb right with difficulty to gain the bottomless groove. Follow this until a move right can be made to the arête, which is climbed on good holds to a stance and flake belay.
2   36 m. Traverse left for 4 metres and climb a rib to a ledge. Continue up the short slab on the left; then a thin crack and easier climbing to the top.

★ **The Neckband**   62 m   VD   1924
Follows the slabby rib at the extreme right end of the crag. Start at the foot of the rib.
1   30 m. Climb the rib and slab to a grassy platform. Move up to a rib on the right, crossing a broad ledge and miniature overhang. Continue up a groove above. Belay.
2   32 m. Climb up a series of large ledges and small slabs, to a steep corner on the extreme right. Go up the corner then scramble to the top.

The Girdle Traverse   60 m   VS   1949
A very poor right to left traverse. Start at the foot of The Neckband.
1   26 m. Climb the rib for 10 metres, then make a short traverse to
    the arête of Nectar; follow this to a good ledge.
2   18 m (4b). Traverse left along the ledge, move up slightly and
    make an awkward traverse left, round a nose to a block belay.
3   16 m (4c). Continue left along the ledge for a further 4 metres to
    a thin crack (peg runner). Finish by either traversing below the
    overhang or, more delicately, across the wall above it. Walk off
    to the left.

★ **Tattered Banners**   87 m   E2   1974
A much better girdle, with some interesting climbing. Start as for
Virgo.
1   35 m (5a). Climb Virgo to the overhang at 10 metres, pull into
    the continuation of the corner on the left. Follow this to below
    the large roof. Traverse left to gain the arête just below a small
    bulge, by some loose flakes. Peg belay. (This is 6 metres below
    and left of the large overhang.)
2   15 m (5c). Move up left to a large block, then descend a little until
    it is possible to move leftwards across the corner of Efrafa to reach
    a small corner. Gain the cracks on the left and go down on
    undercuts until á traverse leads below the overhang to a belay in
    Razor Crack.
3   15 m (5a). Move left to a rib and descend 3 metres, until it is
    possible to move into Gandalf's Groove. Traverse left, and belay
    mid-way across the descending traverse.
4   22 m (5c). Continue the traverse and go up the rib of Gandalf's
    Groove. Step left and finish up the steep crack of Aragorn.

The right-hand gully of Neckband Crag contains a short, clean slabby
wall, which has one route recorded on it.

Route One   20 m   VS   1949
Start at the foot of the highest section of the wall, below an obvious
boss.
    (4c). Climb the slab direct for 10 metres on small holds; make an
    awkward move right level with the top of the boss. Continue direct
    to the top.

Two other routes **Twain Cracks**, (VS, 25 m, 1960) and **Massiacasm**,
(VS, 30 m, 1960) have also been recorded on the main crag at the
extreme left end, however neither of these can now be found.

Crinkle Crag   (250 050)   Alt. 800 m   South East Facing

Opposite Gladstone Knott on the right side of Crinkle Gill and just below the summit of the highest Crinkle, is a large broken-looking crag. The following climb lies on the steepest part between two prominent terraces sloping up to the left.

Terrace Crack   50 m   S   1953
Follows a line of cracks just right of the impressive 25 metre central pillar, which is split by a steep crack. The pinnacle belay of the second pitch, up on the right, is an obvious landmark. Start at a short thin crack just right of the pillar.
1   20 m. Climb the crack to a ledge, go right into a deep corner and climb it, pulling out right into a crack beneath a huge block. Belay above the block.
2   10 m. Go left into a wide crack and follow it to the top of the pinnacle.
3   8 m. Left again into a scoop, and climb it to a difficult landing on a grass ledge on the left.
4   12 m. A couple of short walls lead up to the second terrace.

Gladstone Knott   (256 046)   Alt. 600 m   East Facing

Situated 400 metres from the head of Crinkle Gill, on the left. The crag has five chimney lines but the rock is generally poor with a lot of vegetation and quite slow to dry. The crag cannot be recommended.

Routes are from left to right.

Gladstone's Finger (10 m, M, 1926) climbs a sharp pinnacle two hundred metres to the left of the chimney's on the right of a scree chute. **First Chimney** (D, 1913); **Second Chimney** (D, 1923); **Third Chimney** involves no serious climbing but a lot of vegetation; **Fourth Chimney** (D, 1916) is very deep, black and conspicuous; **Fifth Chimney** (D) starts 15 metres right of Fourth Chimney, a variation start climbs a rock trough to its left.

Crinkle Gill   (257 049)   Alt. 400 m   North and South Facing

Situated in the upper half of Crinkle Gill above Oxendale. The crag is reached in about one hour from the car park at the Old Dungeon Ghyll. Follow the road to Stool End Farm then branch left from the track up The Band into Oxendale. From here a track leads to Crinkle Gill which can be ascended, in dry conditions, until the crag appears on the left above the open middle reaches of the Gill.

The South Gully Wall

The South Gully Wall which faces north, is steep, and takes a condiderable time to dry out after wet weather, particulary the extreme left-hand side. The rock is generally sound, though rather dirty because of the wetness and aspect.

The climbs are described from left to right. Descent can be made down the steep grassy hillside downstream from the crag.

Public Convenience   25 m   E2   1988
Climbs the overhanging square cut groove at the left end of the crag. Frequently wet!
  (5b). Easy broken rock leads leftwards to below the groove. Climb it exiting rightwards to the arête below the top overhang. Easy slabs are followed to an ash tree belay.

Private Investigations   25 m   E2   1985
The stepped right-hand groove just left of the obvious arête of A Naked Edge gives an interesting route.
  (5b). Climb a slab rightwards to below the groove. Up this and over a small overhang to a niche. Exit either left or rightwards and follow easy slabs and grooves to an ash tree belay.

★ **A Naked Edge**   25 m   E4   1985
A good route up the slim groove in the overhanging arête near the left-hand end of the crag.
  (6a). Climb a crack and the fine grooved arête to a niche. The short wall above leads to a left-trending ramp which is followed easily to the top.

★★ **Private Dancer**   25 m   E4   1985
A fine sustained and strenuous climb up the steep wall right of the arête of A Naked Edge. Start below a short slab just right of the arête.
  (6a). Climb the slab and steep groove to gain a crack on the left. Up this to the overhang, pull round on the right and up the steep wall above until possible to gain the bottom of the slanting ramp on the left. Straight up more easily to the top.

Genital Touch   28 m   E5   1985
Steep and bold climbing up the slanting grooves right of Private
Dancer. Start 3 metres right of Private Dancer.
    (6a). Pull up and gain the right slanting slab below the large
overhang. Climb the blank groove on its left, or the left side of
the overhang to gain the slab above. Ascend this rightwards to a
small ledge, then up the blank groove and steep wall above to the
top.

★ **Crimes of Quality**   28 m   E2   1985
The obvious right facing slabby corner. Start at a steep crack 8 metres
right of Genital Touch below the corner.
    (5b). Gain and climb the crack to a ledge. Ascend the slab and
left arête to a tiny ledge below the overhangs. Pull up the steep
grooves above, past a peg runner, to the top.

★ **Deception**   42 m   E3   1987
An interesting and committing route up the undercut wall left of
Private Eye, up which it starts.
    (6a). Climb up into a corner then left onto the notched arête. Up
to an overlap and follow this up and right until a step left can be
made to a thin crack in the middle of a steep wall. Straight up and
over on overhang to easier ground. Move right into the long
groove of Private Eye and up this to a tree belay.

Private Eye   42 m   E4   1985
The striking, slim right facing groove, right of Crimes of Quality,
gained via a subsidiary corner on its left.
    (6a). Gain the lower corner then climb up right to the main
groove. Climb it past a peg runner and continue straight up over
the overlaps to a long groove which leads to a tree belay.

Private Affair   42 m   S   1985
Climbs the gentler wall right of the overhangs.
    Up the wall and left to a traverse leading back right to a large
groove. Up this then right and continue via rocks which become
more broken to the top.

The North Gully Wall

50 metres further up the Gill on the opposite side is a rounded buttress
of good quality compact rock. It faces south and is faster drying than
the South Gully Wall. Descent is best made down the slopes 100
metres higher up the Gill.

Cold Nights   38 m   E2   1985
A good but poorly protected route. Start at a short steep corner below
the left side of the buttress.
    (5c). Difficult moves gain easier climbing above, trend up
rightwards to the start of a left slanting crack system. Follow this,
with easier climbing as height is gained.

★ **Bitter Days**   38 m   E5   †   1985
A bold and delicate route which follows a line of shallow niches on
the right-hand side of the buttress, after a steep strenuous start, 6
metres right of Cold Nights.
    (6b). Straight up steeply on layaways and undercuts to gain a ramp
leading left to an obvious weakness in the centre of the buttress.
Straight up to a niche and continue to the topmost shallow niche.
Pull directly out of this and step right and up to gain a thin crack.
Up to a ledge, left along it then up via crack and groove to the top.

40 metres further up the North side of the Gill from the Bitter Days
buttress is another continuous area of good though moss covered rock
up which the following routes climb.

Oberon   30 m   E1   1987
Pleasant slabby climbing on excellent clean rock. Start at the left side
of the wall at a slight groove line.
    (5b). Up the groove line to a natural chockstone in a crack on the
right. Step left and up onto a slab using a thin crack and continue
to an overlap. Pull over using another thin crack then straight up
the pillar above to the top. Block belay 6 metres back.

Titania   30 m   E1   1987
An interesting climb on good rough rock, 2 metres right of Oberon
an obvious diagonal crack slants up to the right. Start below the left
end of the crack.
    (5b). Climb to the slanting crack, step right gain the thin crack in
the wall above and follow it to a niche. Pull over an overlap to a
ledge, climb up left and from the top of a block climb a steep thin
crack to the top. Block belay 6 metres back.

Kettle Crag   (279 050)   Alt. 300 m   North Facing

This is the lowest crag on the slopes of Pike o' Blisco, facing Wall
End Farm. From the climbing point of view most of the crag is useless
being discontinuous and vegetated, but a wide grassy gully on the right

side has some continuous rock on its left wall, which is clean and of reasonable quality.

Semerikod   22 m   VS   1960
Near the bottom of the gully is a large rightward facing corner-crack capped by overhangs.
>   Climb up over vegetated ledges; a crack then leads to the overhangs which are turned on the right.

Further up the gully are two pinnacles or rock buttresses set out from the crag, the first has a large block on its top, the second is a short distance above this.

Major Slab   30 m   S   1933
Start just left of the lowest rock buttress beside a rowan.
>   Straight up passing an overhang on the right, traverse back left to easier rock leading to the top.

Red Slab   18 m   HS   1933
A pleasant pitch starting level with the block on top of the first rock buttress, at a shallow cave.
>   Pull out left from the cave and climb the slab direct.

Minor Slab   15 m   MVS   1933
A good pitch on sound rock. Start between the two rock buttresses some 10 metres right of Red Slab.
>   Climb direct up the slab to a good ledge. A poor continuation can be made up the broken rock above if desired.

Lightning Crag   (270 039)   Alt. 580 m   West Facing

A small buttress on the west slopes of Pike O'Blisco, directly above Red Tarn. It is similar in character to Black Crag, which is about 400 metres to its right. Approach as for Black Crag but continue to Red Tarn and strike directly up the fellside. From left to right the routes are:-

Fat Boys Crack   18 m   E1   †   1988
The crack near the left-hand side of the crag.
>   (5c). After a difficult start gain the easy slab above then follow the short corner crack to the top.

West Wall   16 m   E5   †   1988
The blank wall just right of Fat Boys Crack, gives difficult delicate climbing.
    (6b). Climb the wall just right of centre and reach left to clip a peg with a sling. Make difficult moves past this then up right to gain the slab above.

★ **Amina**   16 m   E1   †   1988
Climb the grooves in the nose of the buttress.
    (5b). Climb the left side of a flake below the nose or the crack to its left to a ledge at 5 metres. Up the V-crack on the left to a slab. Pull left to a short groove, from its top pull up left to gain the top slab.

Judith   18 m   VS   1988
Climbs the chimney on the right of the groove of Amina. Start at a flake crack below the right side of the buttress.
    (4c). Up the flake crack to a ledge. A short steep wall leads to a glacis, then the chimney and slab above.

Clare   18 m   VS   1988
Start 3 metres right of Judith below the right end of a ledge.
    (4c). Gain the ledge then climb twin cracks to another ledge right of the glacis on Judith. Up the rib on the right then the corner above to finish.

The wall to the right has several vertical cracks protected by an undercut start.

Stephen   16 m   VS   1988
The left most crack line.
    (4c). Gain a projecting ledge then climb the thin crack above.

The Prophet   16 m   E1   †   1988
Twin cracks 2 metres right of Stephen.
    (5b). Gain the cracks direct and follow them to the top.

Gandhi   16 m   MVS   1988
    (4b). The next crack right of The Prophet is gained from the right end of a ledge on its left, and followed to the top.

Gotama   16 m   VS   1988
The right most crack before the gully at the right side of the crag.
    (4c). Climb the gully for 3 metres, step left to gain the crack and climb it past a triangular niche.

Long Scar   (272 036)   Alt. 560 m   South West Facing

This long low crag is the poor neighbour to Black Crag. Situated about 200 metres to its left it can be clearly seen on the approach up the path from Wrynose Pass. The rock is similar to Black Crag but less continuous and more scrappy. The most prominent feature is a gully in the centre with a slabby right wall. Left of the gully the front face has a groove near its left-hand side. This is the line of the first route described. As with Black Crag this outcrop is used by many Outdoor Centres, most of the lines have been climbed but only a selection of the most prominent are included.

Katie's Dilemma   20 m   S   1982
The obvious groove at the left side of the front face.
     Gain the groove from the right and continue up the right-hand corner above a large perched block.

Something Stupid   18 m   VS   1982
Start 4 metres right of Katies Dilemma at a long ledge at the foot of the wall.
     (4c). Gain the ledge and follow a thin crack past a small overhang and flake crack to the top.

Forrudd   18 m   MVS   1982
Start 1 metre right of the long ledge at the base of the wall, at a thin crack.
     (4b). Climb the awkward crack past a tiny niche and continue more easily to the top.

Sam's Saunter   15 m   D   1982
Starts at the foot of the gully in the centre of the crag and climbs the clean right wall.
     Follow a series of indefinite cracks and slight grooves direct.

Platt Gang Groove   16 m   VD   1982
Start 2 metres right of the foot of the gully.
     Climb the right slanting shattered looking groove line in the centre of the wall, avoiding a ledge on the right near the top.

Intruder's Corner   18 m   VD   1982
2 metres right of Platt Gang Groove below the left end of an easy ramp.
     Up slightly rightwards to a grass ledge. Finish up the corner above.

Old Holborn   14 m   M   1982
Start from the base of the easy ramp below the right side of the wall.
    Ascend the corner crack to below a block on a ledge. Step right
around it to a ledge and continue up broken rock to the top.

Twin Cracks Right   12 m   S   1982
At the extreme right-hand end of the crag, just left of the lower rib
are two thin cracks.
    Ascend the right-hand crack to a ledge and continue to the top.

Black Crag   (274 037)   Alt. 580 m   West and South Facing

An outcrop of excellent clean rough rock, situated on the southern
slopes of Pike O' Blisco. Remeniscent of a gritstone edge, it has been
used for many years for bouldering and soloing. Most of the climbs
are short, many little more than boulder problems, but they dry very
quickly, catch any sun going and are quite entertaining.

The crag is most easily reached by following the Red Tarn path from
the Three Shires Stone at the top of Wrynose Pass for ¾ kilometer
then striking rightwards direct up the hillside to the foot of the crag.
This takes about 20 minutes.

West Face

At the extreme left end of the crag is an overhanging wall. The first
routes start here.

Dave's Arête   6 m   E1   1988
    (6a). The problem left-hand arête of the overhanging wall.

★ **Pocket Way**   8 m   E5   †   1988
    (6a). Direct up the centre of the wall on sharp pockets.

Pocket Crack   10 m   E3   1987
    (6a). The thin discontinuous cracks up the right-hand side of the
overhanging wall.

Sleep on my Pillow   10 m   E1   1987
Start below a grassy niche just right of the overhanging wall.
    (5b). An open groove up and right of Pocket Crack is gained by
climbing the thin crack above the niche, and followed to the top.

Nod Off   10 m   S   1987
Start as for Sleep On My Pillow.
   Gain the niche, pull right and follow a crack and wall above.

Noddy   10 m   HVS   1988
   (5c). The problem arête just right of Nod Off is climbed to gain
that route after 5 metres.

Three   16 m   VS   1988
Start 2 metres right of a rightward-facing and leaning corner, which
is choked with vegetation in its lower half.
   (4c). Gain a grass ledge then follow the right-hand crack just right
of the chimney/corner.

Blind   16 m   VS   1988
   (4c). The wall 2 metres right of Three leads to a grass ledge. Gain
the left end of a narrow grassy ledge above. Up to another ledge
then rightwards to the top.

Mice   16 m   VS   1988
The 5 metre high right facing, square-cut groove 4 metres right of
Three.
   (4c). The groove leads to a grass ledge. Up the broken slanting
crack on the right to blocks on a ledge. Finish up the corner above
or wall on the left.

The Real World   16 m   E5   †   1984
An eliminate problem up the protectionless pocketed wall. Start just
right of Mice on a small rock platform.
   (6a). Climb direct past a horizontal break at 3 metres, and up the
wall above on small pockets to an obvious circular hole. Pull up
to the ledge and over the left-hand block to finish up a short
groove.

Slipshod   16 m   VS   1984
The crackline 2 metres right of The Real World.
   (5a). Climb the wall direct past a triangular niche to gain the
crack. Follow this to a block lined ledge, step right and up a short
wall to the top.

★ **Yellow Fever**   16 m   E2   1984
The thin cracks up the centre of the prominent clean wall. Start 3
metres right of Slipshod.
   (5b). Pull up a rib and climb the thin cracks passing the right end
of the block-lined ledge to the top.

★ The First Touch   16 m   E1   1984
The groove line 6 metres right of Slipshod. Start from the left end of
a rock ledge below the right half of the crag.
    (5b). Climb the shallow right facing groove and then leftwards to
the top.

Hold On   10 m   S   1987
    The left-hand thin corner crack starting 2 metres right of The First
Touch.

Stop Showing Off   10 m   HVS   1987
    (5a). The right-hand corner crack starting as for Hold On.

Mind of no Fixed Abode   10 m   HVS   1988
The wall 2 metres right of Stop Showing Off.
    (4c). Climb the centre of the wall then up right to a short open
groove which is followed to the top.

The Last Corner   6 m   HVS   1988
    (5a). The deep square cut overhanging corner.

The Prow   6 m   HVS   1988
The undercut rib above a square cut corner in the tier below the rock
ledge.
    (5a). Climb the crack in either side of the rib at a similar grade.

South Face

The crag turns 90° at The Prow, Black Crag Needle is 5 metres to the
right.

Rope Up   12 m   E1   1988
The wall just left of Black Crag Needle.
    (6a). A difficult start up the centre of the wall, moving up
leftwards. Climb up rightwards towards the top.

The Needle   12 m   VD   c1955
    The wide corner crack to a ledge then ascend the crag side of the
pinnacle to a ledge near its top. A bold step can be made to the
top of the Needle from the main crag.

Needle Arête   12 m   E3   †   1988
The outside arête of the Needle.
    (6a). Climb the arête to a ledge at 5 metres. Gain the arête on
the left and climb it past a peg runner in a horizontal break.

Hang the Gallows High   8 m   E6   †   1988
The outside right arête of the Needle gives a bold and protectionless
eliminate route made serious by the drop below the starting ledge.
   (6a). From a ledge climb the left-hand side of the right arête by
bold layback moves.

Monkey the Needle   8 m   HVS   1988
   (5a). The Hang The Gallows High and inside arête's can be
reached together and climbed monkey-style, getting easier as
height is gained.

To the right of the Needle is an area of easy angled corners and slabs
of about Difficult standard. The next routes start from a grass ledge
20 metres right of the Needle.

Man   6 m   HS   1987
   Climb the short left facing corner with an overhang at its top and
easy slab above.

The   6 m   MVS   1988
   (4b). Ascend the narrow square rib between Man and Guns and
the slab above.

Guns   6 m   S   1988
   The short right-facing corner.

Billy Bunter   8 m   VS   1988
5 metres right of Guns.
   (4c). Gain the wide crack right of the rib with difficulty and follow
it to the top.

8 metres right is a leaning wall with two grooves in its upper half.

Bilko   12 m   E4   †   1987
   (6a). Climb the wall directly below the left-hand groove and enter
it from the left. Climb it and reach up left to finish.

★ **Doberman**   12 m   E3   †   1987
The obvious clean cut groove in the upper part of the wall.
   (6a). Climb directly up the wall, using the right wall for assistance
to gain the groove which is followed to the top.

To the right the crag again becomes very broken. 40 metres to the
right is an impressive steep slab taken by Glass Slipper with an

obvious crack in its left arête. Left of this is a secondary smaller slab taken by:-

Jolly Roger   16 m   HS   1987
Climb the slanting cracks to gain the slab above and finish up leftwards.

Jolly Corner   16 m   D   1988
The corner leads to a ledge at 6 metres. Continue past a second ledge and final short corner.

★ **Ann's Agony**   16 m   HVS   1987
The crack in the left arête of the impressive slab.
(5b). Gain the crack by an awkward undercut start and follow it direct.

★ **Glass Slipper**   16 m   E2   1987
A fine bold pitch on small holds with only marginal protection. Start in the corner on the right of the slab.
(5b). Step left above the overhung base and climb the slab slightly left of centre until a step right is made 5 metres from the top.

Glass Clogs   16 m   S   1987
The slab 5 metres right of Glass Slipper is climbed direct.

There are numerous other short problems between the routes described which give good bouldering. These are left for the individual to discover.

Blake Rigg   (287 040)   Alt. 400 m   East Facing

A large slow drying vegetated crag, which lies on the eastern shoulder of Pike O' Blisco overlooking Blea Tarn. It consists of steep rock walls between large grassy terraces and rakes.

Many wandering climbs have been ascended, despite the fact that there are some good pitches the routes are generally scrappy and do not warrant detailed description. In recent years several routes have been cleaned and claimed on two of the best looking buttresses on the crag.

This area including the crag is a Site of Special Scientific Interest, great care should therefore be taken to avoid disturbing the flora and fauna.

The crag can be reached from the car park to the east of Blea Tarn from which it can be clearly seen, by following the footpath and ascending the hillside direct. This takes about half an hour.

Lower Left Buttress

This buttress is situated at the bottom of and near the left-hand side of the crag. It can be identified by a large holly tree growing below the centre of the buttress. Abseil descent recommended for most routes. The routes are described from left to right.

Too Excess   25 m   VS   1987
Climbs the hanging prow at the left-hand end of the buttress. Start at the foot of the gully to its left.
(4c). Climb diagonally right for 4 metres to a ledge. Up steeply past a flake then continue up the wall just left of the arête. 6 metres of scrambling leads to a thread/spike belay.

Variation   Right-Hand Finish   MVS   1987
(4b). From the flake, traverse right to a ledge on the right side of the arête. Climb an easy groove to the same belay.

Crazy Horse   32 m   E1   †   1987
The steep groove right of the prow. Start beneath the left slanting crack 4 metres left of the holly.
(5b). Pull onto a ledge, surmount an overlap then climb diagonally leftwards for 3 metres to gain the prominent overhanging crack/groove. Climb it curving up leftwards to a ledge on the arête. Follow the right side of an easy groove to a thread/spike belay.

Variation   Left-Hand Start   E2   1987
Start below the hanging prow at the left end of the buttress.
(5c). Climb impending rock rightwards past a peg runner, then traverse right for 3 metres to join the main route below the overhanging crack/groove.

Leningrad   30 m   E4   † ·   1987
A fine route which climbs the thin crack system up the centre of the slabby wall left of the holly. Start 4 metres left of the holly, as for Crazy Horse.
(6a). From a ledge, surmount the overlap and follow the thin crack to a large pocket at mid-height. Step right using two tiny pockets, pull up with difficulty then hand traverse back left on more

pockets and continue until possible to pull over an overlap to the left end of a grass ledge. Easy slab climbing leads up left to a thread belay.

Baby Blue Sky   40 m   HVS   1987
Climbs the obvious wide diagonal crack on the right side of the buttress. Start just right of the holly.
1   26 m (5a). Climb the stepped arête to a tiny right slanting overlap. Follow this to the obvious wide crack which is climbed up leftwards to a ledge and block belay.
2   14 m (4c). Move right to a shallow scoop with a block. Climb the scoop and short wall above, then follow grass ledges right to a belay.

Variation Start   10 m   HVS   1987
Start just right of the original start.
    (5a). Climb the thin curving flake crack to gain the base of the obvious wide diagonal crack.

Time After Time   52 m   E2   †   1987
A scrappy route linking rock pitches at the right-hand end of the buttress. Start 20 metres right of Baby Blue Sky at the lowest point of the buttress, just right of another holly.
1   18 m (4c). Surmount a bulge above a ledge at 3 metres, then follow the slabby rib above direct to a ledge.
2   16 m (5a). Steep rock behind the belay is climbed awkwardly to another ledge. Follow easier rock then scramble back to belay beneath an impressive overhanging crack.
3   18 m (5c). Climb this classic jamming crack to a ledge. Continue up the left leaning overhanging crack, then scramble back 5 metres to belay. Scramble up leftwards and descend well to the left of the buttress.

Right-Hand Buttress

Situated near the right-hand side and at about half-height of the crag. A large buttress slanting up from right to left, with a band of overhangs at half-height. The rock is generally rather dirty and mossy but the routes have been well cleaned.

Olga Korbut   45 m   E4   †   1981
A pleasant route with a difficult crux over the overhangs. Start at the vertical stepped groove near the right side of the face.

Photo – Deer Bield Crack, Deer Bield Crag

1   22 m (6b). Climb the stepped groove for 10 metres. Hand traverse
    left for 5 metres to a crack, climb this to, and through the crux
    overhang. Belay 6 metres above.
2   23 m (5c). Continue up the crack and small groove then undercuts
    lead up left to a good hold up right. Reach up left to a large ledge.
    Up right to another ledge then up to a belay and abseil point.

Variation   Press Gang   25 m   E2   1988
Start at the crack line left of the stepped groove.
1a (5a). Climb the crack direct to the overhang, junction with Olga
    Korbut. Step right, climb the overhang at an obvious weakness,
    then back left to the belay of Olga Korbut.

Nelli Kim   42 m   E2   †   1981
Start as for Olga Korbut.
1   20 m (5b). Climb straight up to the top of the groove, crux. Better
    holds lead up and right to a line of overhangs. Climb this on large
    holds directly above the groove, and move left to belay.
2   22 m (5b). Move right to gain a shallow scoop which is climbed
    to easier ground. Belay and abseil point 5 metres higher.

Variation   The Scoop   20 m   E2   1987
Start just right of the stepped groove.
1a (5a). Climb the easy stepped rib and step left to join Nelli Kim
    below the overhang. Follow this to the stance.

Side Pike   (293 053)   Alt. 320 m   South West Facing

This is situated on the extreme right of Lingmoor Fell, as seen from
the New Dungeon Ghyll Hotel. The crag lies on the east side in the
gap between the Pike and the Fell. The approach is from the cattle
grid at the top of the Blea Tarn road. A path contours the hillside
starting from a stile east of the cattle grid until after a couple of
hundred metres a fence can be followed up the hillside to the foot of
the crag.

The rock is sound though rather dirty in places.

The climbs are described from left to right, the best descent is on the
left.

The left side of the crag is quite steep and split by dirty grooves. There
is a large pinnacle at the foot of the crag below some overhangs.

Photo – Laugh Not, White Ghyll Crag

Tower Climb   30 m of climbing   M   1943
A poor wandering route which starts at the wall below and left of the pinnacle. Climb this then the short groove 4 metres left of Rough Ridge. Ribs, slabs and walks lead to a finish up a short chimney crack on the split blocks above the crag.

Rough Ridge   32 m   VD   1963
Start at a ledge 8 metres left of the pinnacle where a right slanting grassy groove leads to a holly at 6 metres.
   Climb the rib on the right of the groove to the holly. Continue up the groove above, work out to the right-hand rib and follow it to the top.

Marrawhack   32 m   S   1957
Start 3 metres right of Rough Ridge.
   Ascend direct to the holly tree; then traverse right across a steep wall onto the front of the buttress above the overhangs. A short corner crack leads to a tree stump, then easier climbing to the top.

Dunn Cruisin'   30 m   E1   1983
Start directly above the pinnacle.
   (5b). Climb to the overhang, pull up the left-hand side on good holds then finish directly up the rib above to easier ground (Rough Ridge).

Limpet Grooves   22 m   MVS   1947
The deep, dirty overhanging groove is mainly avoided by climbing the right wall. Start 3 metres right of the pinnacle.
   (4b). Ascend the right wall for 4 metres, step left into the groove, climb it for a couple of metres then right to a ledge. Finish up the groove above.

The next routes start from a ledge below the steep central wall 15 metres up and right of Limpet Grooves.

Rudolf Nureyev   30 m   E5   1981
Thin and technically very difficult climbing up the left side of the overhanging wall.
   (6c). Straight up the wall left of Margot Fonteyn to a ledge. Thin cracks in the wall above gain a tiny niche, pull up left and follow the rib then easier climbing to the top.

Margot Fonteyn   30 m   E2   1981
The obvious crack near the centre of the wall gives good sustained climbing.

(5b). Climb the crack to a ledge. Narrow stepped corners past 2 old peg runners lead to an overlap, straight over this then the crack above to a ledge. Easier rock to the top.

The dirty gully on the right gives a poor route **South Wall Buttress** (25 m, VD, 1948). The arête to its right gives a pitch only a little better **Judith** (25 m, S, 1959).

To the right is a short stretch of mossy wall seamed with thin cracks and giving some pleasant short climbs. Numerous routes have been claimed, the following selection are included giving the best climbs.

Crustacean Traverse   40 m   VD
A rising traverse line across the mossy wall. Start just right of a short overhanging groove at the left end of the wall.
Climb up then right along a diagonal line to a junction with Spider Crack at a blunt rib. Finish up the rib above.

Cheroot   25 m   MVS   1959
A direct climb up the left-hand side of the wall and shallow groove above. Start midway between Crustacean Traverse and the obvious crack in the centre of the wall.
(4b). Climb a thin crack to a ledge 2 metres left of a small rowan tree then direct up the broken shallow mossy groove line above.

No Big Cigar   25 m   VS   1988
Start at the crack in the centre of the wall.
(4b). Climb the crack to a small rowan tree, then steep broken rock above in a direct line to the top.

★ Panatella   25 m   VS   1988
A good clean route up the steep cracked wall 2 metres right of the central crack line.
(4c). Climb the wall keeping left of Spider Crack, to a small overlap, pull directly over this then continue up the left side of the mossy wall above to the top.

Spider Crack   32 m   MS   1946
The prominent crack at the right-hand end of the wall.
Climb the rib on the left of the overhanging start then step right into the crack afer 6 metres. Continue up the crack to ledges and finish up the mossy slabs on the left.

Variation   VS
(4c). Gain the prominent crack direct over the overhang at the bottom.

Tinning's Move   30 m   MS   1978
Start 3 metres right of Spider Crack, 10 metres left of the stone wall bounding the right-hand end of the crag.
Climb a short rib to a ledge. Pull over a bulge on the left then slightly right to a shallow corner which leads to a ledge. Finish up easier rock directly above.

Girdle Traverse   75 m   MVS   1959
A left to right girdle along the obvious break. Start as for Limpet Grooves.
1   35 m (4b). Follow Limpet Grooves to the ledge. Continue round to the right, up a series of steps then across ledges below the steep wall of Rudolf Nureyev, to a dirty groove.
2   20 m. Move round the corner and traverse the mossy wall past a small ledge to Spider Crack.
3   20 m. Finish up Spider Crack.

Oak Howe Crag · (304 056)   Alt. 280 m   East Facing

Oak Howe Crack lies high on the east side of the ridge running north from Lingmoor Fell, on the opposite side of the valley from Chapel Stile. It can be reached in about half an hours walking from the Stickle Barn. Follow the track opposite, to Side House Farm, then turn left and follow the obvious path rising gradually across the hillside until the ridge below and right of the crag is reached. Ascend this and then cross the scree to the Needle. The crag can also be reached by following the tracks from Chapel Stile or Elterwater to Spout Crag Quarry then contouring the hillside to the crag, passing below Spout Crag.

The routes are very steep and the rock generally sound and clean. The best descent is down the gully at the left-hand end. The routes are described left to right.

The Gentle Touch   30 m   HVS   1984
A pleasant introduction. Start at a left slanting ramp just right of some large flakes at the left end of the crag.
(5a). Climb the stepped ramp to a slab and follow this leftwards to below a thin crackline. Climb this and the short walls above direct to the top.

Highlander   26 m   E3   1987
Climbs the steep pocketed wall left of the obvious crack of Porridge.
Start as for The Gentle Touch.
    (5c). Climb the ramp of The Gentle Touch until the angle eases
then step up right to the base of the impending wall. Climb the
centre of the wall to a jug/small ledge. Make a long reach up right
to gain a hidden pocket and use this to climb up and rightwards
to finish as for Porridge.

An oak tree grows on the left-hand side of the crag at half height.
The next route takes the slanting line to its left.

Porridge   30 m   E2   1984
Strenuous and awkward climbing. Start at a spike below the oak tree.
    (5c). Follow the left slanting line to the tree. Step left and climb
the wide slanting crack, finishing on its left.

★★ **Going Straight**   30 m   E1   1984
Excellent climbing up the crackline right of the tree. Start 1 metre
right of Porridge.
    (5b). Climb the groove and pull directly over a bulge onto a
sloping ledge. Follow the jagged crack, and grooves above direct
to the top.

Sweeney   36 m   E3   1984
Climbs the left side of the steep central wall. Start 7 metres right of
Going Straight at a shallow groove, 3 metres right of an obvious
slanting corner.
    (5c). Climb the groove to below the overhanging wall. Move left
into the corner then up and left onto a large sloping ledge. Up
the wall trending leftwards then direct to a rightwards slanting line
of grooves/ramps, which are followed to the top.

Minder   40 m   E2   1984
A fine route with steep climbing which takes the right side of the
central wall. Start at a large spike 5 metres right of Sweeney.
    (5c). Step off the spike and climb the shallow grooves to below
the overhanging wall. Move up and right on flakes to a ledge. Up
the short groove to a slab on the right beside some holly trees.
Step up left and traverse left for 8 metres. A short wall and slab
above lead to the top.

★★ The Sting   30 m   E3   1984
An excellent and strenuous route which takes the prominent right
slanting crack across the bulges in the upper half of the wall. Start
below a left slanting break 3 metres left of The Deceiver.
    (6a). Gain the break and follow it to a ledge. Follow the right
    slanting crackline over three bulges, then move right and up to
    the top.

★ The Deceiver   32 m   E4   1984
Steep climbing with an intimidating and delicate upper slab. Start
from the crevassed blocks just left of the Needle below an open
groove.
    (6a). Climb the groove then hand traverse left to a junction with
    The Sting at a spike on the first bulge. Pull up right over a bulge,
    as for The Sting then up left to the foot of a slab. Up this to where
    it steepens then traverse left and pull round the rib. Up this to
    the top.

★★ Crooked Crack   30 m   E3   1984
Strenuous and airy climbing up the overhanging arête behind the
Needle. Start on the boulders just left of the arête.
    (5c). Step up and right to a large sloping ledge below a flake crack
    in the arête. Up a groove on the left then right on undercuts to
    gain the crack. Follow this rightwards up the slab, to a pull out
    right above a bulge. A short rib to finish.

Confidence Trick   36 m   E4   1984
Bold climbing up the wall right of Crooked Crack leads to a steep
finish on its left. Start in a corner behind the boulders right of the
arête of Crooked Crack.
    (6a). Climb the prominent corner crack to a ledge on the right.
    Up and left across the wall to the start of a thin crack. (Crooked
    Crack.) Up this for 6 metres, traverse left to the arête, pull up to
    a slab above then back right to finish up a short rib.

Oak Howe Needle

Oak Howe Needle stands in front of the crag, at its right-hand end
and gives a number of short pitches.

The Needle is split almost east to west, the fissure thus formed giving
a Severe crack/groove pitch on either side. Both pitches lead to the
same crevasse just below the summit; the east in 10 metres; the west
in 7 metres with a bulge to gain the crevasse. From here a short
chimney gains the top.

An easy angled crack on the south side reaches the foot of the final chimney in 5 metres.

A shoulder on the north side of the Needle can be reached either by a dirty groove in the North-West Slabs, or by the steeper and cleaner North-East Wall. From the shoulder a Severe slab just left of the west crack leads to the same final 3 metre chimney.

Spout Crag   (305 054)   Alt. 280 m   East Facing

Situated about 300 metres south (left) of Oak Howe Crag is a line of rather dirty outcrops. Approach as for Upper Spout Crag to the quarry then contour through the woods on the right to the foot of the crag; alternatively traverse leftwards across the steep hillside from Oak Howe Crag. The routes climb the right-hand side of the steep yellowish lower face. The descent from the top of the crag is well to the right.

Crossword   56 m   VS   1970
A serious climb which starts 4 metres right of a holly, below the centre of the steep wall.
1   15 m. Pull over an overhang into a niche and climb a crack until a ledge on the right is gained. Traverse right to a recess. Belay on the right.
2   14 m. Climb the overhanging wall on the left of the recess to a ledge and traverse right to a birch.
3   19 m. Ascend the easier wall on the left, moving right to an oak.
4   8 m. The steep wall behind the oak to the top.

Gurt Gardin Stuff   66 m   VS   1970
Start 10 metres right of Crossword, at a left facing corner, just right of a small briar.
1   30 m. Pull up into a groove and climb the rib on its right to ledges. Pull up the steep wall to a flake on the left and up the steep groove above. Cross pitch 2 of Crossword and continue up to some trees. Go left to a birch below a brown wall.
2   36 m. Move up and to the right to a mossy corner. Climb this then traverse left on an obvious line. Mantelshelf onto a higher line, traverse right and pull out to easier rock. Steeply up left, then up rightwards to the top. Tree belay well back.

Upper Spout Crag   (304 051)   Alt. 370 m   East Facing

This is the crag which lies south of Oakhowe Crag, directly above
Spout Crag Quarry on the easten slopes of Lingmoor Fell. The easiest
approach starts from the camp-site at Chapel Stile. Walk up to
Baysbrown Farm and continue up the quarry track. Go round the
back of the quarry and up the steep hillside to the crag.

The main buttress left of the large impending corner is split by two
obvious crack lines giving good routes.

Descend with care at either end of the crag.

★ **Dinsdale**   36 m   E2   1972
The obvious left-hand crack in the centre of the buttress.
    (5b). Climb the crack through a holly, then an awkward overhang
at 25 metres. Continue more easily up the slab to the top.

★ **Spiny Norman**   45 m   E3   1972
The right-hand crack gives an excellent route. Start just right of the
toe of the buttress.
1 36 m (6a). Climb up for 3 metres and traverse left to a slim
    V-groove. Climb this, then move left onto a slab; move back right
    into the groove (crux) which leads to an overhanging crack. Climb
    this, then move up and leftwards to a small holly. Go across right
    to a large holly and belay.
2 9 m. Finish easily, on the right.

Brian Stalin   30 m   E2   1980
Climbs the obvious crack/groove line 10 metres right of the impending
corner.
    (5c). Scramble up to a ledge below the steep corner and climb it
to a dubious down pointing flake. Move left and pull up steeply
to a large shelf below the V-groove. Climb this to the top.

Elterwater Quarries   (324 048)

A number of routes have been climbed in these quarries but they are
still being worked and any climbing activity is likely to meet with stern
opposition.

Rothay Bridge Crag   (368 039)   Alt. 100 m   East Facing

This steep and vegetated crag is located in delightful woodland above
Rothay Bridge, on the outskirts of Ambleside. Approach from

Ambleside on foot, following the Coniston road out of the village and taking the right turn just after crossing the narrow Rothay Bridge. After a short way, a small road leads up to the left, through a gate. Go through the gate and strike up the steep grassy field to where the angle eases and a wall can be seen below the woodland. Cross the wall with care and head leftwards up through the wood until the crag can be seen. There is only one route of any worth here, but it is a real gem.

★ **Crack in the Woods**   20 m   E4   1981
The climb takes the striking, thin crackline which splits the centre of the smoothest face. Start beneath the crack.

(6a). Scramble up leftwards for a couple of metres and step across onto a good foothold on the slab on the right. A delicate move up leads to the small overhang, and a further move right leads to a jug at the base of the crack. The crack is well protected, but gets progressively harder towards the top, where the final pull over onto the slab, via a poor jam and a pinch proves to be a difficult and frustrating crux.

The groove to the right has been climbed on a top rope but it is loose and unpleasant and not worth the effort.

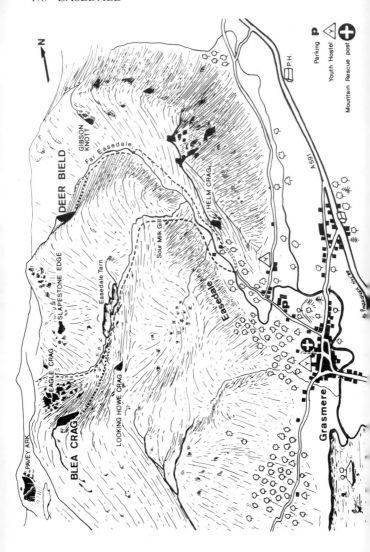

EASEDALE

The main crags in this area are Deer Bield Crag and Blea Crag though several other smaller crags have been developed. They offer a wide range of styles and grades of climbs and are usually less busy than other crags in Langdale, offering a more secluded alternative.

The easiest approach is from Grasmere though those around Blea Crag can be reached in a similar time from Langdale.

The crags are described in an anti-clockwise sequence around the area starting from the hamlet of Easedale.

Helm Crag   (327 087)   Alt. 170 m   South West Facing

The obvious little cag 100 metres above the quarry at the junction of the Helm Crag and Far Easedale footpaths behind the hamlet of Easedale. Marked as Jackdaw Crag on the O.S. map; the central buttress is steep, clean, fairly quick drying and offers some pleasant climbing. Descent is down either side of the crag.

The climbs are described from left to right.

★ **Green Light**   23 m   HVS   1980
A good route up the wall at the left end of the central buttress. Start at a thin crack.
    (5a). Climb the wall passing a small overhang at half height and finish up the blunt arête above.

Beacon Rib   26 m   HVS   1959
A pleasant open climb up the blunt arête. Start below the arête at the lowest point of the crag.
    (5a). Climb on the left of the rib for a couple of metres before gaining the crest, which leads to a ledge. The scoop on the left leads to a mantelshelf to gain a fine platform. Move right to Beacon Crack and finish up this.

★ **Beacon Crack**   24 m   HS
The prominent wide corner-crack containing two large trees. More tree than rock climbing.
    Climb the tree and crack to a ledge, the chimney and holly to a slab and finish up the wide crack above.

Holly Tree Crack   36 m   MS   1924
The steep polished crack facing Beacon Crack and 2 metres to its right.
1   12 m. Climb the crack to a ledge.
2   24 m. Move 3 metres right and climb up over doubtful blocks, past an old tree stump, and continue to a large ledge. Traverse 3 metres right and finish up a short corner.

★ **Flarepath**   30 m   VS   1954
Delicate and quite sustained. The route starts at a steep corner 3 metres right of Holly Tree Crack, crosses that climb and finishes at the top of Beacon Crack.
   (4c). Climb the crack in the corner to a ledge. Follow the open groove on the left for a couple of metres until a move can be made left onto a slab. Delicately up leftwards to a ledge and large detached block, then step left and finish up Beacon Crack.

Atmospheric Phenomena   22 m   E2   1984
A poorly protected eliminate starting at the rib just right of Flarepath.
   (5b). Climb the steep rib left of a small pinnacle to a ledge. Continue up the right side of the steep wall above, just left of pitch 2 of Holly Tree Crack, with an awkward move onto a slab. Finish up Holly Tree Crack.

★ **Flarepath Direct**   28 m   E1
The steep chimney/groove above pitch 1 of Holly Tree Crack. Start 4 metres right of Flarepath at the right-hand corner crack.
1   14 m (4c). Climb the corner to a ledge move left and belay as for Holly Tree Crack.
2   14 m (5b). Follow the open groove on the left, as for Flarepath; then step round the rib on the right into a steep shallow groove. Up this and make a difficult entry into the chimney above, which becomes easier as height is gained.

Spectrum   22 m   VS   1983
Climbs the pillar right of pitch 2 of Holly Tree Crack. Start on the right side of the rib right of Flarepath Direct, just left of the ivy.
   (4c). Climb the wall on large holds to below a short steep groove. Move right, climb the rib and step up onto a slab. Traverse left to a tiny holly in a thin crack, then up passing a slanting groove/overlap to a ledge. Finish up the corner above as for Holly Tree Crack.

The Grouter   28 m   S   1967
Start at a ledge 5 metres up left from the start of Bentley.
   Step left and climb a short crack and groove into a triangular recess. Pull up left then up to an overhung ledge. Traverse right to a steep corner which is climbed to a crevasse. Finish up a short crack behind a pinnacle on the right.

The Brocken Spectre   22 m   E2   1984
Start as The Grouter.
   (5c). Climb the left-slanting crack/groove to a ledge. Pull over the overhang on the right and up a short wall to a ledge. (Peg runner on the girdle on the right.) Finish up the groove above.

Two Star Red   22 m   E3   1980
Takes the overhanging groove on the right side of the impressively steep wall right of The Grouter. Start as The Grouter.
   (6a). Climb the steep wall above into a niche then continue to below a triangular overhang. Pull over this at its widest point to gain a slabby arête which leads to the top.

Bentley   35 m   VD   1954
Makes the most of the rock on the overgrown right-hand side of the crag. Start at a wooded corner 10 metres right of the start of Flarpath Direct.
1   20 m. Climb a rightward slanting flake-crack to a ledge. Continue up the fist wide crack above to a ledge and tree belay below a steep arête.
2   15 m. Step left along the ledge and climb a short crack to below a steep corner. A short gangway on the right of the arête can be used, with a step left round the arête, to gain the same point. Climb the corner over a bulge at the top to tree belays.

Pathfinder   34 m   VS   1983
A pleasant little corner crack which is lost high on the right-hand side of the crag. Best reached from the start of Bentley.
1   22 m. Climb the flake crack as for Bentley to a ledge then scramble up rightwards for 12 metres to below the corner.
2   12 m (4c). Climb the corner and finish up the wall on the right.

Rainbow   76 m   HVS   1969
A left to right girdle of the crag with some impressive positions. Start at the foot of the gully left of Green Light.
1   15 m (5a). Move up and follow the gangway right to Beacon Rib. Go up to a ledge and holly belay on the right.

2   28 m (4c). Cross the wall to ledges on Holly Tree Crack. Follow
    this right and up over doubtful blocks and past a tree stump until
    possible to traverse right across the slab to The Grouter. Follow
    this to the overhang and belay on the ledge on the left.
3   15 m (5a). Follow the horizontal break right to a niche, peg
    runner. Go boldly round the corner descending a little below an
    overhang and on to a ledge and belay.
4   18 m. Move right along the ledge to the short crack on Bentley.
    Climb this and the corner above, as for Bentley, to the top.

Gibson Knott   (317 098)   Alt. 300 m   South West Facing

This steep, vegetation-covered crag lies on the north slopes of Far
Easedale, a little beyond the footbridge over the Gill and 120 metres
above the valley. It is marked on the O.S. map as Horn Crag. It has
two climbs of only moderate interest.

Route 1   62 m (12 m of climbing)   D   1925
Start towards the right-hand end of the crag where a subsidiary
buttress juts out.
1   12 m. Easy scrambling up this leads to a terrace.
2   12 m. Climb slightly right up the steep wall above for 8 metres
    and step left into a very short chimney leading to another terrace.
3   38 m. Easy scrambling through junipers leads to the top.

Route 2   70 m   D   1925
Near the left-hand corner of the crag is a steep 12 metre high chimney
marked by a large triangle of junipers at its foot.
1   8 m. Grass climbing up the left of this triangle lead to the foot of
    the chimney.
2   5 m. The scooped wall on the left to a good ledge.
3   10 m. A 6 metre mossy wall leads to a terrace running leftwards
    to belaying blocks.
4   14 m. Starting left of these blocks climb up a couple of metres and
    make an upward traverse round a corner to the right to a short
    chimney. Climb this and scramble up to a grass terrace.
5   33 m. An easy zig-zag route leads first 12 metres leftwards, then
    rightwards to the top.

Deer Bield Crag   (305 094)   Alt. 400 m   North East Facing

Deer Bield Crag is quite small though impressively steep; more so than first impressions would suggest. It is situated high on the hillside looking out across the quiet upper reaches of Far Easedale.

The easiest approach is from Grasmere village; park in the public car park about ½ kilometre up Easedale Road. Follow the road and signed footpath up the north side of the valley for about 3 kilometres until directly below the crag which is some 150 metres above the path on the left (true right side) of the valley. This takes about one hours easy walking.

There are many excellent routes, mostly in the extreme catagory, on generally sound rock which runs to either good jugs and cracks or minute flake edges.

The crag which steps down and across the hillside can be divided into several distinctly different sections: the left-hand side is a smooth crack seamed wall, covered with vivid green lichen, giving fine steep climbing. To its right is a dank recessed area, above a short section of overhanging grooves; the back corners of the recess are taken by Dunmail and Deer Bield Cracks. Right again is the most prominent feature of the crag, the tall slim buttress taken by one of the areas classic lines, Deer Bield Buttress. This buttress is actually an enormous flake, completely detached and leaning back against the main crag, the fissures on either side are taken by Deer Bield Crack and Deer Bield Chimney. Over the last decade this area has been the scene of several rock falls; the latest and most serious resulting in the loss of the top pitches of several routes and the scarring and removal of holds on their lower pitches. Deer Bield Chimney is now a most dangerous route which is filled with much loose rock and should be avoided.

Right of the chimney the character of the cliff again changes, deep slabby-looking grooves divided by sharp stepped arêtes, which give fine open climbing. The crag now diminishes in size though not in steepness or difficult. Two further truncated and undercut arêtes give short though extremely steep walls taken by some of the hardest routes in the area.

For routes up to Deer Bield Chimney descent is easiest round the left-hand side of the crag. Right of this it is quicker to scramble down to the right.

The routes are described from left to right.

The Pendulum   35 m   E2   1953
The main pitch is steep and somewhat intimidating, with a short
difficult crux section. The climb crosses the smooth and impressively
steep green wall at the left-hand end of the crag by an obvious break
at half-height. Start in a broken corner below the left-hand side of the
wall.
1   22 m (5c). Climb the corner for 6 metres and step onto a small
     ledge on the right. Move up and make some delicate moves right,
     with overhead protection from a peg runner, to gain the gangway
     which is followed to a short overhanging groove. Climb this
     strenuously to a grassy stance on the right.
2   13 m (4c). Move round the arête and mantelshelf onto a flake.
     Step left and continue up to the top.

Limbo   33 m   E3   1980
A steep sustained pitch up the slim ramp/groove in the left-hand side
of the smooth green wall. The groove is guarded by an exasperating
boulder problem start, 4 metres right of The Pendulum.
     (6b). Swing up right from a short crack to gain the base of the
     ramp/groove and a peg runner. Follow the ramp to the traverse
     of The Pendulum, and continue up the crack above, to a large
     grass ledge left of the head wall. Finish up a short steep corner
     on the right.

★★★ **Stiletto**   36 m   E3   1978
A brilliant, sustained and strenuous pitch up the centre of the wall.
Start at a steep groove 7 metres right of The Pendulum, just left of a
large rowan tree.
     (6a). Gain the groove, using the arête on its left, and follow it to
     a good ledge on the right. Continue up the flake on the left and
     crack above to the traverse of The Pendulum. Follow a crack
     through the overhang and wall above to a sloping ledge on the
     right. A thin crack up the overhanging wall leads to a niche; finish
     more easily.

Last Tango   36 m   E5   †   1984
A difficult climb up the thin crackline in the wall right of Stiletto.
Start from the overhung ledge 3 metres right of Stiletto, just right of
a large rowan tree.
     (6b). Bridge up from the tree to gain the first hold on the bulge,
     swing right and climb a faint groove to a good ledge. Stand on a
     large pointed block on the ledge and climb the wall on the right
     to a sloping ledge. Step left and go up to join the traverse of The
     Pendulum. Climb a short continuation crack and step right to a

grass ledge below the headwall. Pull up steeply into a groove and go up left to a good ledge; the short groove/crack above leads to the top.

★ **The Graduate**   45 m   E3   1971
The slim groove in the right-hand side of the smooth green wall gives a fine steep exposed climb. Start at a tall slim spike below a very steep groove, 8 metres right of Stiletto.
1   15 m (5b). Climb the overhanging groove, exit left at its top and up onto a ledge. Follow the crack to easier ground and belay well back in the recess.
2   30 m (6a). Traverse left to a block on the arête and pull up to gain the base of the steep slim groove. Climb this precariously past a peg runner to a ledge on the left at its top. Surmount a bulge on good holds and follow the arête, joining the last couple of metres of The Pendulum.

Dunmail Cracks   50 m   HVS   1952
A serious and rather unattractive climb. It takes the left corner of the dank and forboding amphitheatre left of Deer Bield Buttress. The main difficulty lies in the first pitch which is rather vegetated. Start just right of The Graduate.
1   16 m (5a). A short steep wall leads to a broken-looking groove. Climb this to an overhang, then gain a short crack in the wall on the left with difficulty. Go up to a good ledge and continue over large flakes to another ledge.
2   10 m (4c). A crack at the left end of the ledge, leads to a small ledge on the right. Follow the crack in the corner, formed by a large detached block, with care to a stance.
3   24 m (5a). Climb the outside edge of the steep crack in the corner, which is formed by a huge flake resting on the face, step right to a small ash and continue up the corner above to the top.

Gymslip   56 m   E3   1977
Climbs the unattractive-looking wall in the back of the amphitheatre between Dunmail and Deer Bield Crack's. A serious and technical climb, which is better than appearances suggest. Start as for Deer Bield Crack.
1   18 m (4c). Climb the crack to a flake, traverse left across a slab to a groove which is followed to a good ledge.
2   30 m (5c). Scramble up over blocks for 6 metres to the foot of the deep chimney. Swing up left onto the base of an innocent-looking ramp. Climb this with difficulty and a shallow groove above, a short crack on the left then leads to a ledge. Swing right round the rib to a ledge below the Amen Corner of Deer Bield Crack.
3   8 m (5b). Climb the obvious slanting groove on the left to the top.

** **Deer Bield Crack**   50 m   HVS   1930

"A climb of great character and interest, requiring considerable
energy and perseverance. The famous chimney pitch is probably
unique of its type, and the final overhang is sufficiently problematical
to leave the outcome in doubt until the very end." Thus described the
old guide this test piece of yesteryear which still repulses many
climbers. Start at a small pinnacle slightly up and left of the lowest
point of the buttress.

1   24 m (4b). Up the crack above for 2 metres and stride right to a
    small niche. Move up to a ledge and follow the slab on the left
    for 3 metres and pull round on good holds into a crack line. Follow
    it and the shallow chimney then large dubious blocks to below the
    deep chimney.
2   11 m (5a). The crux. Gain and climb the chimney, by facing right
    and keeping deeply inside as long as possible. Traverse out under
    the overhang where a short very strenuous ascent leads to a small
    ledge on the top.
3   15 m (4c). Continue up the crack which eases after 3 metres to
    below a super Amen Corner. Climb the overhanging crack on the
    right to splendid finishing holds.

** **Deer Bield Buttress**   68 m   E1   ✓   1951

Traditionally one of the 'last great problems' of the district it is still
a fine climb combining considerable technical interest and difficulty
with fine positions. Strenuous in the lower half, more delicate as
height is gained. Start about 3 metres down and right of Deer Bield
Crack at a groove left of the lowest point of the buttress.

1   18 m (5a). Climb the scoop and traverse left under the overhang
    to join Deer Bield Crack. Go up this to a ledge on the right below
    a sharply overhanging crack. Climb this and step left to a belay
    ledge on the edge overlooking Deer Bield Chimney.
2   10 m (5a). Traverse across the slab on the right to an overhanging
    groove. Gain a tiny ledge on its left-hand rib and continue past a
    ledge and short steep section to a stance below 'the long groove.'
3   40 m (5a). Climb the groove taking the right-hand branch where
    it divides, to where it peters out. Move up then traverse delicately
    right to a ledge on the right of the huge pinnacle. The original
    finish was to step left from the top of the pinnacle and climb a
    dubious thin flake/crack to the top (5b). Since the rockfall it is
    now more logical to climb the ramp above, leftwards to its end,
    swing left and scramble up the ridge above and over the bridge to
    the summit.

Variation   El Dorado   36 m   E2   1977
A pleasant alternative which starts below 'the long groove' of pitch 3.
3a (5b). Traverse down and left to a groove in the nose, climb this
    and pull out right at the top. Move across a slab to a shallow
    groove (junction with Peccadillo). Go up and back left to the rib
    and follow this to the top, as for Peccadillo.

★ Peccadillo   54 m   E4   1968
The steep bottomless groove in the lower section of the rib right of
Deer Bield Buttress provides the main interest for this steep and
precarious climb. Start as for Deer Bield Buttres.
1   30 m (6a). Climb straight up the scoop and step round right onto
    a narrow slabby ledge on the face of the buttress. Climb up and
    make a committing and delicate traverse left to gain the base of
    the groove. Climb up to a peg runner, then continue up with
    difficulty to a good spike on the right arête. Move left across the
    slab to join Deer Bield Buttress, and follow this for 6 metres to
    belay at the foot of 'the long groove.'
2   24 m (5b). Climb the wall on the left for 8 metres, then go up a
    shallow groove until moves left can be made onto the arête.
    Follow this to the top.

★ Desperado   65 m   E5   1977
A bold and intricate route up the edge of the smooth face right of
Deer Bield Buttress. Although it lacks independence it gives some
interesting and difficult pitches. Start at the foot of Deer Bield
Chimney, in a corner up and right of Deer Bield Buttress.
1   30 m (6a). Climb the wall diagonally left to gain the narrow slabby
    ledge on Peccadillo. Follow Peccadillo left and up the groove to
    the good spike on the right arête. Pull right onto the face and
    move up to gain a sloping ledge below an overlap. Follow the
    break right for a short distance, then trend left up the wall to a
    ledge below 'the long groove' of pitch 3 of Deer Bield Buttress.
2   20 m (5c). Traverse right to the foot of an obvious groove, climb
    this for 3 metres to a good flake hold. Swing out right onto the
    face and climb, first trending right then direct to the top of the
    huge pinnacle.
3   15 m (4b). Climb the easy ramp above, swing left and scramble
    up the ridge to finish as for Deer Bield Buttress.

Take it to the Limit (E5 (6b), 55 m, 1978) climbed the right edge of
the smooth face right of Desperado, with a detour into the chimney
at half-height at a large projecting block. An enormous rockfall

dislodged this block, which provided a rest and protection for the following moves. This has drastically changed this pitch which still awaits a reascent

● **Deer Bield Chimney**   52 m   S   1908
Although a classic climb of its type, taking the deep chimney line on the right-hand side of the smooth buttress, recent rockfalls from the top of the crag have made the climb dangerous, filling the chimney with much loose rock. It is therefore best avoided.

Imagination   66 m   E5   1977
A difficult route up the arête between Deer Bield Chimney and Hubris; it has a particularly bold and serious second pitch. Start below the arête.
1   20 m (5a). Climb the broken stepped arête, mainly on the right-hand side, to a large glacis below a steep wall. Belay on the left.
2   38 m (6a). Traverse to the right side of the glacis. Climb the steep right wall of the arête, overlooking Hubris, to a good finger hold on the left. Pull up to a good hold, then make a long reach to more holds, and move up to gain the arête itself, where the angle eases. Follow this to a bulge, pull over and continue more easily to the final steep rib which is climbed on its right-hand side on small holds.
3   8 m. Step left and finish up the newly exposed groove at the top of Deer Bield Chimney.

★ **Hubris**   52 m   E1   1956
The first and most prominent of the deep groove lines right of Imagination. Good climbing which is considerably steeper and more difficult than first appearances suggest. Start by scrambling up an easy slabby groove to below a short corner which guards access to the main groove.
1   16 m (5a). Ascend the awkward corner and follow the groove to where it splits.
2   36 m (5a). Continue up the main groove for 3 metres then gain the crack on the left. Climb this, with difficulty where it steepens, into the upper part of the groove. Finish up the easy rib on the right where scrambling leads to a tree.

Variation   An easier finish   38 m
2a   (5a). Follow pitch 2 past the difficult moves to below the mossy groove. Make a delicate step to gain the groove on the right, which is climbed to a tree. Finish up the rib on the right where scrambling leads to the top.

★★ Pearls Before Swine   54 m   E3   1973
An excellent route up the stepped arête between Hubris and Easedale Groove. Sustained and quite bold in parts. Start by scrambling to below a short corner, as for Hubris.

1   45 m (5c). Pull up onto the smooth slab on the right and climb it to the foot of a short steep corner which leads onto the crest of the arête. Climb the corner, (or the arête on the left) stepping right at the top and continue to a good foothold below the first overlap. Move round to the left and make some difficult moves up until it is possible to regain the right-hand side of the arête and a good foot hold. Move up a little and climb a crack on the left of the arête then climb straight up to a large doubtful block on the ridge above the overlap. Pull onto this and continue up the arête to a ledge and nut belay.

2   9 m. Climb easily up the rib above.

Easedale Groove   52 m   S   1961
The slim groove right of Hubris gives a pleasant climb. Start by scrambling to below a short corner, as for Hubris.

1   24 m. Go right along an easy traverse to the rib below and right of the groove. Climb the rib on sloping holds for a couple of metres; then go up to the first overhang that bars access to the groove proper. Pull round the overhang and follow the groove past another overhang to a stance.

2   12 m. Climb up to the roof, make a couple of delicate steps to the right and go up to a tree belay.

3   16 m. Finish easily up rock ribs and grass.

Age Before Beauty   56 m   MVS   1982
The arête between Easedale and Eden Grooves. Start by scrambling to below a short corner, as for Hubris.

1   36 m (4b). Follow Easedale Groove until just above the first overlap, then move right across the wall to gain the arête. Follow this to the tree belay at the top of pitch 2 of Easedale Groove.

2   20 m (4b). Gain the ledge on the right wall and make a high step up onto the arête. Scramble up to the top. Tree belay 12 metres higher.

Eden Groove   62 m   HS   1956
The deep grass-filled groove right of Easedale Groove, is the last and least worthy of the three groove lines splitting the right-hand side of the crag. Start in a grassy bay below an impending wall, at the foot of the groove.

1   15 m. Step off a flake and climb the leftward-slanting corner crack, which leads into the easy-looking groove above. Follow this to its top.

2   12 m. Climb a little slab on the left below the impending wall and pull into the deep groove, which leads to a belay at the foot of a wide crack in the right wall.

3   22 m. Climb the left branch of the groove on its left side to an impending wall which bars the way. Climb a delicate little slab in the corner below the wall, until possible to swing left to a foothold. Step left again, and climb up to a tree in the groove above.

4   13 m. Scrambling leads to the top.

Monkey Puzzle   45 m   S   1946
The first pitch of Eden Groove, then the pleasant slab above on the right lead to the ridge. Traverse right to the arête and ascend the chimney on the right.

★ Dynamo   36 m   E5   1980
A strenuous route up the thin cracks in the right side of the impending wall below and right of Eden Groove. Start at a glacis below the cracks, 4 metres right of Eden Groove.
(6b). Awkward moves gain the cracks which are followed with sustained difficulty to a tiny overhang; a very hard pull left and up gains a good ledge. The slab above is climbed trending leftwards to its top. A short steep groove leads to an easy ridge and pinnacle belay.

Idle Breed   30 m   E5   †   1984
The left side of the very steep buttress at the right-hand side of the crag is climbed by a series of very hard boulder problem type moves. Start below the groove and crack line, about 10 metres right of Dynamo.
(6b). A very steep start using a painfull handjam to gain a small niche. Climb the crack above on the left with a desperate move to gain the slab above. Up rightwards to a corner system which leads more easily to the top.

★★ Pretty in Pink   25 m   E6   †   1986
The thin vertical crack in the right side of the overhanging wall gives an extremely strenuous and sustained 'test piece' which is well protected. Start 3 metres right of Idle Breed below the crack.
(6c). The tiny niche at half-height is gained using layaways and painful finger slots. Continue up the finger crack making an awkward exit onto the slab above. Finish up the wall and short groove.

★ Bravado   32 m   E2   1980

Pleasant climbing up a system of thin ramp and groove lines at the
extreme right-hand end of the crag. Start 3 metres right of Pretty in
Pink at the right-hand end of the impending front wall of the buttress.

    (5c). Climb awkwardly up a slot, then follow the narrow
ramp/groove line above to the foot of a short steep corner. Climb
this to a good platform. The delicate thin groove above is gained
and followed mainly on its right wall to the top.

The Girdle Traverse   100 m   E2   1953

A left to right girdle with some good pitches linked by rather
undistinguished climbing. Start as for Pendulum.

1   22 m (5b). Pitch 1 of Pendulum.
2   28 m (4c). Step round the corner on the right and traverse into
    Dunmail Cracks on doutful rock. Descend the crack to a large
    ledge. Cross to below the chimney pitch of Deer Bield Crack and
    descend to another ledge.
3   10 m (5a). Pitch 2 of Deer Bield Buttress.
4   16 m (5b). Follow pitch 3 of Deer Bield Buttress to a belay on
    top of the pinnacle.
5   24 m (5a). Descend the groove on the right with care to the scree
    filled gully. Ascend the corner above the steep crack and shallow
    groove to the top.

★ The New Girdle   124 m   E3   1978

A much improved girdle from right to left at about half-height. Pitch
2 has suffered from the rockfall above which now makes the descent
of the chimney dangerous. This may change for better or worse in the
future and great care should be taken by any one attempting this
route. Start as for Eden Groove.

1   42 m (5a). Climb Eden Groove for 18 metres to the bottom of a
    long grass-filled groove. Up the wall on the left, traverse round
    the arête beneath a bulge and step down into Easedale Groove.
    Climb up leftwards to the arête of Pearls Before Swine and
    traverse left to the stance at the top of pitch 1 of Hubris.
2   22 m (5c). Climb the steep left-hand branch groove to where the
    angle eases. Traverse left to the arête of Imagination and continue
    into Deer Bield Chimney. Descend, with great care, over loose
    rock for 6 metres to a belay.
3   10 m (5b). Move left out of the chimney onto a slab. Traverse
    horizontally left below an overlap to the foot of 'the long groove'
    of Deer Bield Buttress pitch 3.
4   10 m (5b). Step down and move left to a slab on the arête.
    Traverse into Deer Bield Crack below the chimney and move
    down to large ledges.

5   15 m. Go left along the ledge, follow the obvious ledge across the green wall at the left side of the crag, over a pointed block and belay on Stiletto.
6   25 m (5c). Climb the crack of Stiletto to the sloping ledge below the final wall. Move left round the corner and continue along easy ledges to finish.

Slapestone Edge   (303 089)   Alt. 390 m   South East Facing

An extensive though very broken area of rock which lies due west of and overlooking Easedale Tarn. The following routes, which are quick to dry, lie on the short mossy slabs to the left of the wide gully which splits the centre of the crag.

The routes are described from left to right. Descend to the left of the buttress.

Easedale Ramble   25 m   E1   1988
Start below a flake at 4 metres near the centre of the slabs.
    (5b). Climb the flake to a wide crack, then the clean slab above to a ledge. Finish up the centre of the 'concrete-like' wall above.

Slape Stones   24 m   E1   1988
Start just right of Easedale Ramble and 2 metres left of Sharni Slab.
    (5b). Step up to a triangular pocket then step right. Climb past a horizontal crack to a tiny spike than traverse right and continue boldly to a ledge above. Finish up the mossy slab.

Sharni Slab   25 m   HVS   1988
Start at a small crevassed block below a shallow groove in the centre of the face.
    (5a). Climb direct to the groove, up this to a ledge then finish up a clean wall above.

Eagle Crag   (298 083)   Alt. 450 m   East Facing

About 450 metres right of Blea Crag, is a small though very impressive pillar of rock standing out from the steep hillside. It has a large slanting roof at its base above a short wall.

One route has been climbed up the front face of the pillar.

Too Bleeding Hard   35 m   E5   †   1988
A difficult route up the centre of the wall. Start below a crack in the overhang.

>   (6b). Traverse right, pull up, then back left along the lip of the overhang. Climb the wall to finish up the obvious V-chimney by difficult and painful fist jamming.

Variation   Direct Start   E5   †   1988

>   (6b). The obvious crack in the overhang has been ascended to gain the line direct, passing an in situ sling near the lip, but only with the use of a nut for aid.

Blea Crag   (302 080)   Alt. 450 m   North and North East Facing

A large broken crag situated high on the hillside overlooking Easedale Tarn. It gives fine mainly slabby climbing on excellent rough rock on the many small buttresses scattered around the crag. Its seclusion provides a welcome respite from the crowds on the more popular crags and is particularly useful on those hot summer days when a cool haven is required.

The best approach is from Grasmere village as for Deer Bield Crag. Follow Easedale Road to the gate then cross the river and follow a sign posted footpath up the south side of the valley to Easedale Tarn. A path then leads up towards the left side of the crag. An alternative approach can be made from Langdale. Follow the approach for Pavey Ark to Stickle Tarn then the path round its right side and continue eastwards to the ridge above the crag. Descend round either side of the crag. Each approach takes about 1 hour.

Deep vegetated gullies split the crag into three seperate buttresses. Each buttress is liberally endowed with large vegetated ledges and rakes between clean rock slabs and walls. The majority of the routes lie on fine slabby buttresses along the base of the crag, though several of the older routes find rambling ways to the top.

The Left-Hand Buttress has the excellent Animal Buttress at is base, to its right there are several fine steep groove then a band of overhangs lead rightwards to the left-hand groove. The Central Buttress, which stands forward from the remainder of the crag, is extremely vegetated on its left-hand side. Below the right side is a narrow buttress of smooth rock above a small terrace, this is taken by Bleaberry Buttress. The Right-Hand Buttress has the small Poachers Buttress below its left-hand side facing into the right-hand gully. Further right is a fine area of slabs before the crag deteriorates into more vegetation.

Descents can be made down either side of the main crag or either of the gullies with caution. Descents for each area are given in the description. The climbs are described from left to right.

Left-Hand Buttress
Animal Buttress

The area of slabs on the lower left-hand side of the crag. The upper pitches are above a wide grassy ledge above and to the left of the slabs. Descent is best made down the left-hand side of the crag.

★ **Fruit Bat**   45 m   E1   1984
A good route up the left-hand side of the slab. Start just left of the toe of the buttress.
1   24 m (5b). Climb the steepening slab, gaining good holds in the top horizontal band with difficulty, and continue to the large vegetated ledge.
2   21 m (4c). Walk 15 metres down to the left to a large block below two obvious cracks. Climb a short groove and gain a protruding ledge 3 metres left of the cracks. Continue up the wall above.

★★ **Flying Squirrel**   45 m   HVS   1984
Fine open climbing on excellent rock, following a direct line up the centre of the slab. Start at the toe of the buttress.
1   24 m (5a). A direct line is followed, with a delicate move at half height.
2   21 (4b). Walk down and left, as Fruit Bat, to the large block below the twin cracks. Climb the left-hand crack.

Spider Monkey   45 m   HVS   1984
Pleasant climbing up the right-hand side of the slab. Start just right of Flying Squirrel.
1   24 m (5a). Up the slab towards the left end of a vegetated ledge at half height, follow a crack leftwards and gain the top of a flake above. A short rib leads to the large ledge.
2   21 m (4b). Walk down and left and climb the short corner and crack just right of pitch 2 of Flying Squirrel.

Right of Animal Buttress the prominent slabby corner and ribs are taken by the following routes.

Simon Says   26 m   HVS   1984
The left slanting clean cut groove gives a good pitch. Start at a short rib below the groove, 5 metres right of Animal Buttress.
    (5a). Climb the rib and slab to a vegetated ledge. Up the groove moving right at the top to a tree belay.

No Flange for the Poor   28 m   E2   1985

Excellent, delicate climbing up the rib left of Simon Says. The grade assumes no runners are placed in the adjacent corner. Start from a grassy ledge 3 metres right of Simon Says.

(5b). Climb the short steep wall to some sloping ledges then step left to the vegetated ledge below the corner of Simon Says. Climb direct up the unprotected arête finishing left of a short crack near the top.

★ **No Rest for the Wicked**   24 m   E3   1984

A fine bold pitch up the narrow slab right of the corner of Simon Says with minimal protection. Start on the grassy ledge below a short steep wall as for No Flange For The Poor.

(5c). Climb the wall to some sloping ledges then traverse right to a crack. Up and left to a flat spike, then to a good foothold on the left arête. Delicate moves up and right to a crack, then back left steeply and straight up to an awkward finish directly below the tree.

Sorbo   52 m   VS   1964

The second pitch climbs the obvious left facing corner above the vegetated ledge splitting the crag at about 18 metres. Start beside a juniper on a ledge 3 metres right of No Rest For The Wicked.
1   25 m (4c). Climb the flake crack on the left or the groove above the juniper then trend right to the left end of a ledge, which is followed rightwards for about 6 metres.
2   27 m (4b). The short groove on the left leads to a ledge, follow the pleasant groove above to the top.

Fifteen metres right of No Rest For The Wicked a wide vegetated rake slants up to the right below a series of square cut overhangs in the lower tier of the Left-Hand Buttress of the crag. The rake leads to a wide gully above the fan of vegetated rock in the centre of the crag, and provides a rather awkward descent.

Blea Rigg Climb   38 m   VD   1908

An unsatisfactory route up the left side of the square cut overhangs. Start by scrambling up the vegetated rake to a square cut scoop below the left end of the overhangs.
1   10 m. Climb the scoop, exit left onto a ledge then up right to a block belay below an overhang.
2   28 m. Traverse right to the arête, and up on its right side to a ledge. Follow the groove, chimney and grassy gully to the top.

★ **Chameleon**   40 m   E3   1984
Strenuous climbing through the square cut overhangs leads to delicate
climbing up the slabby wall above. Start at a crack below the
overhangs, 4 metres right of Blea Rigg Climb, and just left of a large
rock spike.
(6a). Climb the crack to the overhang and pull over with difficulty
into a shallow groove. Trend up and right to another groove which
leads to easier slabs and the top.

Erne   20 m   E1   1984
An excellent little pitch up the clean wall in the gully reached by
scrambling some 30 metres up and right of Chameleon. Start below
a thin crack near the left side of the wall.
(5b). Climb the crack to a horizontal break, move right and climb
the twisting crack to the next break. Up the wall above on small
holds to the top.

Central Buttress

Fifty metres right of the scree below the central fan of vegetated rock
is a narrow buttress of clean smooth rock, just right of a holly and
juniper filled groove and above a small subsidiary terrace. The next
three routes start here. Descend down the wide grassy gully 20 metres
to the right.

★ **Offcomers Slab**   30 m   E5   1987
Very delicate climbing up the steep slab left of the corner. A fine
route with a particularly bold and committing move above the pcg.
Start at the left rib.
(6b). Climb the slab past some small wire placements to an in-situ
thread at the bulge. Move left and up to a peg runner and small
spike. Continue up and then rightwards to reach the large spike
on Another Bleeding Controversy. Finish up the groove and slab
above to a grassy corner.

Another Bleeding Controversy   30 m   E3   1987
A direct line up the corner above the start of Bleaberry Buttress.
(5c). Climb the stacked blocks and continue up the ramp and
groove passing a tiny sapling to a good spike. Climb the thin crack
in the bulge above to gain a slab and belay in the grassy corner
above.

Bleaberry Buttress   70 m   HVS   1964
An interesting climb though rather vegetated in parts. Start up a
prominent groove containing a pillar of three blocks.
1   28 m (5a). Climb to the top of the blocks. Swing right onto a block
    on the rib and pull up into a niche above. Move up and right and
    follow two short scoops to a ledge. Two short slabs lead to a
    bilberry terrace.
2   17 m (5a). The slab in the impending wall behind the terrace is
    traversed to the rib on the left, step left round this to where
    steeper easier rock leads to a grass ledge. A bold pitch.
3   25 m (4c). The scoops directly ahead, then the arête on the left
    lead to the top.

Pam's Wall   24 m   E4   1988
A superb pitch up the wall above Offcomers Slab. It provides a fitting
continuation to this route and can easily be reached by scrambling up
left from its belay. This point can also be reached by scrambling up
leftwards from the wide grassy gully to the right of the buttress. Start
on ledges below the cleaned line on the right side of the wall.
    (6a). Sustained climbing leads past a peg runner at 18 metres to
    a large ledge. Thread belay well back.

Sinister Footwear   26 m   HVS   1988
The groove system just right of Pam's Wall.
    (5a). Follow the groove system past a bulge and smooth wall.
    Continue up easier rock to the large ledge and belay as for Pam's
    Wall.

Right-Hand Buttress
Poachers Buttress

The right-hand side of the crag is split by a wide grassy gully,
Right-Hand Gully, rising full height of the crag. Near its lower
right-hand side is a short slabby wall set at right angles to the main
crag with a slabby groove to its left and prominent arête on its right.

Iguana   18 m   VS   1987
A poor filler in.
    (4c). Climb the clean cut groove which gradually steepens and
    runs into vegetation near the top.

The Ivory Wall   20 m   E5   1987
Superb climbing up the poorly protected wall. Start beside the twin
hairline cracks just left of the arête.

(6a). Climb the wall direct on small finger holds (skyhook used at 6 metres for protection) to some good wires in the horizontal break right of a small overlap. Follow the horizontal fault line left then pull up to good finishing holds.

The Hunted   22 m   E4   1987
The arête gives a fine though unprotected climb which rapidly eases as height is gained. Start below the left side of the arête.
   (5c). From the obvious foothold step round onto the right side of the arête and climb it using small flakes. Continue up the easier angled arête above to the top.

The Prey   22 m   HVS   1987
A pleasant route up the wall and slabs 3 metres right of the arête. Start from a ledge just right of the obvious niche.
   (5a). Climb direct up the wall and over a slight bulge to gain the easier slabs above, which lead to the top.

Low on the extreme right-hand side of the Right-Hand Buttress is a slabby buttress of light coloured rock of excellent quality. This is about 30 metres right of the large grassy Right-Hand Gully splitting the right side of the crag. A large silver birch tree at the top of the buttress provides a convenient belay for most routes. The best descent is to abseil from the same tree, though it is possible to descend down the right-hand side of the buttress. The following routes start from a narrow vegetated ledge below the left side of the slabs:-

★ **Mussolini**   24 m   E2   1987
A good pitch starting below the thin vertical crack near the left side of the slabs.
   (5c). Climb the crack to a resting place at its end. Go up and right past an obvious flake to the left end of the overlaps near the top. Climb a short groove and traverse right to a ledge and tree belay.

Hermann Goering   24 m   E2   1987
Delicate climbing up the slab just right of Mussolini, giving a pleasant eliminate.
   (5c). Straight up the slab, use a slanting crack to surmount a bulge and continue up the centre of the slab above to join Mussolini at the prominent flake. Finish as Mussolini.

★ **Asterix The Gaul**   24 m   HVS   1987
An enjoyable mixed route starting 3 metres right of Mussolini at a thin crack.

(5a). Climb the crack to a ledge. The thin crack above is followed to its end then climb up rightwards to below an overlap. Step right to its centre and pull over to a slim ledge. Up the short wall above to a ledge and tree belay.

Death Camp   18 m   E5   1987
Bold, poorly protected climbing on tiny rugosities. Start 5 metres right of and at a higher level than Asterix The Gaul, below a rock scar at 8 metres. A peg runner in the shallow groove on the right protects the first moves.
(6a). Precarious moves up the slab just right of a hairline crack gain small holds below the scar. Step left and pull up into the vague scoop above. Easier climbing up the groove above to a tiny overlap, pull over on large holds and up a short wall to a ledge and tree belay.

S.S. Scoop   20 m   E3   1988
A delicate poorly protected route with a worrying but short crux section up the vague scoop right of Death Camp. Start as for Raindancer.
(5c). The light coloured slabs lead up to poor wires on the right, near the foot of Raindancer's groove. Make an increasingly delicate series of moves leftwards into the scoop, and climb this to better holds. Move left to the top of Death Camp and follow it to the tree belay.

Raindancer   20 m   HVS   1987
Awkward moves up the shallow crackline just left of the groove of Obelix and Co. Start directly below the crack.
(5b). Climb up over short slabs and easy ledges to below the crackline. Climb the crack to a good ledge.

Obelix and Co.   20 m   HVS   1987
The obvious right facing groove in the upper half of the right-hand side of the slab.
(4c). Climb the easy slabs to gain the groove which is followed to an overhang. Finish on the right.

Looking Howe Crag   (309 082)   Alt. 370 m   East Facing

Also know as the Hidden Buttress, this small crag is composed of excellent rough, grey rock – reminiscent of parts of Pavey Ark. Like its bigger neighbour, Blea Crag, it provides climbing in a beautiful and quiet setting, despite the proximity of the ever popular Easedale Tarn. The easiest approach is to strike up leftwards from a point just beyond the tarn outlet towards a vague ridge which leads up to the base of the buttress in about ten minutes. It should be noted that the major part of the crag cannot be seen from the approach as it is hidden by a broken ridge.

The first two routes lie on the area of rock right of the broken ridge.

The Brazen Hussey   19 m   S   1987
   Climb the obvious cleaned groove right of the broken ridge then the slab to the right.

Hidden Treasure   19 m   S   1987
Start at the foot of the groove right of The Brazen Hussey.
   Climb the groove to gain the top of the pedestal and climb the clean and pleasant slab direct.

Left of the broken ridge is the best section of the crag, a compact and attractive wall.

Hidden Pleasures   19 m   E1   1987
The left-hand crack/ramp/crack line.
   (5c). Make a hard move up the initial crack, assisted by a conspicuous sharp nobble, and gain the ramp. Follow this and the upper crack with less difficulty.

Hidden Secrets   18 m   E1   1987
   (5b). The right-hand crack and wall above are followed with continuous interest on excellent rock.

Bouldering Areas

Langdale has some excellent bouldering locations, some of which present problems of a length which almost pushes them into the route category. All the places described are worth a visit and are all close to Chapel Stile.

Chapel Stile Boulders   (322 058)

A series of short outcrops above the village providing a good selection of problems of all grades and of varying lengths. They can be well seen from the patio at the front of 'Wainright's' or from outside the Post Office. Of particular note is one of the higher outcrops which has some good pocketed slabs and some steep walls. Access is from behind the small council estate on the road out to Walthwaite. Park either in the village, or as for Raven Crag, Walthwaite, and walk along the road to the rear of the aforementioned estate until a piece of open fell allows access to the crags.

Copt Howe   (316 058)

An excellent variety of short routes and problems on superb, rough rock, virtually unique in Langdale. The lowest section has some problems with undercut starts, the right-hand crack at (5b) and a very low level traverse at (6a) being particularly good. The upper slabs, recognisable by the red streak on its right are very fine. Of particular note are a grey slab in the centre and the red steak itself. Dozens of variations have been climbed here. Round the back of the knoll containing these crags is another area worth a visit. Facing north, it is rather less attractive than the slabs, but Greenbank's Crack (S) - the main groove, and a traverse of the wall to its right on pockets prove very worthwhile.

Access is as follows; leave Chapel Stile and pass Thrang Brow, the rows of white cottages on the right. A short way further on, the road levels and turns to the left. The crag can then be seen up on the right. Limited parking is available on the roadside beneath the crag, opposite a house called Thrang Close. A short walk up a well worn path leads to the crags.

This is a very popular training area with groups, but it has suffered badly from erosion in recent years. As with many other areas in this guide, please treat it with respect.

Langdale Boulders   (324 058)

Continuing past Copt Howe, a large, pocketed slab is passed on the roadside on the right. Just past here, the Langdale Boulders can be seen through some metal fencing on the left. Park on the right just past a gate which gives access to them. The boulders are on enclosed agricultural land, and access is by kind consent of the farmer. Therefore, please ensure that the gate is shut, that no litter is left and that walls are not damaged.

Best problems are the crack which splits the upper boulder at (5b), wall problems at either side (6a/6b), a low level traverse on the rear of the boulder (6a), and the bottom side of the lower boulder (5c to 6a). Lots of other possibilities exist.

Climbing Walls

Although artificial walls are not particularly numerous in Cumbria it has two of the top ten climbing wall in the Country, and a number of other walls are currently under construction or being planned and should be opened in the near future. Only the best or most readily accessible are described here:

Ambleside: Charlotte Masons College.   BMC rating ★★
Good access, minimal regulations, low cost and excellent climbing. Unfortunately it tends to get very busy and has no changing facilities. Tickets available from Rock and Run and, The Golden Rule Hotel.
Access check; Tel: Charlotte Mason Collage (0966 33066)
Distance from Langdale 6km. (4 miles).

Carlisle: The Sands Centre.   BMC rating ★★
Good access, minimal regulations, low cost and good climbing. There are excellent changing and shower facilities included in the price and alternative sports available. Tickets obtained at the Centre.
Access check; Tel: The Sands Centre (0228 27555)
Distance from Langdale 76km. (48 miles).

Whitehaven Sports Centre: BMC rating ●
Good access, minimal regulations, low cost, rather poor climbing. An afterthought on the rear of the centre, it is very small but high and lacks adequate facilities. Tickets available at the centre.
Access check; Tel: Whitehaven Sports Centre (0946 5666)
Distance from Langdale 56km. (35 miles).

203

RAVEN CRAG – WALTHWAITE

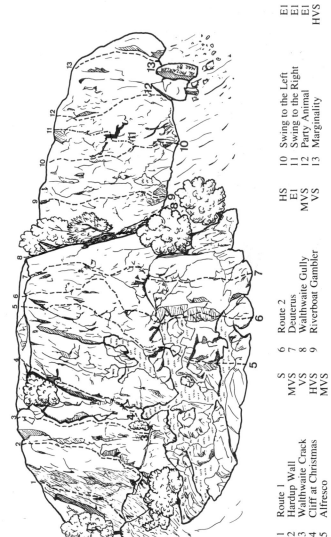

1	Route 1	S
2	Hardup Wall	MVS
3	Walthwaite Crack	VS
4	Cliff at Christmas	HVS
5	Alfresco	MVS

6	Route 2	HS
7	Deuterus	E1
8	Walthwaite Gully	MVS
9	Riverboat Gambler	VS

10	Swing to the Left	E1
11	Swing to the Right	E1
12	Party Animal	E1
13	Marginality	HVS

204

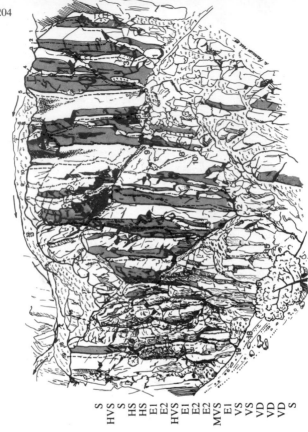

WHITE GHYLL
Lower Crag

1	Russett Groove	S
2	Ethics of War	HVS
3	Heather Groove	S
4	Not Again	HS
5	Inferno	HS
6	Man of Straw	E1
7	Sahara	E2
8	Laugh Not	HVS
9	Do Not	E1
10	Slip Knot Variations	E2
11	Antarctica	E2
12	Slip Knot	MVS
13	The Palestinians	E1
14	Moss Wall	VS
15	Shivering Timber	VS
16	Garden Path	VD
17	Question Not	VD
18	Why Not	VD
19	Hollin Groove	S

205

WHITE GHYLL
Upper Crag

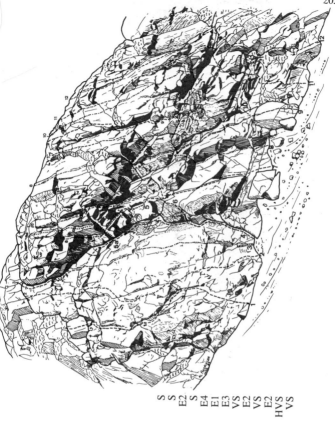

1	The Slabs, Route 2	S
2	The Slabs, Route 1	S
3	Dead Loss Angeles	E2
4	White Ghyll Chimney	S
5	Warrior	E4
6	Chimney Variant	E1
7	Paladin	E3
8	Haste Not	VS
9	Haste Not Direct	E2
10	The Gordian Knot	VS
11	Eliminot	E2
12	Tapestry	HVS
13	White Ghyll Wall	VS

206

PAVEY ARK – General View

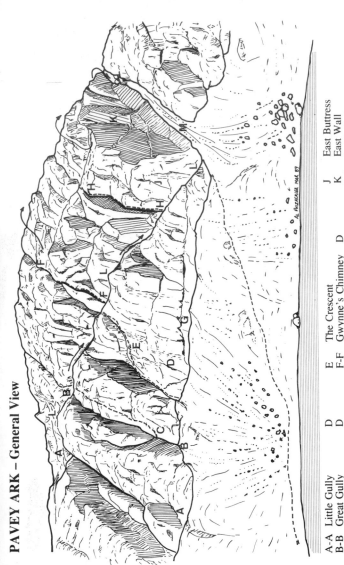

A. PIAZACISA MAR 89

A-A Little Gully
B-B Great Gully
C   Stony Buttress

D   The Crescent
E   Gwynne's Chimney   D
F-F The Barrier   D
G

J   East Buttress
K   East Wall
L-L Jack's Rake
M   East Gully

PAVEY ARK – Central Area

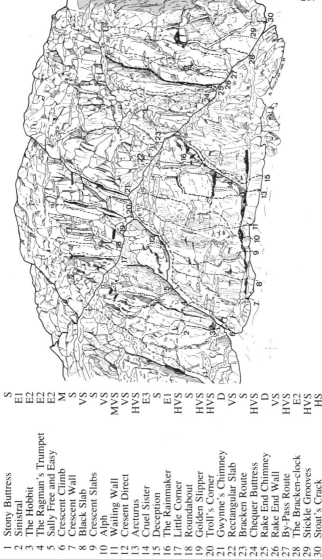

1	Stony Buttress	S
2	Sinistral	E1
3	The Hobbit	E2
4	The Ragman's Trumpet	E2
5	Sally Free and Easy	E2
6	Crescent Climb	M
7	Crescent Wall	S
8	Black Slab	VS
9	Crescent Slabs	S
10	Alph	VS
11	Wailing Wall	MVS
12	Cresent Direct	VS
13	Arcturus	HVS
14	Cruel Sister	E3
15	Deception	S
16	The Rainmaker	E1
17	Little Corner	HVS
18	Roundabout	S
19	Golden Slipper	HVS
20	Troll's Corner	HVS
21	Gwynne's Chimney	D
22	Rectangular Slab	VS
23	Bracken Route	S
24	Chequer Buttress	HVS
25	Rake End Chimney	D
26	Rake End Wall	VS
27	By-Pass Route	HVS
28	The Bracken-clock	E2
29	Stickle Grooves	HVS
30	Stoat's Crack	HS

PAVEY ARK
East Wall

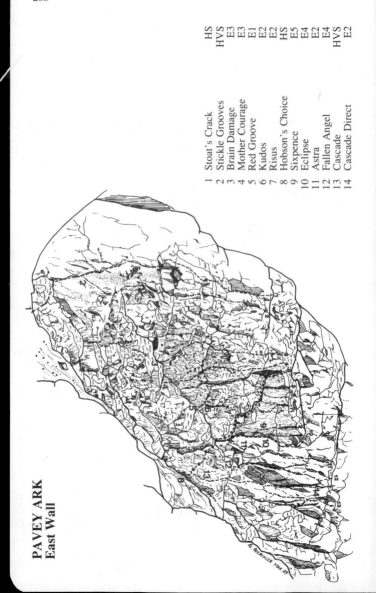

1	Stoat's Crack	HS
2	Stickle Grooves	HVS
3	Brain Damage	E3
4	Mother Courage	E3
5	Red Groove	E1
6	Kudos	E2
7	Risus	E2
8	Hobson's Choice	HS
9	Sixpence	E5
10	Eclipse	E4
11	Astra	E2
12	Fallen Angel	E4
13	Cascade	HVS
14	Cascade Direct	E2

MIDDLEFELL & RAVEN CRAG BUTTRESSES

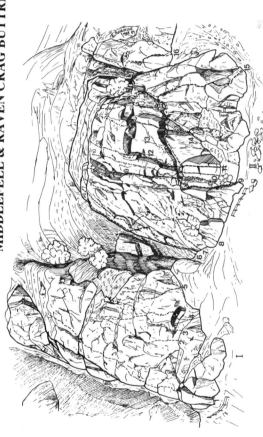

I	Middlefell Buttress		5	Bryson's Flange	E2	11	Pluto	HVS
II	Raven Crag Buttress		6	The Patella Pinch	E1	12	Trilogy	E5
1	Middlefell Buttress	D	7	Evening Wall	S	13	R 'n' S Special	E5
2	Bradley's Damnation	HVS	8	Oak Tree Wall	MS	14	Fine Time	E4
3	Mendes	VS	9	Holly Tree Direct	VS	15	Bilberry Buttress	VS
4	The Power of Imagination	E4	10	Kalashnikov	E4	16	Centipede	S

210

GIMMER CRAG
South East & West Faces

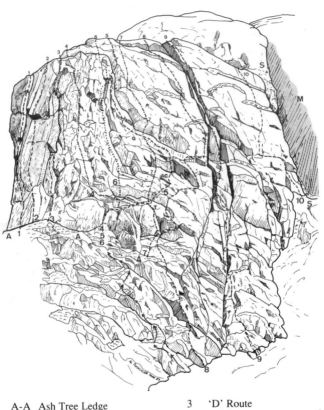

A-A	Ash Tree Ledge		3	'D' Route	S
T	Thompson's Ledge		4	'A' Route	MS
G	The Gangway		5	'B' Route	S
AC	Amen Corner		6	'C' Route	S
→	To Ash Tree Ledge		7	Crow's Nest Direct	VS
S-S	South East Gully		8	Bracket and Slab Climb	S
M	Main Wall		9	Gimmer Chimney	VD
1	'F' Route	VS	10	Chimney Buttress	S
2	Spring Bank	E1		

GIMMER CRAG
West & North West Faces

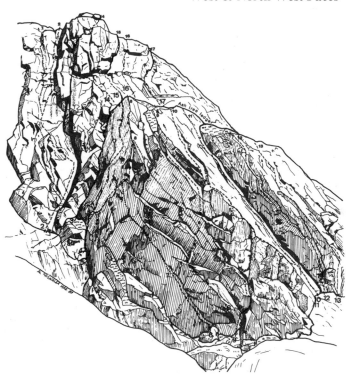

1	Dight	E1	9	Joas	VS
2	The Crack	VS	10	Ash Tree Slabs	VD
3	Samaritan Corner	HS	11	Ash Tree Corner	VS
4	Asterisk	HS	12	Crystal	E1
5	North-West Arete	MVS	13	Introduction	HS
6	Langdale Cowboys	E3	14	Kipling Groove	HVS
7	Langdale Cowboys		15	'F' Route	VS
	Continuation	E4	16	Whit's End Direct	E1
8	Intern	HVS	17	'D' Route	S

212

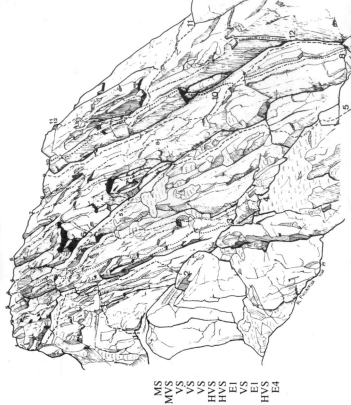

GIMMER CRAG
North West Face

1	Juniper Buttress	MS
2	Godiva Groove	MVS
3	The Dream Merchants	VS
4	Carpetbagger	VS
5	Hiatus	VS
6	Grooves Superdirect	HVS
7	Inertia	HVS
8	Dight	E1
9	The Crack	VS
10	Gimmer String	E1
11	Kipling Groove	HVS
12	Midnight Movie	E4

213

FLAT CRAGS

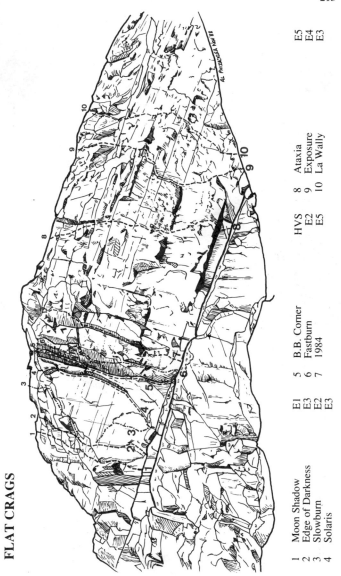

1	Moon Shadow	E1	5	B.B. Corner	E1
2	Edge of Darkness	E3	6	Fastburn	E2
3	Slowburn	E2	7	1984	E3
4	Solaris	E3			

8	Ataxia	HVS
9	Exposure	E2
10	La Wally	E5

	E5
	E4
	E3

AL PATZCOLA NOV 88

NORTH BUTTRESS

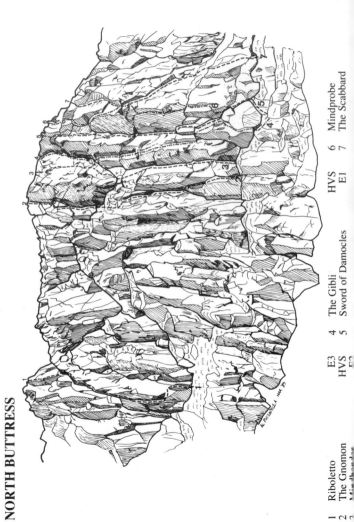

1 Riboletto   E3
2 The Gnomon   HVS
3   E3

4 The Gibli   HVS
5 Sword of Damocles E1

6 Mindprobe   E3
7 The Scabbard   VS

BOWFELL BUTTRESS

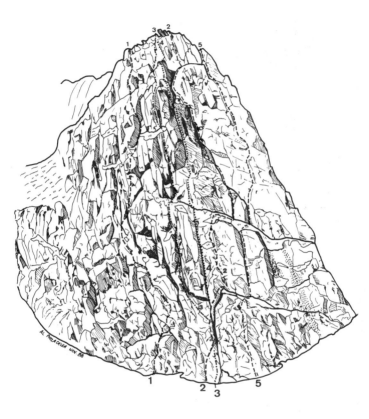

1	Sinister Slabs	HS
2	Bowfell Buttress	VD
3	Rubicon Groove	E1
4	The Central Route	HS
5	Bowfell Buttress Eliminate	E1

NECKBAND CRAG

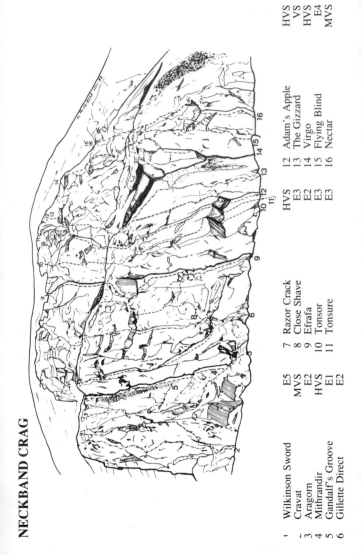

1	Wilkinson Sword	E5
2	Cravat	MVS
3	Aragorn	E2
4	Mithrandir	HVS
5	Gandalf's Groove	E1
6	Gillette Direct	E2

7	Razor Crack	HVS
8	Close Shave	E3
9	Efrafa	E2
10	Tonsor	E3
11	Tonsure	E3

12	Adam's Apple	HVS
13	The Gizzard	VS
14	Virgo	HVS
15	Flying Blind	E4
16	Nectar	MVS

217

HELM CRAG

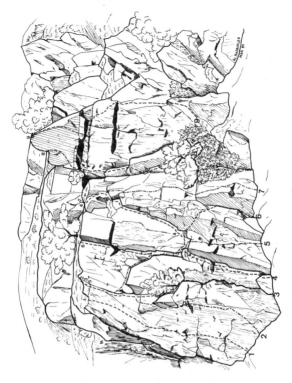

1	Green Light	HVS
2	Beacon Rib	HVS
3	Beacon Crack	HS
4	Holly Tree Crack	MS
5	Flarepath	VS
6	Flarepath Direct	E1
7	Spectrum	VS
8	The Grouter	S
9	Two Star Red	E3

DEER BIELD CRAG

1	The Pendulum	E2
2	Limbo	E3
3	Stiletto	E3
4	Last Tango	E5
5	The Graduate	E3
6	Dunmail Cracks	E2
7	Gymslip	E3

8	Deer Bield Crack	HVS
9	Deer Bield Buttress	E1
10	Peccadillo	E4
11	Desperado	E5
12	Deer Bield Chimney	—
13	Imagination	E5
14	Hubris	E1

15	Pearls Before Swine	E3
16	Easedale Groove	S
17	Eden Groove	HS
18	Dynamo	E5
19	Idle Breed	E5
20	Pretty in Pink	E6
21	Bravado	E2

BLEA CRAG

I	Left-Hand Buttress				
II	Central Buttress				
III	Right-Hand Buttress				

A	Animal Buttress		3	Another Bleeding	E3
B	Poachers Buttress			Controversy	E2
1	Sorbo	VS	4	Mussolini	HVS
2	Chameleon	E3	5	Raindancer	

GRADED LIST OF CLIMBS

These lists which first appeared in the F&RCC guides in 1986, when the Borrowdale edition was published are designed to give an idea of the comparative difficulty of leading each route taking account of such factors as protection, rock quality and sustained nature as well as technical difficulty.

The compilation of these lists is not a precise science; everyone has their own idea on relative ratings of routes, how much bias to put on protection, rock quality, difficulty, etc. The more people that are asked to comment the more variations arise and arguments ensue.

No one person has done all of the routes in a sufficiently short period of time to give an across the board consensus in any grade, let alone all grades thus anomalies will exist this should be borne in mind when condemning the compiler because the position of a route does not align with ones expectations or wishes.

At best the list will give an indication of the hardest and easiest routes in each grade; at worst a good check list for the 'compulsive ticker.' No doubt it will also provide a basis for arguments in the pub or hut but please remember not to take it too seriously.

E6
** Pretty in Pink (6c)	Deer Bield Crag	190
** Centrefold (6b)	Raven Crag Buttress	95
The Beatles (6a)	Middle Scout Crag	33
Hang the Gallows High (6a)	Black Crag	165

E5
*** Sixpence (6b)	Pavey Ark	79
** Ataxia (6b,4c)	Flat Crags	137
* Desperado (6a,5c,4b)	Deer Bield Crag	187
Razor's Edge (6b)	Neckband Crag	153
Rudolf Nureyev (6c)	Side Pike	170
1984 (6b,5a)	Flat Crags	137
Too Bleeding Hard (6b)	Eagle Crag	193
Warlock (6b)	Far East Raven Crag	106
Stars and Bars (6a)	Pavey Ark	79
Imagination (5a,6a)	Deer Bield Crag	188
* Bitter Days (6b)	Crinkle Gill	158
* Wilkinson Sword (6b)	Neckband Crag	149
* Offcomers Slab (6b)	Blea Crag	196
The Watch (4c,5c,6a,5b)	Raven Crag Buttress	94
** R'n'S Special (6a)	Raven Crag Buttress	95
*** Trilogy (6a)	Raven Crag Buttress	95
Idle Breed (6b)	Deer Bield Crag	190

E5 (Continued)

★ Dynamo (6b)	Deer Bield Crag	190
Last Tango (6b)	Deer Bield Crag	184
Into the Light (6b)	Raven Crag, Walthwaite	27
★ Supernova (6a,4c)	Pavey Ark	80
Genital Touch (6a)	Crinkle Gill	157
★ Pocket Way (6a)	Black Crag	162
The Real World (6a)	Black Crag	163
West Wall (6b)	Lightning Crag	160
Death Camp (6a)	Blea Crag	199
★ The Ivory Wall (6a)	Blea Crag	197

E4

★ Peccadillo (6a,5b)	Deer Bield Crag	187
Jagged Edge (6a)	Neckband Crag	149
Kalashnikov (5c,6a)	Raven Crag Buttress	94
★ Fine Time (6b)	Raven Crag Buttress	95
★ Heartsong (6b)	Pavey Ark	81
★ Elvis (6a)	Middle Scout Crag	33
Solstice (6a,4c)	Pavey Ark	78
Skinhead (6b)	Middle Scout Crag	32
★★ Private Dancer (6a)	Crinkle Gill	156
★ Afterburner (6a)	Flat Crags	137
★ The Deceiver (6a)	Oak Howe Crag	174
★ Pam's Wall (6a)	Blea Crag	197
Black Hole (6b,4c)	Pavey Ark	80
Obscured by Clouds (6a)	Pavey Ark	66
Elton John (6b)	Middle Scout Crag	33
★ Crack in the Woods (6a)	Rothay Bridge Crag	177
★ Coma (6a,6a)	Pavey Ark	76
★★★ Fallen Angel (6a)	Pavey Ark	80
★★ Midnight Movie (5b,6b,6a)	Gimmer Crag	124
★ Warrior (6a)	White Ghyll Crag	47
The Power of Imagination (6b)	Middlefell Buttress	90
★★ Eclipse (6a,4c)	Pavey Ark	79
★ Flying Blind (6a)	Neckband Crag	153
Confidence Trick (6a)	Oak Howe Crag	174
Private Eye (6a)	Crinkle Gill	157
★ Exposure (6a)	Flat Crags	138
Olga Korbut (6b,5c)	Blake Rigg	168
★ A Naked Edge (6a)	Crinkle Gill	156
Bilko (6a)	Black Crag	165
★ Armalite (5c)	Middlefell Buttress	188
Leningrad (6a)	Blake Rigg	167
Perfect Head (5c)	Middlefell Buttress	88
The Hunted (5c)	Blea Crag	198

E3

Limbo (6b)	Deer Bield Crag	184
★ Deception (6a)	Crinkle Gill	157

E3   (Continued)

⋆ The New Girdle (5a,5c,5b,5b,-,5c)	Deer Bield Crag	191
⋆ Mythical M.M. (6a)	Raven Crag Buttress	100
Finger Swing (6b)	East Raven Crag	104
⋆ Close Shave (6a)	Neckband Crag	151
⋆⋆⋆ Stiletto (6a)	Deer Bield Crag	184
Langdale Cowboy's (5c,5b)	Gimmer Crag	123
⋆⋆⋆ Mother Courage (5c)	Pavey Ark	77
Two Star Red (6a)	Helm Crag	181
Solaris (6a)	Flat Crags	136
⋆ The Graduate (5b,6a)	Deer Bield Crag	185
The Fine Art of Surfacing (6a,6a)	White Ghyll Crag	47
⋆ Spiny Norman (6a)	Upper Spout Crag	176
⋆⋆ Big Brother (5b,5c,5a)	Pavey Ark	64
⋆ No Rest for the Wicked (5c)	Blea Crag	195
Edge of Darkness (6a)	Flat Crags	135
⋆⋆ Brain Damage (5c,5c)	Pavey Ark	76
Muscle Wall (6a)	Raven Crag Buttress	98
Tonsor (6b)	Neckband Crag	152
⋆⋆⋆ Pearls Before Swine (5c)	Deer Bield Crag	189
⋆⋆ The Sting (6a)	Oak Howe Crag	174
Abba (6a)	Middle Scout Crag	32
Blondie (6a)	Middle Scout Crag	33
Gymslip (4c,5c,5b)	Deer Bield Crag	185
⋆ Rock Around the Clock (5c,6a,5c,5b)	Pavey Ark	74
La Wally (6a)	Flat Crags	138
Crescent Superdirect (5c)	Pavey Ark	61
⋆ Chameleon (6a)	Blea Crag	196
Death Star (5c,5a)	Pavey Ark	72
Maggie's Farm (5c)	Pavey Ark	65
⋆ Mindprobe (5b,5c,5b)	North Buttress	141
⋆ Riboletto (6a,4c)	North Buttress	140
⋆⋆ Eastern Hammer (6a)	Gimmer Crag	120
Enormous Room (6a)	Gimmer Crag	119
⋆⋆ Cut Throat (6a)	Neckband Crag	150
Needle Arête (6a)	Black Crag	164
S.S. Scoop (5c)	Blea Crag	199
⋆⋆ Crooked Crack (5c)	Oak Howe Crag	174
Book of Reasons (4c,5c,4c)	Pavey Ark	66
Baldy's Wall (6b)	Far West Raven Crag	84
Highlander (5c)	Oak Howe Crag	173
Tonsure (6a)	Neckband Crag	152
⋆ Doberman (6a)	Black Crag	165
Sweeney (5c)	Oak Howe Crag	173
Tenderfoot (6a)	Middle Scout Crag	33
Pocket Crack (6a)	Balck Crag	162
Another Bleeding Controversy (5c)	Blea Crag	196
⋆⋆⋆ Cruel Sister (5b,5c,5a)	Pavey Ark	64
Short Man's Route (6a)	Lower Scout Crag	32

E2

** Paladin (5c)	White Ghyll Crag	47
* Risus (5b,5c)	Pavey Ark	78
* Breaking Point (5a,5c,5c)	Gimmer Crag	125
** Startrek (5c,5b,4c)	Pavey Ark	82
Centipede Direct (6a,5c)	Raven Crag Buttress	99
* Antarctica (6a)	White Ghyll Crag	40
Brian Stalin (5c)	Upper Spout Crag	176
Marilyn Monroe Please (6a)	Raven Crag Buttress	100
* Kudos (5b,5c)	Pavey Ark	78
Sahara (6a)	White Ghyll Crag	39
* Sunshine Crack (5c)	Flat Crags	135
** Cascade Direct (5c)	Pavey Ark	81
Longhair (6a)	White Ghyll Crag	39
Minder (5c)	Oak Howe Crag	173
Absence of Malice (4b,5a,5c,4a)	Gimmer Crag	113
Karma (4a,5c)	White Ghyll Crag	44
Marilyn 60 Today (6a,5c)	Far West Raven Crag	85
* Eliminot (5c,5b,4b)	White Ghyll Crag	45
** Equus (5c)	Gimmer Crag	120
Cold Nights (5c)	Crinkle Gill	158
Sally Free and Easy (5b,5a,5c)	Pavey Ark	60
Out from the Darkness (4a,6a)	Raven Crag, Walthwaite	28
* Tattered Banners (5a,5c,5a,5c)	Neckband Crag	154
** Haste Not Direct (4c,5c)	White Ghyll Crag	46
Slip Knot Variations (5c,5c)	White Ghyll Crag	40
Efrafa (5c,-)	Neckband Crag	151
Sexpot (5c)	Raven Crag Buttress	100
* Walk Tall (5c)	Middlefell Buttress	88
The Broken Spectre (5c)	Helm Crag	181
Jerusalem (5c)	Far East Raven Crag	107
Porridge (5c)	Oak Howe Crag	173
* Aragorn (5c)	Neckband Crag	150
* Dinsdale (5b)	Upper Spout Crag	176
Pianola (5b)	Far East Raven Crag	105
The Pendulum (5c,4c)	Deer Bield Crag	184
** White Ghyll Eliminate (4b,5c,5a)	White Ghyll Crag	46
Don't Look Back! (5c)	West Raven Crag	87
* Dead Loss Angeles (5b)	White Ghyll Crag	49
Potluck (5c)	Raven Crag Buttress	100
** Sweeney Todd (5c)	Neckband Crag	149
Andy Pandy (5c)	Millbeck Crag	54
Bryson's Picnic (5c)	Thrang Quarry	30
Slaphead's Groove (5c)	Far West Raven Crag	85
The Ragman's Trumpet (5b,-)	Pavey Ark	60
The Girdle Traverse (5b,4c,5a,5b,5a)	Deer Bield Crag	191
** Astra (5c)	Pavey Ark	80
** Fastburn (5b)	Flat Crags	137

E2   (Continued)

Father of Night (5a,5b,5c)	Pavey Ark	70
Rhythm Killers (5c)	Raven Crag, Walthwaite	29
The Pillar (5c)	Stickle Barn Crag	52
★★ The Bracken-clock (5a,5c,5b,4a)	Pavey Ark	74
★★★ Gillette Direct (5c)	Neckband Crag	150
The Hobbit (5b,-)	Pavey Ark	59
★ Bravado (5c)	Deer Bield Crag	191
Atmospheric Phenomena (5b)	Helm Crag	180
★ Crimes of Quality (5b)	Crinkle Gill	157
Hermann Goering (5c)	Blea Crag	198
★ Bryson's Flange (5c)	Middlefell Buttress	90
Time after Time (4c,5a,5c)	Blake Rigg	168
★ Mussolini (5c)	Blea Crag	198
Public Convenience (5b)	Crinkle Gill	156
Poacher Right-Hand (5b)	Gimmer Crag	119
Private Investigation (5b)	Crinkle Gill	156
Nelli Kim (5b,5b)	Blake Rigg	169
Yellow Fever (5b)	Black Crag	163
★ Slowburn (5b)	Flat Crags	136
No Flange for the Poor (5b)	Blea Crag	195
Mindbender (5b)	North Buttress	141
★ Glass Slipper (5b)	Black Crag	166
Margot Fonteyn (5b)	Side Pike	170

E1

★★ Springbank (5c)	Gimmer Crag	118
Potty (5c)	Raven Crag Buttress	101
★ Bowfell Buttress Eliminate (5b,4c,4b, 5b,5b)	Bowfell Buttress	145
★ Flarepath Direct (4c,5b)	Helm Crag	180
★ Hogweed Direct (5c,5b)	Far West Raven Crag	86
★ Whit's End Direct (5b)	Gimmer Crag	118
Blade Runner (5c,5b)	Far West Raven Crag	86
Madonna (5b)	Middle Scout Crag	33
Gimmer Gorilla (5b)	Gimmer Crag	111
★ Amina (5b)	Lightning Crag	160
Rope Up (6a)	Black Crag	164
The Rib (5c,5a)	Pavey Ark	71
Fat Boys Crack (5c)	Lightning Crag	159
Dave's Arête (6a)	Black Crag	162
Dead Loss G.G. (5b)	White Ghyll Crag	49
Bill (5b)	Millbeck Crag	54
Do Not (5b,5a)	White Ghyll Crag	40
Confidence Trick (5b)	Lower Scout Crag	32
★ Waste Not, Want Not (5b)	White Ghyll Crag	39
★ Ben (5b)	Millbeck Crag	54
Babylon (4a,5b)	Far East Raven Crag	106
Feet of Clay (5b)	White Ghyll Crag	38

E1   (Continued)

Barman's Saunter (5c)	East Raven Crag	103
★ Muscle Crack (5c)	Raven Crag Buttress	98
★★ Going Straight (5b)	Oak Howe Crag	173
Jokers Slab (5b)	East Raven Crag	104
★★ Poker Face (4b,5b,4a,)	Pavey Ark	68
Sleep on my Pillow (5b)	Black Crag	162
Rubicon Groove (-,5b,4c,4c)	Bowfell Buttress	144
Basher's Bulge (5b)	Lower Scout Crag	31
Swing to the Right (5b)	Raven Crag, Walthwaite	29
★ Dight (5b,5a)	Gimmer Crag	126
★ The Palestinians (5b)	White Ghyll Crag	41
The New Partnership (5b)	Lower Scout Crag	31
Titus Groan (5b)	White Ghyll Crag	41
Hidden Pleasure (5c)	Looking Howe Crag	200
★★ Sword of Damocles (4b,5b,5a)	North Buttress	141
The Patella Pinch (5a,5b)	Raven Crag Buttress	91
★★ Aardvark (5c,-)	Pavey Ark	69
Half Moon (5c)	Pavey Ark	62
Gimmer High Girdle (5a,5b)	Gimmer Crag	126
★ Chimney Variant (5b,-)	White Ghyll Crag	40
Party Animal (5b)	Raven Crag, Walthwaite	29
Slapestone (5b)	Slapestone Edge	192
Men at Work (5b)	East Raven Crag	103
Swing to the Left (5b)	Raven Crag, Walthwaite	29
Variation Girdle Traverse (4a,5a,4c,4c,4a)	White Ghyll Crag	50
Easedale Ramble (5b)	Slapestone Edge	192
★ Deer Bield Buttress (5a,5a,5a)	Deer Bield Crag	186
★ Intern (5b,5a)	Gimmer Crag	123
★ Rainmaker (5b)	Pavey Ark	65
★ Hubris (5a,5a)	Deer Bield Crag	188
Campaign Crack (5b)	Raven Crag Buttress	98
★ Gandalf's Groove (5a)	Neckband Crag	150
★ Man of Straw (5b)	White Ghyll Crag	39
★ The First Touch (5b)	Black Crag	164
Erne (5b)	Blea Crag	196
Hidden Secrets (5b)	Looking Howe Crag	200
Titania (5b)	Crinkle Gill	158
Moon Shadow (5b)	Flat Crags	135
Crazy Horse (5b)	Blake Rigg	167
The Prophet (5b)	Lightning Crag	160
Dunn Cruisin' (5b)	Side Pike	170
★ Frankie Goes to Kendal (5b)	Far East Raven Crag	105
Olympus (5a)	Raven Crag, Walthwaite	27
★ Fruit Bat (5b,4c)	Blea Crag	194
★ Gimmer String (4b,4c,5b)	Gimmer Crag	125
★ Flat Iron Wall (5a)	Flat Crags	136

E1 (Continued)

	Oberon (5b)	Crinkle Gill	158
	Sinistral (5a)	Pavey Ark	59
	Shower of Vegetation (5b)	Middlefell Buttress	90
	Crystal (5a)	Gimmer Crag	122
	Deuterus (5b)	Raven Crag, Walthwaite	27
★	Red Groove (5a,4c)	Pavey Ark	77

HVS

★★★	Razor Crack (5a,4c)	Neckband Crag	151
	Caustic (4b,5b)	Far East Raven Crag	106
★	B.B. Corner (5a,5a)	Flat Crag	136
	Pollster (5a)	Thrang Quarry	30
★★	Deer Bield Crack (4b,5a,4c)	Deer Bield Crag	186
	Right Wall Eliminate (5b,5b)	Bowfell Buttress	146
	Dancin' Barefoot (4b,5b,5a,5a)	Gimmer Crag	127
★★	Mithrandir (5a)	Neckband Crag	150
	Noddy (5c)	Black Crag	163
	Mendes Traverse (5a,-)	Middlefell Buttress	90
	The Gamekeeper (5b,-)	Middlefell Buttress	90
	The Gnomon (5b,4b)	North Buttress	140
	Marginality (5a)	Raven Crag, Walthwaite	30
★	Ann's Agony (5b)	Black Crag	166
	Bradley's Damnation (5b,-)	Middlefell Buttress	89
	Tapestry (5a,5a,4b)	White Ghyll Crag	45
	Brown Trousers (5a)	East Raven Crag	104
★★	Poacher (5a,4c)	Gimmer Crag	119
	Flower Pot Man (5b)	Far West Raven Crag	85
	D.G. Corner (5b)	Middlefell Buttress	88
★★★	Arcturus (5b,5a,5a)	Pavey Ark	63
	Rope Not (5a)	White Ghyll Crag	43
★★	The Girdle Traverse (4b,4c,-,-,5a,4c,4b,4b)	Gimmer Crag	132
★★★	Kipling Groove (-,4c,5a)	Gimmer Crag	120
	Kneewrecker Chimney (4b,4b,5a)	Raven Crag Buttress	97
	Perhaps Not (-,4b,5a,4b)	White Ghyll Crag	44
★★	Inertia (5a,5a)	Gimmer Crag	129
	Crackpot (5a)	Raven Crag Buttress	101
	The Gibli (4c,5b,-,4c)	North Buttress	141
★	Green Light (5a)	Helm Crag	179
	Recount (4c)	Thrang Quarry	30
	Samarkand (4b,5b)	Far East Raven Crag	107
	Troll's Corner (4c,5a,4b)	Pavey Ark	68
	Virgo (5a,-)	Neckband Crag	152
	Festerday (5b)	East Raven Crag	102
★★	Pluto (4c,4b,5a)	Raven Crag Buttress	94
★	Grooves Superdirect (5a,5b)	Gimmer Crag	128
★	Cascade (4c,5a,4b)	Pavey Ark	81
	Swastika (4c,4c,5a,-,4c)	North Buttress	142
★	By-Pass Route (4c,5a,4c)	Pavey Ark	73
	Nutcracker Cleft (5a,4b,4b)	Raven Crag Buttress	96
	Bleaberry Buttress (5a,5a,4c)	Blea Crag	197

HVS   (Continued)

Old Man's Crack (5a)	Millbeck Crag	54
Beacon Rib (5a)	Helm Crag	179
Return of the Giant Hogweed (4c,5a)	Far West Raven Crag	86
Cliff at Christmas (5b)	Raven Crag, Walthwaite	26
Raindancer (5b)	Blea Crag	199
Digitalis (5a,5a,5a)	Pavey Ark	67
** Laugh Not (5a)	White Ghyll Crag	39
* Nazareth (5a,5a)	Far East Raven Crag	107
Rainbow (5a,4c,5a,-)	Helm Crag	181
* The Chopper (5a)	East Raven Crag	103
* Stickle Grooves (5a,-,4c,4c)	Pavey Ark	74
Main Wall Left-Hand	Stickle Barn Crag	52
Proportional Representation (5a)	Raven Crag, Walthwaite	29
Monkey the Needle (5a)	Black Crag	165
Sinister Footwear (5a)	Blea Crag	197
Militant Tendancy (5a)	Raven Crag, Walthwaite	29
Baby Blue Sky (5a,4c)	Blake Rigg	168
The Last Corner (5a)	Black Crag	164
Before the Storm (5a)	Far West Raven Crag	84
* Rectangular Rib (5a,4c)	Pavey Ark	70
The Shroud (5a)	Far East Raven Crag	105
Hanging Corner (5a,-)	Flat Crag	138
Adams Apple (5a,4c)	Neckband Crag	152
Stop Showing Off (5a)	Black Crag	164
The Prow (5a)	Black Crag	164
* Asterix the Gaul (5a)	Blea Crag	198
Dunmail Cracks (5a,4c,5a)	Deer Bield Crag	185
Little Corner (5a)	Pavey Ark	66
The Prey (5a)	Blea Crag	198
Andromeda (5a,4c,4c)	Pavey Ark	75
* Ethics of War (5a)	White Ghyll Crag	38
Mind of no Fixed Abode (4c)	Black Crag	164
** Flying Squirrel (5a,4b)	Blea Crag	194
Chequer Buttress (-,5a,4c)	Pavey Ark	71
Sharni Slab (5a)	Slapestone Edge	192
Simon Says (5a)	Blea Crag	194
* Golden Slipper (4b,4c,4a)	Pavey Ark	67
* The Rib Pitch (5a)	Pavey Ark	73
The Gentle Touch (5a)	Oak Howe Crag	172
Meson (5a)	Raven Crag, Walthwaite	27
Deadly Dave's Demonic Groove (5a)	Far Far East Raven	109
Spider Monkey (5a,4b)	Blea Crag	194
The Girdle Traverse (-,4c,5a)	Millbeck Crag	54
Grooves Traverse (4c,5a)	Gimmer Crag	128
Obelix and Co (4c)	Blea Crag	199
Casket (5a)	East Raven Crag	103
* Protus (5a)	Raven Crag, Walthwaite	27

VS

★ Joas (4c,4c,4c)	Gimmer Crag	122
White Ghyll Traverse (4c,4a,-,4b,4a, 4a,4c,4b,-,4c,4a,4a)	White Ghyll Crag	50
★ Right-Hand Wall (-,4c,4b)	Bowfell Buttress	146
Slipshod (5a)	Black Crag	163
Crossword	Spout Crag	175
Nadir (4b,4c)	Raven Crag Buttress	93
Ramrod (4c)	East Raven Crag	102
Annie's Song (4c)	Far West Raven Crag	84
The Scabbard (4c,4c,4b)	North Buttress	142
Black Slab (5a,-)	Pavey Ark	61
★ Rectangular Slab (4c,4b,5a)	Pavey Ark	69
I Crashed a Vulcan Bomber (5a,4b)	Far West Raven Crag	85
★★★ 'F' Route (4c)	Gimmer Crag	119
Shivering Timber (-,4c,-)	White Ghyll Crag	41
The Girdle Traverse (-,4b,4c)	Neckband Crag	154
Sport for All (4c)	Far West Raven Crag	85
★★★ Rake End Wall (4b,4c,4c,4a)	Pavey Ark	72
Hot Pot (4c)	Raven Crag Buttress	100
The Dream Merchants (4c,4c,4c)	Gimmer Crag	129
Gurt Gardin Stuff	Spout Crag	175
Girdle Traverse (-,4c,4b,4a,4a,4b)	Far East Raven Crag	108
★ Holly Tree Direct (4c,4c,4c)	Raven Crag Buttress	93
★ Whit's End (4c,4c,4c)	Gimmer Crag	118
The Gizzard (4c,4c)	Neckband Crag	152
Stalag (4c,4b,4b)	Pavey Ark	68
Salmon Leap (-,4c)	Upper Scout Crag	35
★ Crow's Nest Direct (4c,4b,4c)	Gimmer Crag	114
Naztron (4a,4c)	White Ghyll Crag	44
Swine Knott Chimney	Swine Knott	51
Spectrum (4c)	Helm Crag	180
★ Panatella (4c)	Side Pike	171
★ Crescent Direct (4c,4b)	Pavey Ark	62
★★ Haste Not (4b,4c,4b)	White Ghyll Crag	46
The Girdle Traverse	Swine Knott	51
★★ Billberry Buttress (4b,4c,4b)	Raven Crag Buttress	96
★ Damascus (4c,4b)	Far East Raven Crag	107
★★★ The Crack (4b,4c,4c)	Gimmer Crag	126
Riverboat Gambler (4c)	Raven Crag, Walthwaite	29
★★ Mendes (-,4c,4a)	Middlefell Buttress	89
★ Flarepath (4c)	Helm Crag	180
No Big Cigar (4b)	Side Pike	171
★ Ash Tree Corner (4c)	Gimmer Crag	122
Hitcher (4a,4c)	White Ghyll Crag	43
Girdle Traverse of Lower North West Face (-,4c,-)	Gimmer Crag	124
Evening Oak Variations (4c,4b)	Raven Crag Buttress	91
Trambiolina (4c)	Middlefell Buttress	90

VS   (Continued)

Too Excess (4c)	Blake Rigg	167
The Girdle Traverse (-,-,4b,4b)	Raven Crag, Walthwaite	28
★ Sign of Four (4c)	East Raven Crag	104
Main Wall Rib	Stickle Barn Crag	52
★ Baskerville (4c)	East Raven Crag	103
Alph (4b,4b,4c,4a)	Pavey Ark	62
Flat Crag Corner (-,4c)	Flat Crags	136
Walthwaite Crack (4c)	Raven Crag, Walthwaite	26
Carpetbagger (4b,4b,4b)	Gimmer Crag	129
Pathfinder (-,4c)	Helm Crag	181
Semerikod	Kettle Crag	159
Route One (4c)	Neckband Crag	154
Iguana (4c)	Blea Crag	197
Judith (4c)	Lightning Crag	160
★ Moss Wall (-,4c)	White Ghyll Crag	41
Sooty (4c)	Millbeck Crag	54
★★ The Gordian Knot (4b,4c,4b)	White Ghyll Crag	45
Mice (4c)	Black Crag	163
Blind (4c)	Black Crag	163
Sorbo (4c,4b)	Blea Crag	195
Billy Bunter (4c)	Black Crag	165
Stephen (4c)	Lightning Crag	160
Granny Knot Direct (-,4b)	White Ghyll Crag	42
Main Wall Crack	Stickle Ghyll Crag	53
Clare (4c)	Lightning Crag	160
★ Hiatus (-,-,4b,4b)	Gimmer Crag	127
★ Rowan Tree Groove (4b)	East Raven Crag	102
★ Roundabout Direct (-,4c,-)	Pavey Ark	67
Three (4c)	Black Crag	163
Gotama (4c)	Lightning Crag	160
Langdale Ferret (4c)	Far West Raven Crag	86
Nineveh (4b)	Far East Raven Crag	106
Something Stupid (4c)	Long Scar	161
Waller's Crack	Harrison Stickle	83
Shizen Groove (4b)	East Raven Crag	103
★★ White Ghyll Wall (-,4c,4b)	White Ghyll Crag	44

MVS

Wailing Wall (4c,4a,4b,4b)	Pavey Ark	63
Porkers' Parade	Swine Knott	51
Ashen Traverse (4c,-,-,4c)	Gimmer Crag	132
Bowfell Buttress Girdle (-,-,-,-,-,4c,4b)	Bowfell Buttress	147
Nocturn (4b,4b,4b)	Gimmer Crag	130
★★ Slip Knot (4a,4b)	White Ghyll Crag	40
Peascod's Route (4a,4b)	Far East Raven Crag	107
Godiva Groove (-,4b,4b)	Gimmer Crag	132
Gandhi (4b)	Lightning Crag	160
Age Before Beauty (4b,4b)	Deer Bield Crag	189
Barry's Traverse (4b,4c)	Gimmer Crag	121

MVS (Continued)

★★ North-West Arête (4b) — Gimmer Crag — 124
 ★ Cravat (4b) — Neckband Crag — 149
 Minor Slab — Kettle Crag — 159
 The (4b) — Black Crag — 165
 Walthwaite Gully (4b,4c) — Raven Crag, Walthwaite — 28
 Limpet Groove (4b) — Side Pike — 170
 Hardup Wall (4b) — Raven Crag, Walthwaite — 26
 Cheroot (4b) — Side Pike — 171
 Porcupine (4b,4b) — Raven Crag, Walthwaite — 28
 ★ Jingo (4b) — East Raven Crag — 101
 Nectar (4b,-) — Neckband Crag — 153
 Girdle Traverse (4b,-,-) — Side Pike — 172
 Forrudd (4b) — Long Scar — 161
 Alfresco (4b) — Raven Crag, Walthwaite — 26

HS

 Jungle Wall — East Raven Crag — 102
 Eden Groove — Deer Bield Crag — 189
 White Rabbit — Middlefell Buttress — 87
★★ Asterisk — Gimmer Crag — 124
 ★ The Central Route — Bowfell Buttress — 144
 Grondle Grooves — Gimmer Crag — 111
★★ Stoats Crack — Pavey Ark — 75
 ★ Watson Wall — East Raven Crag — 104
 Sinister Slabs — Bowfell Buttress — 143
 Bachelor Crack — Gimmer Crag — 111
 Lichen Groove — Gimmer Crag — 116
 ★ Route 2 — Raven Crag, Walthwaite — 26
 Granny Knot — White Ghyll Crag — 43
 Oh Heck Direct — Lower Scout Crag — 31
 Hobson's Choice — Pavey Ark — 78
 ★ Beacon Crack — Helm Crag — 179
 'E' Route — Gimmer Crag — 116
 Musgraves Traverse — Gimmer Crag — 117
 Jolly Roger — Black Crag — 166
 Sun Street — West Raven Crag — 87
 Diphthong — Gimmer Crag — 116
 Samaritan Corner — Gimmer Crag — 124
 Introduction — Gimmer Crag — 122
 Red Slab — Kettle Crag — 159
 Man — Black Crag — 165
 Zebedee — Millbeck Crag — 53
 Sweep — Millbeck Crag — 53

S

 ★ Revelation — Raven Crag Buttress — 97
 Heathery Groove — Stickle Barn Crag — 52
★★★ Bracket and Slab Climb — Gimmer Crag . — 112

S (Continued)

Private Affair	Crinkle Gill	157
★★ Crescent Slabs	Pavey Ark	61
★★ 'C' Route	Gimmer Crag	115
Left Chimney	Stickle Barn Crag	52
Slanting Grooves	Swine Knott	51
★ The Slabs, Route 2	White Ghyll Crag	49
★ Evening Wall	Raven Crag Buttress	92
Stoney Buttress	Pavey Ark	59
Terrace Crack	Crinkle Crag	155
★ Pallid Slabs	Gimmer Crag	131
Far from the Stickle Barn	Far West Raven Crag	86
Monkey Puzzle	Deer Bield Crag	190
★ 'D' Route	Gimmer Crag	117
Glass Clogs	Black Crag	166
★ White Ghyll Chimney	White Ghyll Crag	48
Chimney Buttress	Gimmer Crag	112
Paleface	Gimmer Crag	131
★★ The Slabs, Route 1	White Ghyll Crag	49
Main Wall Scoop	Stickle Barn Crag	53
Easedale Groove	Deer Bield Crag	189
Not Again	White Ghyll Crag	38
Raven Girdle	Raven Crag Buttress	97
Marrawhack	Side Pike	170
Major Slab	Kettle Crag	159
★ Inferno	White Ghyll Crag	38
Borstal Buttress	Cambridge Crag	139
The Grouter	Helm Crag	181
● Jaundice	Raven Crag Buttress	98
Crescent Wall	Pavey Ark	60
★★ 'B' Route	Gimmer Crag	115
Twin Cracks Right	Long Scar	162
Roundabout	Pavey Ark	66
Pianissimo	Far East Raven Crag	105
Ornithology	East Raven Crag	103
Bluebell Arête	Raven Crag Buttress	99
The Slab	Lower Scout Crag	31
Hyphen	Gimmer Crag	119
★★ Centipede	Raven Crag Buttress	99
Siamese Chimneys	North Buttress	140
Deception	Pavey Ark	65
Russet Groove	White Ghyll Crag	37
Katie's Dilemma	Long Scar	161
Stewpot	Raven Crag Buttress	100
Heather Groove	White Ghyll Crag	38
Bluebell Gully	Raven Crag Buttress	98
Nod Off	Black Crag	163
Deadly Dave's Demon Rib	Far Far East Raven	108
Brazen Hussy	Looking Howe Crag	200
Grey Corner	Bowfell Buttress	147

S   (Continued)

Flat Crags Climb	Flat Crags	138
Hidden Treasure	Looking Howe Crag	200
⋆ Hollin Groove	White Ghyll Crag	42
North Gully	Bowfell Buttress	148
Right of Peascod's Route	Far East Raven Crag	108
Cub's Crack	Lower Scout Crag	31
Guns	Black Crag	165
Bracken Route	Pavey Ark	71
Hold On	Black Crag	164
Grey Rib	Bowfell Buttress	147
Ledge and Groove	Bowfell Buttress	145
Junction Arête	White Ghyll Crag	37
⋆ Route 1	Raven Crag, Walthwaite	26
● Walthwaite Chimney	Raven Crag, Walthwaite	26

MS

⋆ 'A' Route	Gimmer Crag	115
⋆ Mamba	East Raven Crag	101
⋆ Savernake	Raven Crag Buttress	96
Juniper Buttress	Gimmer Crag	130
Oak Tree Wall	Raven Crag Buttress	92
Wall End	Gimmer Crag	131
⋆⋆ The Original Route	Raven Crag Buttress	93
Spider Crack	Side Pike	171
Holly Tree Crack	Helm Crag	180
Tinning's Move	Side Pike	172
Orchid	Tarn Crag	56

VD

⋆⋆⋆ Bowfell Buttress	Bowfell Buttress	143
⋆⋆ Route 1	Upper Scout Crag	34
Blea Rigg Climb	Blea Crag	195
The Cambridge Climb	Cambridge Crag	139
⋆⋆ Ash Tree Slabs	Gimmer Crag	122
⋆⋆ Gimmer Chimney	Gimmer Crag	112
⋆ Speckled Band	East Raven Crag	102
Garden Path	White Ghyll Crag	62
Bently	Helm Crag	181
Question Not	White Ghyll Crag	42
Why Not	White Ghyll Crag	42
Cartwheel	Gimmer Crag	121
Crustacean Traverse	Side Pike	171
Cook's Tour	Pavey Ark	70
Platt Gang Groove	Long Scar	161
⋆ Holly Tree Traverse	Raven Crag Buttress	92
Right-Hand Wall Traverse	Bowfell Buttress	146
Scout's Belt	Upper Scout Crag	35
Blandish	Tarn Crag	56
Herdwick Buttress	Gimmer Crag	122

VD (Continued)

Mary Ann	Flat Crags	135
⋆ Route 1.5	Upper Scout Crag	34
⋆ Main Wall Climb	Gimmer Crag	110
⋆ Cub's Wall	Lower Scout Crag	31
Heather Slab	Tarn Crag	55
Right-Hand Chimney	Stickle Barn Crag	53
Intruders Corner	Long Scar	161
Interlude	Gimmer Crag	121
Subsidiary Ridge	East Raven Crag	104
Porphyry Slab	Harrison Stickle	83
The Needle	Black Crag	164
⋆ The Neckband	Neckband Crag	153
⋆ Route 2	Upper Scout Crag	34
⋆⋆ Oliverson's Variation and Lyon's Crawl	Gimmer Crag	117
Rough Ridge	Side Pike	170
Left Wall	Stickle Barn Crag	52
Harristickorner	Harrison Stickle	83
Cub's Groove	Lower Scout Crag	31
Zero Route	Upper Scout Crag	35
Ramblers Hangover	Upper Scout Crag	35

D

⋆⋆⋆ Middlefell Buttress	Middlefell Buttress	89
⋆⋆ Rake End Chimney	Pavey Ark	72
The Plaque Route	Bowfell Buttress	143
⋆ Gwynne's Chimney	Pavey Ark	69
Jolly Corner	Black Crag	166
⋆ Great Gully	Pavey Ark	58
Sam's Saunter	Long Scar	161
⋆ Route 2	Tarn Crag	55
South-East Lower Traverse	Gimmer Crag	113
⋆ Route 1	Tarn Crag	56
Merlin Slab	Pike O'Stickle	133
Route 2	Gibson Knott	182
Prelude	Gimmer Crag	114
Rib and Wall	Tarn Crag	56
West Buttress	Tarn Crag	55
Bumble Arête	Far West Raven Crag	85
Route 1	Gibson Knott	182

M

⋆ Crescent Climb	Pavey Ark	60
Tower Climb	Side Pike	170
⋆ Little Gully	Pavey Ark	58
Old Holborn	Long Scar	162

FIRST ASCENTS

Alternate and Varied leads are indicated respectively by (alt) and (var).

1870/80	**Jack's Rake** R Pendlebury	
	Date indefinite.	
1882	**Great Gully** W P Haskett-Smith	
1882	**North Gully** W P Haskett-Smith	
1882	**North-West Gully** W P Haskett-Smith	
1986 June	**Little Gully** W P Haskett-Smith	
1892 April	**Gwynne's Chimney** H A Gwynne and party	

W P Haskett-Smith had previously descended the Chimney.
18 March 1923. Variation, R S T Chorley, H P Cain, W G Pape.

1898 Oct 1	**Rake End Chimney** C W Barton	
1902 May 24	**Bowfell Buttress** T Shaw, G H Craig, G R West, C Hargreaves and L J Oppenheimer	

30 September 1916. Alternative start, H M Kelly.
20 September 1919. Variation by Chimney, T H Somervell, L Somervell.

1902 Nov 2	**Gimmer Chimney** E Rigby, J Sandison, A S Thomson	
1902 Nov 2	**South-East Lower Traverse** E Rigby	
1903 April 7	**'A' Route** E Rigby, D Leighton, J Sandison	
1907 April	**Crescent Climb** F Botterill, W E Palmer	

The Gully portion of this climb was ascended by C W Barton, 24 October 1899.

1907 May 26	**Oliverson's Variation** C H Oliverson, G C Turner, F B Kershaw	
1907 May 26	**Lyon's Crawl** H B Lyon, J Stables, A S Thomson	
1907 July 7	**'B' Route** H B Lyon, J Stables, A S Thomson	
1907 Sept 22	**Junipall Gully** Fell and Rock Party	
	Names not recorded.	
1908 Oct	**Blea Rigg Climb** G C Turner, J Stables	
1908 Oct	**Deer Bield Chimney** J Stables, G C Turner	
1910 March 22	**Gibson's Chimney** H Bishop, C D Yeomans	
1910 March 28	**Bennison's Chimney** W E Bennison, A E Burns, T H Seaton, C D Yeomans	
1911 Sept 24	**Middlefell Buttress** J Laycock, S W Herford, A R Thomson	
1913 May 13	**First Chimney** H Bishop, C D Yeomans	
1916 Oct 2	**Fourth Chimney** H M Kelly	
1918 Aug 3	**'C' Route** A P Wilson, C H Jackson, A Brundritt	
1919 May 31	**'D' Route** G S Bower, P R Masson	
	Gritstone techniques introduced to Langdale by a Black Rocks expert.	
1920 April 18	**Stony Buttress** G S Bower, A W Wakefield	
1920 June 19	**Crescent Slabs** G S Bower, A W Wakefield	
1920 June 20	**Ash Tree Slabs** G S Bower, A W Wakefield	
1921 Jan 30	**Harristickorner** G S Bower, J C Appleyard	
1921 July 28	**Route 1**, Tarn Crag J A Garrick, W L Tulip	
1922 June 8	**Juniper Buttress** C F Holland, A S Piggott, M Wood	

1922 Sept 6	**The Cambridge Climb** W T Elmslie, A de St C Walsh
1922 Oct	**Route 1**, Upper Scout Crag F Graham
1922 Oct	**Route 2**, Upper Scout Crag F Graham
	Variation, 8 July 1950. J R Files, M Moxey.
1923 April 19	**Second Chimney** W T Elmslie, A de St C Walsh
1923 Aug 8	**Bracket and Slab Climb** H B Lyon, J Herbert
	The chimney was first climbed as an alternative to Gimmer
	Chimney by H M Kelly and J B Meldrum 18 May 1918.
1923 Aug 10	**White Ghyll Chimney** H B Lyon, J Herbert, H P Cain
	10 April 1948. Variation to Pitch 2, J D Teare.
1923 Sept 3	**Chimney Buttress** H B Lyon, G Ackerley, J Herbert
1924 Aug 11	**'E' Route** J A Wray, G Basterfield
1924 Aug 11	**Right-Hand Wall** M de Selincourt, B Ritchie
1924 Sept 1	**The Neckband** M de Selincourt
1924 Sept 7	**Holly Tree Crack** M de Selincourt
1924	**Crescent Wall** M de Selincourt
1925 March 18	**Herdwick Buttress** F Graham
1925 April	**Routes 1 & 2**, Gibson Knott A R Thomson, A Dibona
1926 May 13	**Pallid Slabs** G S Bower, A W Wakefield, H V Hughes
1926 June 27	**Diphthong** M Wood, G S Bower, A B Reynolds, F Frischmann
	Incorporating a Direct Finish by J R Files, J E B Wright 22 July
	1934.
1926 Aug 15	**Gladstone's Finger** W T Elmslie, D Duncan, T Baird
1927 July 10	**Hiatus** G S Bower, A B Reynolds, A W Wakefield, G G Macphee
	First climbed on a rope from above by G Basterfield, J R Tyson
	in 1926.
	1931. Variation Finish, A W Bridge, A B Hargreaves.
1928 May 5	**The Crack** A B Reynolds, G G Macphee
	4 April 1928. First ascended with a rope from above by A B
	Reynolds and H G Knight.
1928 May 6	**Borstal Buttress** A B Reynolds, G G Macphee, R C Abbatt
1928 May 13	**Asterisk** H S Gross, G Basterfield, B Tyson
1928	**Joas** G G Macphee, A B Reynolds
1929 Aug 8	**Musgrave's Traverse** J A Musgrave, N Ridyard
1930 Feb 16	**Deer Bield Crack** A T Hargreaves, G G Macphee
	The party reported the climb to be Severe!.
1930 Aug 10	**The Original Route** S Watson, D Usher, R Holmes, W Cowen, N Middleton
1930 Sept 15	**The Slabs, Route 1** G Barker, A T Hargreaves
1931 April 30	**The Plaque Route** H M Kelly, B Eden-Smith
1931 May 20	**The Centre Route** H M Kelly, B Eden-Smith
1932 Sept 24	**Sinister Slabs** A T Hargreaves, G G Macphee
1933 June 28	**Stoats' Crack** B R Record, J R Jenkins
	9 August 1945. Variation to pitch 3, H A Carsten, E H Phillips.
1933 July 21	**Major Slab, Minor Slab, Red Slab** J Wharton, F G Stangle
1933	**The Slabs, Route 2** S Cross, E Fallowfield, C Tatham
	21 August 1947. Variation Start, A Gregory, J W Tucker.

1936 Sept. 21	**Barry's Traverse** R V M Barry, E G Harper	
1936 Sept. 21	**Grooves Traverse** R V M Barry, E G Harper	
1938 April 17	**Hyphen** A Mullan, G Parkinson	
1939 April 16	**Zero Route** S Thompson, J Diamond	
1939 May 6	**Deception**, Pavey Ark S H Cross, A M Nelson	
	September 1959. Variation Start, J A Austin, J M Ruffe.	
1939 Aug 26	**Wailing Wall** S H Cross, A T Hargreaves, R Hargreaves. A M Nelson	
1940 April 18	**Prelude** A H Griffin, L K Griffin, J Diamond	
1940 Sept 15	**North-West Arête** R J Birkett, V Veevers	
1940 Sept 15	**The Gordian Knot** J W Haggas, E Bull	
1940 Sept 29	**Interlude** J Ashton, J Diamond, J Brady	
1940 Oct 13	**Wall End** J Ashton, J Diamond, J Apted, L Kellett	
1940 Oct 13	**Paleface** J Ashton, J Apted, L Kellett, J Diamond	
1940	**Crow's Nest Direct** S Thompson, P White, A Mullan, V Bolton, J Ashton	
	13 January 1946. Alternative Start, Green Gambit, A R Dolphin, A B Gilchrist.	
1941 May 4	**'F' Route** R J Birkett, V Veevers	
1941 June 27	**Bilberry Buttress** C F Rolland, J F Renwick	
1941 Aug 3	**Bachelor Crack** R J Birkett, V Veevers, J Craven	
1942 May	**Bowfell Buttress Girdle** S H Cross, A T Hargreaves, R Hargreaves, A Cross	
1942 June 17	**Bracken Route** G B Elliott, A Mullan, S A Williams	
1942 Aug 11	**Porphyry Slab** J R Jenkins, J A Martinez, M S Taylor	
1943 March 14	**Cook's Tour** J Cook, G B Elliott	
	The last two pitches were climbed as an extension to Gwynne's Chimney by G B Elliott and T Nicholson in September 1942.	
1943 Sept 5	**Savernake** J E Q Barford, M P Ward	
1943	**Tower Climb** A F Airey	
1945 Feb 26	**Peascod's Route** W Peascod, J Pugh	
1945 May 5	**Ledge and Groove** R D Stevens, G Stoneley	
	The upper part had been climbed from the gully by G B Elliot and H M Elliott, 1 May 1942.	
1945 Aug 1	**Hollin Groove** R J Birkett, L Muscroft	
1945 Aug 9	**Rake End Wall** H A Carsten, E H Phillips	
1945 Sept 24	**Nocturne** A R Dolphin, J W Cook	
	14 April 1946. Groove Variation Start, D D Davies, B Black. 22 April 1946. Direct Start, A R Dolphin, D D Davies, D C Birch.	
1946 Jan 15	**Monkey Puzzle** A R Dolphin, A B Gilchrist	
	The tree which gave the route its name and character has long since disappeared.	
1946 May 5	**Ashen Traverse** D D Davies, J M Hirst	
1946 May 9	**White Ghyll Wall** R J Birkett, L Muscroft, T Hill	
1946 June 23	**White Ghyll Traverse** R J Birkett, L Muscroft, T Hill	
1946 July 21	**Spider Crack** R Bumstead, D J Hewitt, R L Plackett	
1947 May 25	**Slip Knot** R J Birkett, L Muscroft	
1947 May 25	**Limpet Grooves** A R Dolphin, M Dwyer	

1947 May 26	**Garden Path** A R Dolphin, M Dwyer	
1947 May 27	**Whit's End** A R Dolphin, M Dwyer	
	Pitch 3 was added by R Smith and J Moriarty, 1959.	
1947 June 23	**Protus** D C Birch, A R Dolphin	
1947 June 23	**Deuterus** A R Dolphin, D C Birch, J W Cook	
1947 July 12	**Oak Tree Wall** A Gregory, J Woods	
1947 July 12	**Cartwheel** J A Mullan, A C Cain, J Lancaster	
1947 July 20	**Junction Arête** L Muscroft, R J Birkett	
1947 Aug 10	**Heather Groove** R J Birkett, L Muscroft, J Craven	
1947 Aug 31	**Hobson's Choice** J W Cook, A R Dolphin (alt)	
1947 Sept 4	**Scout's Belt** J Lancaster, E Kelly, A C Cain	
1947 Oct 4	**Route 1.5** R A Ewin, J R Files	
	Easter 1957. Ramsbottom Variation. R A Brayshore, N K T Froggatt.	
1947 Oct 6	**Evening Wall** A Gregory, J W Tucker, J Woods	
1948 March 13	**Raven Girdle** A Gregory, J Ward, J W Tucker	
1948 March 13	**South Wall Buttress** S Taylor, J W Hughes	
1948 March 29	**Revelation** A Gregory, B Black, J Woods	
1948 April 23	**Introduction** D J Cameron, A B Durrant	
1948 May 9	**Haste Not** R J Birkett, L Muscroft	
1948 May 15	**Samaritan Corner** A R Dolphin, J B Lockwood, J Bloor	
1948 May 16	**Alph** A R Dolphin, J B Lockwood, J Bloor	
	14 July 1971. Variation pitch 2, D M Hardwick, J Mitchell, J Greybrook.	
	23 April 1972. Direct Start, D Miller, J A Austin, R Matheson.	
1948 May 17	**Kipling Groove** A R Dolphin, J B Lockwood	
	First ascended on a top rope. Much bolder in conception than its contemporaries. The climb was a remarkable lead for the period. Variation. Direct Finish, 12 September 1959, A McHardy, R Fayer.	
1948 May 23	**Granny Knot** R J Birkett, L Muscroft	
1948 May 29	**Bluebell Gully** A Gregory, T W Tucker, J Ward, C Peckett	
1948 July 10	**Centipede** A Gregory, C Peckett	
1948 Sept 4	**Rambler's Hangover** W Kelsie, D McKelvie	
1948 Sept 18	**Bluebell Arête** A Gregory, J Renwick	
1948 Oct 20	**Pianissimo** W Kelsie, D McKelvie	
1948 Dec 12	**Route 2**, Tarn Crag A Gregory, J Renwick	
1949 Feb 6	**Why Not** L Muscroft, R J Birkett (alt)	
1949 April 24	**Watson Wall** A R Dolphin, J Bloor	
1949 April 24	**Baskerville** A R Dolphin, J Bloor	
1949 May 2	**Lichen Groove** A C Cain, J Lancaster	
	A route closely corresponding to this was climbed solo by J M Edwards some ten years before, but could not be identified exactly.	
1949 May 15	**Perhaps Not** R J Birkett, L Muscroft (alt)	
	Variation, Short Cut, J D Johnston, 4 April 1957.	
1949 June 4	**Grey Corner** R D Stevens, J Stevens	
1949 June 5	**Grey Rib** R D Stevens, J Stevens	
1949 June 7	**Kneewrecker Chimney** A R Dolphin, J Bloor	

1949 June 19	**Do Not** R J Birkett, L Muscroft
	This was the second pitch only, climbed as an alternative finish to
	Slip Not. The independent start was added by K Heaton and A
	Heaton on 9 October 1949. The direct start climbed by L Brown
	and P Muscroft on 29 October 1960; a foot loop was used on the
	10-foot crack. Now free.
1949 June 23	**Dons' Delight** A G N Flew, J R Rauldon
1949 June 25	**Nectar** K Heaton, J Umpleby, J A Jackson
1949 June 25	**Holly Tree Traverse** A Gregory, C H Peckett, J Woods
	Variation Finish, C H Peckett. J Woods.
1949 June 25	**Route 1**, Neckband Crag K Heaton, J Umpleby, J Jackson
1949 June 26	**Stewpot** A Gregory, A R Dolphin
	Variation Start. 5 October, 1957 R Marshall, C W Burman.
1949 June 27	**Heather Slab** J W Cook
1949 July 3	**Rib and Wall** A Gregory, J Woods
1949 July 3	**Orchid** A Gregory, J Woods, J Renwick
1949 July 3	**Blandish** A Gregory, J Woods, J Renwick
1949 Aug 28	**Grooves Superdirect** A R Dolphin, J Bloor
	Pitch 1 added 3 July 1970 by M Mortimer and J A Austin.
	The groove direct by M Mortimer, Easter 1976.
1949 Aug 28	**West Buttress** A Gregory, J Woods
1949 Sept 4	**The Girdle Traverse**, Gimmer Crag A R Dolphin, J W Cook
	The outcome of much wandering. On the 5 July a complete
	traverse of the crag had been achieved by J W Cook, J G Ball
	and L J Griffin, following an easier, and inferior, line across the
	North-West face via the second pitch of Godiva Groove.
1949 Sept 7	**The Girdle Traverse**, Neckband Crag K Heaton, S Vernon
1949 Sept 18	**Russet Groove** A R Dolphin, K Heaton (alt)
1949 Sept 18	**Inferno** K Heaton, A R Dolphin (alt)
1949 Oct 8	**The Gizzard** K Heaton, A Heaton
1950 Jan 7	**Godiva Groove** C M G Smith, L J Griffin
1950 June 11	**Girdle Traverse**, Pavey Ark A R Dolphin, J B Lockwood
	4 June 1950. Traverse as far as Jack's Rake. A R Dolphin, H
	Schofield, A D Brown.
1950 May 28	**Mamba** A R Dolphin, J Bloor
1950 May 28	**Speckled Band** J Bloor, P T, J Renwick
1950 May 28	**Jungle Wall** A R Dolphin, J Lancaster
1950 July 1	**Question Not** C Peckett, J Renwick
1950	**Cravat** H Drasdo, N Drasdo
1951 June 24	**Deer Bield Buttress** A R Dolphin, A D Brown
	A R Dolphin's solution to a long standing problem.
	Variation, El Dorado, J Eastham, E Cleasby, 30 July 1977.
1951 Oct 7	**Rubicon Groove** A R Dolphin, A D Brown
	Well named! A remarkably bold first ascent.
1951 Oct 14	**Babylon** A R Dolphin, F M Ball
1951 Oct 21	**Nineveh** A R Dolphin, P Tuke, D Bennett
1952 Feb 9	**Girdle Traverse** Far East Raven Crag P J Greenwood, D Gray, H Drasdo

1952 April 20   **Chequer Buttress**   A R Dolphin, A D Brown
The party traversed into Rake End Chimney just above the little slab for a belay, and returned along the Girdle. The route was not popular and it was not until 1965 that a new way was found. 21 June 1970. Variation Finish, M Bebbington, J A Austin, S Wood.

1952 July 27   **Holly Tree Direct**   H Drasdo, E Mallinson
31 August 1963. Variation, J A Austin, E Metcalf.

1952 Aug 16   **Shivering Timber**   A R Dolphin, J Wilkinson

1952 Aug 23   **Siamese Chimneys**   D Hopkin, A R Dolphin, P J Greenwood

1952 Aug 23   **Sword of Damocles**   P J Greenwood, A R Dolphin (alt), D Hopkin
It was not thought that the 'sword' would last long. In fact it remained for another 26 years.

1952 Aug 24   **Dunmail Cracks**   P J Greenwood, A R Dolphin (alt), N V Stephenson

1952 Sept 4   **Bradley's Damnation**   P Woods, P J Greenwood (alt)

1952   **Nutcracker Cleft**   V Ridgeway, P J Greenwood (alt)

1953 Feb 2   **Mendes**   P Woods, J Sutherland

1953 May 30   **Jaundice**   P J Greenwood, M Watson

1953 May 31   **The Pendulum**   R Moseley
Moseley abseiled down and placed a peg which was used for aid. Climbed free, E Cleasby, 23 June 1977.

1953 July 6   **Jericho Wall**   P Wood, F Carr (alt)
Original route finished up Babylon.
Direct Finish added later; this has now collapsed and the route is best avoided.

1953 July 9   **Not Again**   T Parker, M Dawson, A C Cain

1953 Oct 3   **Dight**   R Moseley, R Greenall
The party started out from the Bower and completed their ascent unaware that only the first half was new, the top pitch had been led by A R Dolphin as part of the Girdle.
The modern way on pitch 2 was climbed by J A Austin, E Metcalf, 25 May 1963.
Pitch 1 and the variations were added by G Gibson and D Beetlestone, August 1979 and called Outside Tokyo.

1953 Oct 17   **Laugh Not**   J Brown, R Moseley, T Waghorn
A tension traverse was used to cross the slab under the big roof. Now free.
Direct Finish by A Faraday, A Barber 5 April 1967 now incorporated in Sahara.

1953 Oct 18   **The Girdle Traverse**, Deer Bield Crag   D Whillans, R Moseley

1953 Oct 25   **The Girdle Traverse**, Raven Crag Walthwaite   A C Cain, R Brooks, R Miller

1953   **Terrace Crack**   D M Oxtoby, R L Lockwood

1954 Feb 6   **Alfresco**   A C Cain, P J Greenwood

1954 March 28   **Flarepath**   P J Greenwood, A C Cain

1954 March 28   **Bentley**   D Ball, P J Greenwood, A C Cain

1954 April 17   **Merlin Slab**   J Umpleby, G Hope

1954 April 18   **Cave Buttress**   J Umpleby, G Hope

1954 April 18	**Chip Groove** J Umpleby, G Hope	
1955	**Evening Oak Variations** Pitch 1 E Metcalf, Pitch 2 G Oliver, F Carrol, P Ross, A Campbell, 1958	
	The pitches were originally the Variation Start to Evening Wall and Variation Finish to Oak Tree Wall.	
1955 circa	**The Needle** E J Hodge, J Lynam	
1956 Jan 5	**Hubris** H Drasdo, A J Norton	
	An epic ascent! Pegs were used for both aid and protection. A young sapling which fortuitously hung down over the crux is, alas, no longer with us. Now free.	
1956 April 14	**Stickle Grooves** J A Austin, R B Evans (alt)	
1956 May 20	**Girdle Traverse of Lower North-West Face**, Gimmer Crag C E Davies, B Wright	
1956 May 27	**Eden Groove** R B Evans, J A Austin (alt)	
1956 July 31	**Stickle Slab** J Umpleby, G Hope	
1957 March 3	**Grondle Grooves** C R Allen, N J Soper (alt)	
1957 May 18	**Walthwaite Gully** J A Austin, J M Ruffe	
	Variation, Left-Hand Finish by B Rogers, D Bates, T Walkington 18 July 1987.	
1957 May 19	**Rowan Tree Groove** J A Austin, J M Ruffe, R Jackson	
1957 May 26	**Cascade** J A Austin, R B Evans	
1957 Nov 9	**Marrawhack** F Holmes, M Cheevers	
1957	**Eliminot** J Brown, J Smith	
	On pitch 2 the team traversed the long 'sandwiched' slab to join up with White Ghyll Wall.	
	The overhang exit was found by J A Austin and I Roper on 14 August 1966.	
1958 June 1	**By-Pass Route** J A Austin, J M Ruffe	
	Easter 1971. Variation pitch 3, R Valentine, P L Fearnehough. 20 April 1980, Alternative Start. R Graham, A Hyslop.	
1958 June 1	**The Rib Pitch** J A Austin, J M Ruffe	
1958 June 29	**Stalag** J A Austin, R B Evans (alt)	
1958 June 29	**Roundabout** R B Evans, J A Austin (alt)	
1958 July 5	**Swine Knott Buttress** R Warner, A L Atkinson, P Turnbull, H Middleton	
1958 July 19	**The Girdle Traverse**, Swine Knott A L Atkinson, R Warner (alt)	
1958 July 19	**Golden Slipper** J A Austin, R B Evans	
1958 July	**Salmon Leap** A H Greenbank, M Thompson	
1958 July	**Swine Knott Chimney** A L Atkinson, R Warner, H Middleton	
1958 July	**Slanting Grooves** D B Jack	
1958 Summer	**Pluto** A L Atkinson, J R Warner	
	This route was a much improved version of an old traverse below the main overhang by P Woods, 2 January 1953 which was known as M. & B. Traverse. Pitch 3 had been climbed by E Metcalf and J Ramsden in 1957 as a finish to Bilberry Buttress. Green Groove Finish was climbed by R Matheson and M Matheson, Summer 1972.	
1959 May 2	**Virgo** G Oliver, F Carrol	
1959 July 30	**Right of Peascod's Route** D Brown, D C Ivins	

1959 Aug 8	**Moss Wall** G Oliver, D Laws
	A cunning solution to a problem which had baffled tigers for years.
1959 Aug 26	**Inertia** L Brown, R G Wilson, C E M Yates
	The party traversed left on what was to become the Girdle using a sling on a spike for aid to finish up Grooves Superdirect. The second pitch was added 25 May 1963 by E Metcalf and J A Austin.
1959 Sept 5	**Schizen Groove** M Burke, G Woodhouse
1959 Sept 17	**Girdle Traverse**, Side Pike D Evans, J A Hartley (alt)
1959 Sept 20	**Trolls Corner** J A Austin, J M Ruffe
1959 Sept 27	**Caustic** R P Grounds, C Harkins
1959 Sept	**Beacon Rib** D G Farley, B A Fuller
1959 Nov 15	**Judith**, Side Pike P Callaghan, P Seddon
1959 Nov 15	**Cheroot** P Seddon, P Callaghan
1960 April 23	**The Gnomon** L Brown, G Lund
1960 May 2	**Mendes Traverse** B Kershaw, R Brown
1960 May 5	**Twain Cracks** B Kershaw
1960 May 6	**Massiacasm** B Kershaw
1960 May 14	**Sermerikod** B Kershaw, R Brown
1960 May 20	**Rectangular Slab** J A Austin, E Metcalf
	E Metcalf led pitch 1.
1960 May 27	**Astra** J A Austin, E Metcalf (alt), D G Roberts
	A peg was used for aid. Now free.
1960 May 28	**The Scabbard** J A Austin, E Metcalf (alt)
1960 May 28	**Flat Crag Corner** E Metcalf, J A Austin (alt), D G Roberts
1960 July 3	**Red Groove** J A Austin, E Metcalf
	The party attempted to traverse left from the niche using pegs and tension!
	Direct Start.
1960	**Hitcher** N Drasdo, F P Jenkinson
1961 May 14	**Easedale Groove** R B Evans, L S Howell, A Evans
1961 Oct 1	**Block and Rib** J Gaymore, D Hall
1962 April 28	**Arcturus** J A Austin, E Metcalf (var)
1963 May 18	**Swastika** J A Austin, E Metcalf (alt)
1963 May 26	**Intern** P Fearnehough, J Oliver, J Hesmondhalgh
	The first pitch only. The second pitch was climbed by J A Austin, I Roper, 19 March 1966.
1963 Whit	**The Gibli** N J Soper, J A Austin (alt)
1963 July 15	**Gimmer String** J A Austin, E Metcalf, D Miller
	All the pitches had been climbed previously: – the Direct Start to Kipling Groove had been led by J Brown in 1952; the Rib had been climbed from the Crack with the aid of a peg; R Smith and J Moriarty had linked Kipling Groove and the Rib with the aid of another peg. It only remained to remove the aid pegs and string it together.
	The Direct Start climbed by E Cleasby, M Lynch Easter 1986.
1963 July 21	**Poacher** J A Austin, E Metcalf (alt)
1963 Sept 8	**Forget-me-not** M Sinker, R Isherwood
1963 Nov 18	**Rough Ridge** A H Greenbank, J A Austin

1964 June 21	**Bowfell Buttress Eliminate** J A Austin, D G Roberts	

Earlier in the year R B Evans and A H Greenbank had climbed as far as the Girdle. The Direct Finish was climbed by P Livesey in 1975.

| 1964 July 4 | **Gandalf's Groove**   J A Austin, F P Jenkinson |

Variation Finish, I Williamson, J White 21 July 1983.

| 1964 July 5 | **Sorbo**   N J Soper, J A Austin (alt) |

Cleaned and reclimbed with start described by J White, D White, 1984.

| 1964 July 12 | **Bleaberry Buttress**   J A Austin, N J Soper (alt), D G Roberts |
| 1965 April 3 | **Man of Straw**   J A Austin, D G Roberts |

The lower level exit was first led by J Syrett in 1970 rendering the use of a peg at the top of the groove unnecessary.
The original exit from the top of the groove is also free.

| 1965 July 10 | **Rainmaker**   J A Austin, I Roper, A H Greenbank |

A peg was used for aid. Now free.

1966 April 30	**Chimney Variant** J A Austin, I Roper, D Miller
1966 April 30	**Roundabout Direct** J A Austin, D Miller, I Roper, H Wiggins
1966 July 16	**Poker Face** J A Austin, K Wood
1966 Aug 6	**Variation Girdle Traverse**, White Ghyll J A Austin, K Wood (alt)
1966 Aug 26	**Razor Crack** J A Austin, K Wood
1966 Sept 17	**Ramrod** J A Austin, I Roper, T Parker
1966 Nov	**Sherlock** D Mitchell, F John
1967 July 9	**The Shroud** W Day, G Kershaw
1967 July 9	**Reckless Necklace** R Dixon, P Knowles
1967 July 22	**The Gamekeeper** D Harding, E Grindley

A similar line was climbed in this area by B Kershaw circa 1960.

1967 Summer	**The Grouter** J A Austin, I Roper (alt)
1968 May 5	**Porcupine** N Halligan, P Maughan, P Chapman
1968 May 16	**Meson** P Chapman, N Halligan
1968 June 9	**Carpetbagger** N Allinson, N J Soper (alt)

A Direct start was added by J A Austin, M Mortimer.

| 1968 July 7 | **Peccadillo**   C Read, J Adams (var) |

Tension from a peg, a preplaced peg and long sling and a nut were used for aid.
Climbed free by P Botterill, S Clegg, 29 May 1977.

| 1968 July | **Gillette Direct**   K Wood, J A Austin |

Incorporating the Direct Finish, added by W Lounds and party in 1969.
Variation, Gillette the original finish by K Wood, A Austin.

| 1968 Aug 2 | **Andromeda**   N J Soper, N Allinson (alt) |

On the first ascent the party climbed the first 6 metres of Stoats' Crack, before swinging onto the wall.
1 nut used for aid on pitch 1.
Climbed free and variation finish added P Ellis, D Hannon 24 August 1968.

1968 Aug 8	**Oh Heck Direct** D Briggs, A Kelly
1969 April 20	**East Buttress Girdle** C H Taylor, I Roper (alt)
1969 May 18	**Crescent Direct** J A Austin, D G Roberts

1969 July	**Rainbow** R D Barton, J L Cardy
1969 Aug 17	**B.B. Corner** K Wood, F Booth
1969 Summer	**The Hobbit** J Fullalove, R Wood
	Some aid used.
	Climbed free by M Burbage, A Liddell on second ascent.
1970 June 14	**The Bracken-clock** J A Austin, N J Soper, A Faller
	Named after an insect (phyllopertha porticola), which was infesting the crag on that day.
	A peg was used for aid on pitch 2, but this pitch was led free by R Valentine the following year.
1970 June 21	**Little Corner** J A Austin, M Bebbington, S Wood
1970 July 20	**Crossword** E Cross, N J Soper (alt)
1970 July 20	**Gurt Gardin Stuff** N J Soper, E Cross (alt)
1970 Sept 26	**Paladin** R Matheson
	Aid was used on the first ascent but the route was climbed free subsequently by R Matheson March 1971.
1971 May 2	**The Ragman's Trumpet** R Valentine, J A Austin
	Drier variation start incorporated in description.
1971 May 2	**Haste Not Direct** J A Austin, R Valentine
	The first complete ascent. Pitch 1 had been climbed as a direct start to Haste Not by P Allison and N Smithers in 1962. Pitch 2 was added by J A Austin and C E Davies, 4 July 1965.
1971 May 9	**White Ghyll Eliminate** A Evans, D Parker, G Miller
	A sling was used for aid on the first ascent, but was dispensed with by J A Austin the following April during work for the guide.
1971 July 14	**The Graduate** R Matheson, G Fleming, J Poole (alt)
	Two points of aid were used, one of which was a pre-placed peg and sling. The route had been climbed previously but not recorded because considerable aid had been used.
	The first free ascent was made by J Lamb and P Smith, 19 June 1979.
1971 July 18	**Flat Iron Wall** J A Austin, F Wilkinson (alt)
1971 Aug 10	**Sinistral** P Long, S Michniewski
1971 Aug 20	**Longhair** P Livesy, J Shackleton
1971 Summer	**Sally Free and Easy** P Livesey
	One point of aid was used.
	Climbed free by P Botterill, J Adams 27 April 1975.
1971 Summer	**Mary Ann** J Umpleby, P Grindley, J Slockett
1971 Summer	**Naztron** L Dickenson, S Southern
1971 Sept 2	**Granny Knott Direct** R Sager, R Meakin, G Thompson
1971 Sept 4	**Slip Knot Variations** H I Banner, D Ladkin
	A point of aid was used on each pitch.
	Pitch 2 climbed free by J Lamb, C Read 1974.
	All now free.
1971 Sept 11	**Cascade Direct** P Long, A D Barley
	Originally named The Sun.
	Three points of aid were used.
	First free ascent was made by P Whillance and J Moore on 3 May 1975.

1971 Sept	**Aragorn** A Evans, D Parker *Two points of aid were used.* *Climbed free R Valentine, J Adams, P Long Spring 1974.*
1972 April 20	**Cruel Sister** R Matheson, S Golvin *A controversial ascent because one of the two points of aid used* *was a pre-placed peg with a long sling.* *The first free ascent was by J Lamb, P Botterill, 19 February* *1975.*
1972 May 20	**Tapestry** R Matheson, M R Matheson, N B Lett
1972 June	**Fine Time** P Livesey, J Hammond *A pre-placed peg and sling were used for aid* *The upper half is a free version of the old aid route Kaisergebirge* *Wall.* *First completely free ascent, P Botterill, J Lamb, 23 June 1979.*
1972 Aug	**Mithrandir** J Hartely, R Sager
1972 Sept 22	**Dinsdale** T W Birkett, M R Myers *One point of aid was used..* *Climbed free by E Cleasby, M Lynch 30 August 1975.* *The climb has become much harder since the removal of a* *wedged block in the wide crack.*
1972 Sept 29	**Spiny Norman** T W Birkett, R Gill *Much aid was used. The first free ascent was by M Berzins and B* *Berzins in 1976.*
1972 Sept 30	**Aardvark** P Long, D J Harding *One point of aid was used.* *First free ascent P Whillance, J Moore August 1975.* *Named in the hope that it would be the first route in alphabetical* *order.*
1972 Sept	**Risus** E Grindley, N J Soper, D J Harding *A peg was used for aid.* *First free ascent P Livesey, R Fawcett Sept 1972.*
1972 Oct 2	**Whit's End Direct** J A Austin, R Valentine
1972 Oct 21	**Fallen Angel** E Grindley, I Roper (alt) *A peg for aid and a peg for a rest were used on the main pitch.* *The first free ascent was by J Lamb and P Botterill on 3 April* *1974.*
1973 July 1	**Joker's Slab** J Hartley, R Crosbie
1973 Aug 23	**Brain Damage** E Grindley, G Higginson, P Long *A peg for resting was used on pitch 2.* *Now free.*
1973 Aug 25	**Mindprobe** K Myhill, K Jones
1973 Sept 9	**Pearls Before Swine** P Long, D J Harding
1974 March 31	**Tattered Banners** P Long, E Grindley (var)
1974 Spring	**Adam's Apple** J Adams, R Valentine, P Long
1974 May 22	**Eastern Hammer** P Livesey, A Manson *Replaces the old aid route If, climbed by P Ross in 1960.*
1974 June 22	**Efrafa** E Grindley, J A Austin, T Parker *Better use of the available rock than a previous route called* *Swordblade, climbed by A D Barley and R Barley, on 14 June* *1970 using 2 points of aid.*

1974 Oct 13	**Rectangular Rib** M G Mortimer, M G Allen
1975 June 15	**1984** E Cleasby, T W Birkett (alt)
	Much aid used to surmount the overhang.
	First free ascent M Berzins, B Berzins (alt), 27 April 1980.
1975 June 15	**Right Wall Eliminate** T W Birkett, E Cleasby (alt)
	One point of aid on pitch 2.
	Now Free.
1975 Aug 31	**Titus Groan** R Sager, J Hartley
1976 April 21	**Equus** E Cleasby
	The alternative finish now incorporated in the description was added by M G Mortimer, M G Allen, 8 May 1976, though part of this had been climbed earlier by G Cram.
1976 April 26	**Eclipse** P Whillance, P Botterill, S Clegg
	One sling for resting was used on pitch 1.
	Climbed free by M Berzins, E Cleasby 8 May 1976.
1976 May 8	**Gimmer High Girdle** M G Mortimer, M G Allen
1976 June 26	**Startrek** M Berzins, B Berzins (alt)
1976 June	**Across Not** A Hyslop, I Greenwood
1976 July 3	**Breaking Point** P Livesey, J Sheard, J Lawrence, G Price
	The first pitch had been climbed by E Cleasby and M Lynch Easter 1976.
1976 July 8	**Mother Courage** E Cleasby, R Matheson
	A peg was used for a rest.
	Climbed free by J Peel, D Hollows 22 August, 1976.
1977 April 17	**Gymslip** D Armstrong, P Whillance (alt)
1977 May 1	**R'n'S Special** G Summers, E Cleasby
	One nut for aid was used.
	Climbed free by D Cuthbertson, M Hamilton 30 July 1977.
1977 May 14	**Enormous Room** M Berzins, B Berzins
1977 May 26	**Kudos** P Sanson, W Lounds
1977 May	**Big Brother** R Fawcett, C Gibb, I Edwards
1977 June 1	**Desperado** P Whillance, D Armstrong
1977 June 4	**Warrior** E Cleasby, R Matheson
	The Rampant Finish was climbed with 2 points of aid by A Evans in 1972. Climbed free, Summer 1978 by M Berzins, C Sowden.
1977 June 5	**The Rib** M G Mortimer, M G Allen
1977 June 18	**Solstice** M Berzins, B Berzins
	One rest sling was used.
	Climbed free by M Berzins 1987.
1977 June	**Wast-Not, Want-Not** W Lounds, P Sanson
1977 July 16	**Obscured by Clouds** P Whillance, D Armstrong
1977 July 19	**Imagination** E Cleasby, R Matheson
	A controversial ascent. The route was top-roped prior to leading.
1977 July 28	**Ethics of War** E Cleasby (solo)
	Upper part of rib previously climbed by A Parkin, P Clarke 1975.
1978 April 4	**Stiletto** P Whillance, D Armstrong
1978 April 29	**Digitalis** P Clarke, M Tolley, M Dale

1978 May 6	**The New Girdle**. Deer Bield Crag D Armstrong, P Whillance (alt)
1978 May 13	**Cut-throat** M Berzins, B Berzins
1978 May 21	**Death Star** T W Birkett, J Adams
	The first pitch was protected by a runner pre-placed high in Rake End Chimney. It has since been led without this runner.
1978 June 3	**Feet of Clay** M G Mortimer, S Foster, M G Allen
1978 June 24	**Tinning's Move** A Evans, G Milburn (alt), J Moran
1978 July 14	**Solaris** M Berzins, C Sowden
1978 July 15	**Take it to the Limit** P Whillance, D Armstrong (alt)
1978 July 16	**Flying Blind** T W Birkett, K W Forsythe
1978 Summer	**Heartsong** R Fawcett, C Gibb
1978 Summer	**The Horror** R Fawcett
	The first free ascent of the old aid route by P Ross, P Myers 1965. A large block on the main overhang has now fallen off and the route has not been reclimbed.
1978	**Basher's Bulge** M Atkinson, J White
	Probably done before.
1979 May 30	**Trilogy** J Lamb, E Cleasby
	The first complete, free ascent.
	Originally an aid route of the same name by G West, I Hadfield, R Huges, Easter 1957.
	Climbed free to an escape left below the big overhang by D Hollows and J Peel, 1977.
1979 June 1	**Spring Bank** M G Mortimer, E Cleasby (var), M G Allen, M Lynch, J Lamb
1979 June 1	**Poacher Right-Hand** M G Mortimer, M G Allen
	Incorporates the original finish to Poacher by E Metcalf, J A Austin, 21 July 1963.
1979 June 10	**Karma** E Cleasby, I Greenwood
1979 June 10	**Mindbender** R Kenyon, R Bennett
1979 June 11	**Wilkinson Sword** R Fawcett, C Gibb
1979 June 27	**Not Much** J Whittock, R Rutland
	Probably climbed before.
1979 June	**Fastburn** E Cleasby, I Greenwood
1979 June/July	**Coma** J Lamb, P Botterill (var)
1979 July 11	**Slowburn** B Berzins, M Berzins
1979 July 12	**Ataxia** M Berzins, B Berzins (var)
1979 Aug 10	**Armalite** E Cleasby, R Matheson
1979 Aug 10	**Walk Tall** E Cleasby, R Matheson
1979 Aug 10	**D.G. Corner** R Matheson, E Cleasby
1979 Aug	**Dead Loss Angeles** G Gibson, D Beetlestone
1979 Aug	**Outside Tokyo** G Gibson, D Beetlestone
1979 Summer	**Supernova** R Fawcett, C Gibb
1979 Sept 31	**Dancin' Barefoot** P Clarke, R Kidd (var)
1979 Oct 21	**The Dream Merchants** P Clarke, R Kidd
1979 Oct 21	**Centrepiece** R Kidd, P Clarke
1980 Feb	**Green Light** P Whillance (solo)
1980 April 13	**The Fine Art of Surfacing** A Hyslop, T W Birkett, R Graham
	Pitch 1 added by R Graham, T W Birket 18 May 1982.

1980 April 26	**Close Shave**	M Berzins, B Berzins
1980 April	**Dead Loss G.G.**	R Graham, A Hyslop, T W Birkett
1980 May 3	**Exposure**	B Berzins, M Berzins
1980 May 3	**Brian Stalin**	P Whillance, R Parker
1980 May 3	**Two Star Red**	P Whillance, R Parker
1980 May 10	**Limbo**	P Botterill, D Armstrong
1980 May 11	**Tonsor**	P Whillance, R Parker
1980 July 16	**Centipede Direct**	P Freyburger, T Walkington

Pitch 1 climbed as a Direct Start to Centipede after prior top roping. Pitch 2 climbed as a Variation to Centipede by parties unknown.

1980 July 21	**Dynamo**	P Whillance, P Botterill
1980 July 21	**Bravado**	P Botterill, P Whillance
1980 July	**Kalashnikov**	E Cleasby, I Greenwood, A Phizacklea

Doubt remains as to whether this climb has yet had a proper ascent. On this attempt a traverse was made left into Holly Tree Direct and the top bulges not ascended. This is claimed to have been climbed later.

1980 Sept 6	**Olympus**	B Rogers, L Greenwood
1980 Oct 4	**The Watch**	I Dunn, R Graham (alt)
1981 April 2	**Elvis**	T Walkington, A Trull

Climbed with 2 rest points.
First free ascent N Dixon, I Dunn April 1982, 1 nut runner pre-placed.

1981 April 9	**Ben**	T Walkington, E Penman

Variation Finish by T Walkinton on 20 April 1981 using a pre-placed nut and sling for aid.

1981 April 9	**Old Man's Crack**	E Penman, T Walkington
1981 April 10	**Bill**	T Walkington, A Trull
1981 April 14	**Sooty**	T Walkington, A D Murray
1981 April 15	**The Girdle Traverse**, Millbeck Crag	T Walkington, J Metcalf, J W Garnett
1981 April 17	**Langdale Cowboys**	R Graham, T W Birkett (alt)

Pitch 1 claimed by M Danson, I Williamson October 1980 and by J Lamb 1 June 1979.
Continuation of Pitch 1 beyond pull right onto Intern by P Craven, J Dunne 5 May 1984.

1981 April 18	**Andy Pandy**	T Walkington
1981 April 18	**Sweep**	A Sattenstall, T Walkington
1981 April 18	**Zebedee**	A Sattenstall, T Walkington
1981 April 23	**Ash Tree Corner**	R Graham, J Graham
1981 April	**Tenderfoot**	P Botterill, J Lamb
1981 May 5	**Finger Swing**	T Walkington
1981 June 1	**Crystal**	T W Birkett, A Atkinson, D Lyle
1981 June 3	**Rudolf Nureyev**	T Walkington

Climbed with several rests after prior top roping.
First free ascent T Walkington 12 September 1983, after many attempts and top rope practicing.

1981 June 12	**Margot Fonteyn**	T Walkington, R T Hamilton

1981 June 18	**Warlock** B Berzins, M Berzins	

Free climbs an old aid route which used 6 pegs for aid climbed by M J Burke, G Woodhouse 11 July 1959.

1981 June 28   **Nelli Kim**   T Walkington, D Nottage
Variation pitch 1 The Scoop climbed by K Phizacklea, J Daly 6 December 1987 during a 'first ascent' of virtually the same line, which had not then been recorded.

1981 June 28   **Olga Korbut**   T Walkington, D Nottage
Several rests taken at the overhang.
Climbed free T Walkington 17 September 1988.
Variation pitch 1 Press Gang climbed by J Daly, K Daly 11 June 1988 during a 'first ascent' of virtually the same line, which had not then been recorded.

1981 July 12   **Sixpence**   A Atkinson, K Forsythe
Climbed using several rest points.
First free ascent C Hamper, T W Birkett 9 July 1983 and renamed Equinox.

1981 Aug 2   **Black Hole**   B Berzins, M Berzins

1981 Aug 10   **The Palestinians**   A Hewison, C Robinson

1981 Aug 14   **Barman's Saunter**   M Furniss (solo)

1981 Aug 23   **Sahara**   S Howe, C Dale, D Kay

1981 Sept 8   **The Beatles**   T Walkington
Climbed with several rest points after prior top roping.
Climbed free after top rope practice and pre-placing runners N Dixon, D Wakelord 1983.
Climb free after pre-placing 1 peg runner P Cornforth 1987.

1981 Nov 5   **Antarctica**   R Graham, S Hubbard

1981   **Crack in the Woods**   E Cleasby, M Danson
An old aid route, climbed free.

1982 May 14   **Age Before Beauty**   R Wightman, S Stean

1982 May 19   **Abba**   T Walkington

1982 May 21   **Blondie**   T Walkington, D Mounsey

1982 Spring   **Midnight Movie**   R Graham, T W Birkett (alt)

1982   **Twin Cracks Right**   D Oddy

1982   **Old Holborn**   D Worrall

1982   **Intruder's Corner**   D Worrall, R Linton

1982   **Platt Gang Groove**   D Worrall, R Linton

1982   **Sam's Saunter**   R Linton, D Worrall

1982   **Forrudd**   D Oddy

1982   **Something Stupid**   D Oddy, D Potter

1982   **Katie's Dilemma**   R Linton, D Worrall
These 8 climbs were first recorded by these parties but all have almost certainly been climbed previously.

1983 May 28   **Bryson's Flange**   I Williamson, J White, P Cornforth

1983 June 6   **Muscle Wall**   T Walkington, B Rogers

1983 June 6   **Campaign Crack**   J White, P Cornforth, I Williamson

1983 June 9   **Recount**   R Graham, A Hyslop

1983 June 9   **Pollster**   A Hyslop, R Graham

1983 June 10   **Bryson's Picnic**   A Hyslop, I Williamson, A Phizacklea

1983 June 11   **Crackpot**   T Walkington, D Mounsey

1983 June 12	**Nazareth** B Rogers, A Kenny
1983 June 12	**Dunn Cruisin'** A Phizacklea, R Wightman
1983 June 16	**Potty** T Walkington, D Finn
1983 June 22	**Deadly Dave's Demon Rib** T W Birkett, D Mounsey
1983 June 22	**Deadly Dave's Demonic Groove** T W Birkett, D Mounsey
1983 June 26	**Spectrum** B Rogers, A Kenny, D Mounsey
1983 June	**Pathfinder** R McHaffie, A McKinney
1983 July 15	**Marilyn Monroe Please** T Walkington, D Mounsey
1983 July 21	**Sweeney Todd** I Williamson, J White
1983 July 29	**Sexpot** T Walkington, D Mounsey
1983 Aug 7	**Absence of Malice** D Jewell, C Brown, T W Birkett, R Graham (alt)
1983 Aug 7	**Gimmer Gorilla** R Graham, T W Birkett
1983	**Maggie's Farm** M Berzins, C Sowden
1983	**The Power of Imagination** J White, J Metcalfe
1984 May 2	**Idle Breed** C Gore
1984 May 5	**The New Partnership** C R Davis, M Hicks
	Done many times before.
1984 May 31	**Simon Says** A Feely, I Williamson
1984 June 7	**Crooked Crack** P Whillance, D Armstrong
1984 June 7	**Going Straight** P Whillance, D Armstrong
1984 June 8	**Atmospheric Phenomena** B Rogers, T Walkington, D Bates
1984 June 8	**No Rest for the Wicked** I Williamson, A Tilney
1984 June 16	**The Brocken Spectre** B Rogers, T Walkington, M Lovatt, D Seddon
1984 June 19	**Last Tango** P Whillance, R Parker
1984 July 1	**Men at Work** B Rogers, A Kenny, T Walkington
1984 July 1	**The Sting** P Whillance, D Armstrong
1984 July 1	**Sweeney** D Armstrong, P Whillance
1984 July 2	**Yellow Fever** R Greewood, C Ensoll, P Donnelly
1984 July 2	**The First Touch** R Greenwood, C Ensoll, P Donnelly
1984 July 5	**Frankie Goes to Kendal** B Rogers, F Booth
1984 July 6	**Centrefold** T W Birkett, I Cooksey, R Graham
1984 July 14	**The Real World** R Greenwood, R Cooper
	Top roped only.
	Climbed free by D Bates solo 17 May 1988.
1984 July 14	**Slipshod** R Greenwood, R Cooper, P Donnelly
1984 July 17	**Father of Night** B Swales, D Cobley
1984 July 23	**Minder** T Furniss, P Whillance
1984 July 24	**Confidence Trick** P Whillance, D Armstrong, T Furniss
1984 July 27	**Porridge** D Armstrong, M Hamilton, P Whillance
1984 July 27	**The Gentle Touch** D Armstrong (solo)
1984 July 29	**The Deceiver** P Whillance, D Armstrong, M Hamilton
1984	**Fruit Bat** I Williamson, J White, P Cornforth
1984	**Flying Squirrel** J White, D White, P Cornforth, I Williamson
1984	**Spider Monkey** P Cornforth, J White, I Williamson
1984	**Chameleon** J White, I Williamson
1984	**Erne** J White, D White
1984	**Shower of Vegetation** P Cornforth (solo)

1985 June 3	**Private Investigations** J White, T W Birkett
1985 June 3	**Private Dancer** T W Birkett, J White
1985 June 6	**Private Affair** T W Birkett (solo)
1985 June 14	**Genital Touch** P Cornforth, T W Birkett
1985 June 14	**Crimes of Quality** J White, P Cornforth, T W Birkett
1985 June 14	**Private Eye** T W Birkett, J White
1985 June 15	**No Flange for the Poor** M Dale (solo)
1985 June 16	**A Naked Edge** T W Birkett, P Cornforth
1985 June 26	**Rock Around the Clock** M Dale, R Brookes
	1st pitch added by M Dale (solo) on 7 August 1988.
1985 July 4	**Bitter Days** T W Birkett
1985 July 4	**Cold Nights** T W Birkett
1986 May 11	**Flower Pot Man** C Crowder, T Walkington
1986 May 11	**Slaphead's Groove** T Walkington, C Crowder
1986 May 14	**Before the Storm** D Bates
1986 May 24	**Baldy's Wall** T Walkington
1986 May 24	**Annie's Song** B Rogers, A McCarthy, D Wood, T Walkington
1986 May 31	**Sport For All** T Walkington, J Cooper, B Rogers
1986 May 31	**I Crashed a Vulcan Bomber** J Cooper, B Rogers, T Walkington
1986 May	**Bumble Arête** T Walkington and friends
	Climbed previously.
1986 June 1	**Marilyn 60 Today** T Walkington, B Rogers, J Cooper
1986 June 1	**Hogweed Direct** B Rogers
1986 June 1	**Return of the Giant Hogweed** B Rogers, T Walkington
1986 June 1	**Far from the Stickle Barn** B Rogers, G McColl
1986 June 1	**Langdale Ferrets** T Walkington, B Rogers
	Direct Finish, 1986.
1986 June 2	**Blade Runner** B Rogers, T Walkington
1986 June 14	**Sun Street** J Coooper
1986 July 18	**Mythical M.M.** T Walkington, B Rogers
1986 Aug 4	**Potluck** A Moore
1986 Aug 17	**White Rabbit** T Walkington, A Wallace
1986 Aug 19	**Trambiolina** T Walkington, I Conway
1986 Aug 23	**Pink Panties** T Walkington, B Rogers, J Kelly
	A Variation Finish to Brown Trousers, a route for which the first ascent details are not known.
1986 Sept 9	**Pretty in Pink** P Ingham
1986 Oct 4	**Book of Reasons** A Dunhill, M Dale (alt)
1987 May 5	**Tonsure** J Swarbrick, P Rigby
1987 May 10	**The Hunted** J White, I Williamson
1987 May 10	**The Ivory Wall** J White, I Williamson
1987 May 19	**Highlander** J Daly, K Phizacklea
1987 May 23	**Mussolini** A Tilney, A Rowntree
1987 May 23	**Asterix The Gaul** A Rowntree, A Tilney
1987	**Hermann Goering** I Williamson, J White
1987 May 24	**Razor's Edge** M Berzins, C Sowden
1987 May 24	**Jagged Edge** C Sowdon, M Berzins
1987 May 25	**Another Bleeding Controversy** C Sowden, M Berzins

1987 May 25	**Offcomers Slab** M Berzins, C Sowden *These two routes were stolen from the locals who had been systematically cleaning and climbing the crag, despite the fact that abseil ropes had been left in place from the previous days cleaning.*
1987 May 26	**Iguana** I Williamson, J Billingham, J White
1987 June 11	**Party Animal** I Williamson, J White
1987 June 14	**Swing to the Right** I Williamson, J Billingham
1987 June 17	**Swing to the Left** I Williamson, J White
1987 June 19	**Proportional Representation** J White, G Hussey
1987 June 19	**Militant Tendancy** J White, I Williamson
1987 June 19	**Marginality** J White, G Hussey
1987 June 19	**Riverboat Gambler** J Daly, K Daly
1987 June 21	**Deception**, Crinkle Gill L Steer, T W Birkett
1987 June 21	**Oberon** T W Birkett, L Steer
1987 June 21	**Titania** T W Birkett, L Steer
1987 June 21	**Obelix and Co** A Rowntree, R Faragher, A Tilney
1987 June 21	**Raindancer** R Faragher, A Tilney, A Rowntree
1987 June 24	**The Prey** I Williamson, J White
1987 June 24	**Death Camp** J White, I Williamson
1987 June	**Hidden Treasure** I Williamson, J White, J Billingham
1987 June	**Hidden Pleasure** I Williamson, J White, J Billingham
1987 June	**Hidden Secret** I Williamson, J Billingham
1987 June	**The Brazen Hussey** G Hussey, J White, I Williamson
1987 July 12	**Out from the Darkness** B Rogers, A Kenny
1987 July 18	**Walthwaite Gully Left-Hand** B Rogers, D Bates, T Walkington
1987 Aug 3	**Baby Blue Sky** K Phizacklea, J Daly (alt) *Variation Start, J Daly, K Phizacklea 15 August 1987.*
1987 Aug 8	**Too Excess** J Wilkinson, J Daly, K Phizacklea *Variation, Right-Hand Finish, K Phizacklea, J Daly 3 August 1987.*
1987 Aug 19	**Crazy Horse** J Daly, K Phizacklea *Variation, Left-Hand Start, J Daly, K Phizacklea 2 August 1987.*
1987 Aug 19	**Leningrad** K Phizacklea, J Daly
1987 Aug 29	**Time After Time** K Phizacklea, J Daly (alt)
1987 Sept 18	**Glass Clogs** D Bates (solo)
1987 Sept 27	**Stop Showing Off** J Cooper, T Walkington
1987 Sept 27	**Hold On** J Cooper (solo)
1987 Sept	**Nod Off** J Cooper (solo)
1987 Sept	**Man** D Linney, R Spencer
1987 Sept	**Jolly Roger** J Cooper (solo)
1987 Oct 2	**Pocket Crack** T Walkington
1987 Oct 2	**Bilko** T Walkington, J Cooper
1987 Oct 2	**Doberman** T Walkington
1987 Oct 2	**Ann's Agony** T Walkington, A Cammack
1987 Oct 2	**Glass Slipper** T Walkington, A Cammack
1987 Oct 3	**Sleep on my Pillow** J Cooper, T Walkington, R Spencer, D Linney

1988 April 9	**Mind of no Fixed Abode**	J Cooper, T Walkington, B Rogers, D Birkett
1988 April 13	**Madonna**	T Walkington, J Kelly
1988 April 24	**Rope Up**	T Walkington
1988 April 24	**Needle Arête**	T Walkington, J Cooper
1988 April 24	**Fat Boys Crack**	B Rogers, J Cooper
1988 May 6	**West Wall**	T Walkington
1988 May 6	**Judith**, Lightning Crag	T Walkington, A Cammack
1988 May 6	**Clare**	T Walkington, A Cammack
1988 May 6	**Stephen**	T Walkington, A Cammack
1988 May 15	**Stars and Bars**	M Berzins, A Manson
1988 May 15	**Dave's Arête**	D Bates (solo)
1988 May 17	**Hang the Gallows High**	D Bates (solo)
1988 May 17	**Monkey the Needle**	D Bates (solo)
1988 May 21	**No Big Cigar**	D Armstrong (solo)
	Probably done before.	
1988 May 21	**Panatella**	D Armstrong (solo)
	Probably done before.	
1988 May 21	**Pianola**	D Armstrong (solo)
	Probably done before. Old peg runner in situ.	
1988 May 22	**Public Convenience**	D Armstrong, J Williams
1988 May 25	**Pocket Way**	T Walkington
1988 May	**La Wally**	P Rigby, A Greig
1988 May	**Hanging Corner**	P Rigby (solo)
1988 May	**Elton John**	T Walkington, D Birkett
1988 June 11	**Edge of Darkness**	D Armstrong, J Williams
1988 June 11	**Moon Shadow**	D Armstrong, J Williams
1988 June 11	**Sunshine Crack**	D Armstrong, J Williams
1988 June 19	**Afterburner**	D Armstrong, A Murray, J Williams
1988 June 19	**Riboletto**	P Rigby, A Greig
1988 June 22	**Amina**	T Walkington, S Hubball
1988 June 22	**The Prophet**	S Hubball, T Walkington
1988 June 22	**Gandhi**	S Hubball, T Walkington
1988 June 22	**Gotama**	S Hubball, T Walkington
1988 June 23	**Noddy**	T Walkington (solo)
1988 June 23	**Three**	T Walkington (solo)
1988 June 23	**Blind**	T Walkington (solo)
1988 June 23	**Mice**	T Walkington (solo)
1988 June 23	**The Prow**	T Walkington (solo)
1988 June 23	**The**	T Walkington (solo)
1988 June 23	**Guns**	T Walkington (solo)
1988 June 23	**Billy Bunter**	T Walkington (solo)
1988 June 25	**The Last Corner**	T Walkington, J Kelly
1988 June	**Jolly Corner**	J Cooper (solo)
1988 June	**S.S. Scoop**	J White, M Scrowston
1988 June	**Pam's Wall**	J White, M Scrowston
1988 June	**Sinister Footwear**	M Scrowston, J White
1988 June	**The Patella Pinch**	J White, M Scrowston
1988 July 21	**Perfect Head**	M Van Gulik
1988 July	**Short Mans Route**	J White (solo)

1988 July	**Confidence Trick** J White, M Scrowston
1988 Summer	**Too Bleeding Hard** C Sowden, M Berzins
	1988, Direct Start, C Sowden, M Berzins using 1 nut for aid.
1988 Sept 10	**Into the Light** D Birkett, P Ramsden, B Rogers
	After much top rope practicing.
1988 Oct 16	**Sharni Slab** A Phizacklea, J Lockley
1988 Oct 16	**Slape Stones** A Phizacklea, J Lockley
1988 Oct 16	**Easedale Ramble** A Phizacklea, J Lockley
1988 Nov 5	**Black Slab** J Daly, K Phizacklea
1988 Nov 5	**Crescent Superdirect** K Phizacklea, J Daly
1988 Nov 7	**Half Moon** J Daly, K Phizacklea
1988 Dec 19	**Cliff at Christmas** J White, I Williamson, J Billingham
1989 Feb 5	**Don't Look Back!** J Cooper (solo with a back rope)

Note

Details of the first ascents of the following routes are not known, any information or claims should be sent to the editor.

Routes 1 and 2 Raven Crag, Walthwaite, Hardup Wall, Walthwaite Crack, Walthwaite Chimney, Cub's Groove, Cub's Crack, Cub's Wall, The Slab, Route 1.5 variation, Rope Not, all routes on Stickle Barn Crag, Waller's Crack, Middlefell Buttress variations, Nadir, Muscle Crack, Confidence, Hotpot, Jingo, Festerday, Casket, The Chopper, Ornithology, Brown Trousers, Sign of Four, Subsidiary Ridge, Eighty-Foot Slab, Samarkand, Jerusalem, Damascus, Main Wall Climb, Grondle Groove variation, Carpetbagger variation, Flat Crags Climb, Bowfell Buttress variation, Right-Hand Wall Traverse, Fifth Chimney, Crustacean Traverse, Oak Howe Needle, Beacon Crack, Flarepath Direct, Hubris variation.

Dates for the first free ascent of the following routes are also unknown: The Hobbit, Rainmaker, Brain Damage, Astra, Hubris.

MOUNTAIN ACCIDENTS

Procedure for Climbers in the Lake District

There has recently been considerable change in the procedures for mountain rescue in the Lake District. This change has been brought about by many factors, including the increase in the number and availability of rescue teams, the developments and improvements in equipment and techniques, and the increased availability (thanks to the R.A.F.) of helicopters for mountain rescue purposes.

Consequently, only minor casualties should come within the scope of treatment and evacuation by the climber's companions. The rule for all other cases is to make the casualty safe, to initiate the treatment, and to send expeditiously for a Mountain Rescue Team.

Sending for Help

A reliable member of the party should be sent for the Rescue Team, with full information about the nature of the injuries and the position of the incident (including, if possible, the map reference). **He should then find the nearest telephone, dial 999, and ask for the Police**, who will notify the most readily available team. The sender of the message should stay by the telephone until he receives instructions from the Team Leader, who may want further information or may want his help to guide the team to the incident.

General Treatment

Pending the arrival of the rescue team, basic first-aid treatment should be given. The patient should be examined as far as is possible without unduly exposing him. Wounds should be covered and external bleeding controlled by pressure of dressings. Application of tourniquets can be very dangerous and often make haemorrhage worse; they should only be used by experts and then only in extreme cases. Fractures should be immobilised by the most simple method available. The patient, if shocked, or suffering from actual or potential exposure, should then be put in a sheltered place, protected from the rain and wind, wrapped in as many layers of clothing as possible, encased in a 'poly bag' or other impermeable material, and, if conscious and not suffering from abdominal injuries, given warm drinks containing glucose. If available a tent should be erected around him.

The majority of cases will respond to this treatment and their condition should have improved by the time the team arrives. The more serious cases, where such an improvement may not occur, ..

include head injuries, spinal fractures, chest and abdominal injuries with possible internal haemorrhage, and multiple injuries with consequent severe shock. They require urgent expert treatment, and every effort should be made to stress the urgency and the nature of the injuries when the 999 call is made. The use of a helicopter, by courtesy of the R.A.F., can be quickly obtained through the Mountain Rescue Team Leader and the Police.

Treatment of special cases

Fractures of the limbs are usually best treated, in the case of the arm, by padding it and bandaging it to the chest, and in the case of the leg, by padding it and bandaging it to the other leg.

Severe head injuries run the risk of death from asphyxia with deepening unconsciousness. The position of the patient, his head and tongue should be adjusted to facilitate breathing. Apparently less severe head injuries should be continually and carefully observed as the condition of the patient can rapidly deteriorate.

Fracture of the spine, if suspected, means that the patient should not be moved and should be made to keep still. If he is in a dangerous position, a difficult decision will have to be made as to whether or not to move him. If he has to be moved to save his life, then obviously every care should be taken to prevent movement of the spine.

Internal haemorrhage should be suspected if the patient has sustained blows to the chest or abdomen. It is confirmed if, despite the measures adopted for the treatment and prevention of shock, his condition progressively deteriorates. All steps should be taken to facilitate the rapid arrival of doctor, team and, if possible, helicopter. A record should be kept of pulse rate to facilitate subsequent diagnosis.

Lack of help. The most difficult decision has to be made when the patient is severly injured, possibly unconscious, and there is only one climbing companion present. He should try to summon help from nearby climbers or walkers by shouting, giving the distress call on his whistle, flashing a torch, or sending up a red flare. If there is no response then he has to assess the relative dangers of leaving the patient, or of failing to get help, and should act decisively in the interest of the patient.

256

INDEX

	Page		Page
'A' Route	115	Bentley	181
A Naked Edge	156	Big Brother	64
Aardvark	69	Bilberry Buttress	96
Abba	32	Bilko	165
Absence of Malice	113	Bill	54
Across Not	43	Billy Bunter	165
Adam's Apple	152	Bitter Days	158
Afterburner	137	Black Crag	162
Age Before Beauty	189	Black Hole	80
Alfresco	26	Black Slab	61
Alph	62	Blade Runner	86
Amina	160	Blake Rigg	166
Andromeda	75	Blandish	56
Andy Pandy	54	Blea Crag	193
Ann's Agony	166	Blea Rigg Climb	195
Annie's Song	84	Bleaberry Buttress	197
Another Bleeding Controversy	196	Blind	163
Antarctica	40	Block and Rib	37
Aragorn	150	Blondie	33
Arcturus	63	Bluebell Arête	99
Armalite	88	Bluebell Gully	98
Ash Tree Corner	122	Book of Reasons	66
Ash Tree Slabs	122	Borstal Buttress	139
Ashen Traverse	132	Bowfell	134
Asterisk	124	Bowfell Buttress	143
Asterix The Gaul	198	Bowfell Buttress Eliminate	145
Astra	80	Bowfell Buttress Girdle	147
Ataxia	137	Bowfell Links	148
Atmospheric Phenomena	180	Bracken Route	71
		Bracken-clock, The	74
'B' Route	115	Bracket and Slab Climb	112
B.B. Corner	136	Bradley's Damnation	89
Baby Blue Sky	168	Brain Damage	76
Babylon	106	Bravado	191
Bachelor Crack	111	Brazen Hussey, The	200
Baldy's Wall	84	Breaking Point	125
Barman's Saunter	103	Brian Stalin	176
Barry's Traverse	121	Brocken Spectre, The	181
Basher's Bulge	31	Brown Trousers	104
Baskerville	103	Bryson's Finish	103
Beacon Crack	179	Bryson's Flange	90
Beacon Rib	179	Bryson's Picnic	30
Beatles, The	32	Bumble Arête	85
Before the Storm	84	By-Pass Route	73
Ben	54		
Bennison's Chimney	82	'C' Route	115

	Page
Cambridge Climb, The	139
Cambridge Crag	138
Campaign Crack	98
Carpetbagger	129
Cartwheel	121
Cascade	81
Cascade Direct	81
Casket	103
Casteration Crack	89
Caustic	106
Cave Buttress	134
Centipede	99
Centipede Direct	99
Central Route, The	144
Centrefold	95
Centrepiece	111
Chameleon	196
Chequer Buttress	71
Cheroot	171
Chimney Buttress	112
Chimney Variant	48
Chip Groove	134
Chopper, The	103
Clare	160
Cliff at Christmas	26
Close Shave	151
Cold Nights	158
Coma	76
Confidence	99
Confidence Trick (Lower Scout)	174
Confidence Trick (Oak Howe)	32
Cook's Tour	70
Crack in the Woods	177
Crack, The	126
Crackpot	101
Cravat	149
Crazy Horse	167
Crescent Climb	60
Crescent Direct	62
Crescent Slabs	61
Crescent Superdirect	61
Crescent Wall	60
Crimes of Quality	157
Crinkle Crag	155
Crinkle Ghyll	155
Crooked Crack	174
Crossword	175
Crow's Nest Direct	114

	Page
Cruel Sister	64
Crustacean Traverse	171
Crystal	122
Cub's Crack	31
Cub's Groove	31
Cub's Wall	31
Curtain Wall	89
Cut-throat	150
'D' Route	117
D.G. Corner	88
Damascus	107
Dancin' Barefoot	127
Dave's Arête	162
Dead Loss Angeles	49
Dead Loss G.G.	49
Deadly Dave's Demon Rib	108
Deadly Dave's Demonic Groove	109
Death Camp	199
Death Star	72
Deceiver, The	174
Deception (Crinkle Gill)	157
Deception (Pavey Ark)	65
Deer Bield Buttress	186
Deer Bield Chimney	188
Deer Bield Crack	186
Deer Bield Crag	183
Desperado	187
Deuterus	27
Dight	126
Digitalis	67
Dinsdale	176
Diphthong	116
Do Not	40
Doberman	165
Don's Delight	148
Don't Look Back!	87
Dream Merchants, The	129
Dunmail Cracks	185
Dunn Cruisin'	170
Dynamo	190
'E' Route	116
Eagle Crag	192
Easedale Groove	189
Easedale Ramble	192
East Buttress Girdle	82
East Raven Crag	101

	Page		Page
Eastern Hammer	120	Frankie Goes to Kendal	105
Eclipse	79	Fruit Bat	194
Eden Groove	189		
Edge of Darkness	135	Gamekeeper, The	90
Efrafa	151	Gandalf's Groove	150
Eighty Foot Slab	105	Gandhi	160
El Dorado	187	Garden Path	42
Eliminot	45	Genital Touch	157
Elterwater Quarries	176	Gentle Touch, The	172
Elton John	33	Gibli, The	141
Elvis	33	Gibson Knott	182
Enormous Room	119	Gibson's Chimney	82
Equus	120	Gillette Direct	150
Erne	196	Gimmer Chimney	112
Ethics of War	38	Gimmer Crag	109
Evening Oak Variations	91	Gimmer Gorilla	111
Evening Wall	92	Gimmer High Girdle	126
Exposure	138	Gimmer String	125
		Girdle Traverse (Far East Raven)	108
'F' Route	119	Girdle Traverse (Pavey Ark)	82
Fallen Angel	80	Girdle Traverse (Side Pike)	172
Far East Raven Crag	105	Girdle,Traverse of Lower North-West Face	124
Far Far East Raven Crag	108	Girdle Traverse, The (Deer Bield Crag)	132
Far from the Stickle Barn	86	Girdle Traverse, The (Gimmer)	54
Far West Raven Crag	84	Girdle Traverse, The (Millbeck Crag)	154
Fastburn	137	Girdle Traverse, The (Neckband Crag)	191
Fat Boys Crack	159	Girdle Traverse, The (Raven Crag, Walthwaite)	28
Father of Night	70	Girdle Traverse, The (Swine Knott)	51
Feet of Clay	38	Gizzard, The	152
Festerday	102	Gladstone's Finger	155
Fifth Chimney	155	Gladstone Knott	155
Fine Art of Surfacing, The	47	Glass Clogs	166
Fine Time	95	Glass Slipper	166
Finger Swing	104	Gnomon, The	140
First Chimney	155	Godiva Groove	129
First Touch, The	164	Going Straight	173
Flarepath	180	Golden Slipper	67
Flarepath Direct	180	Gordian Knot, The	45
Flat Crag Corner	136	Gotama	160
Flat Crags	134	Graduate, The	185
Flat Crags Climb	138	Granny Knot	43
Flat Iron Wall	136		
Flower Pot Man	85		
Flying Blind	153		
Flying Squirrel	194		
Forget-me-Not	48		
Forrudd	161		
Fourth Chimney	155		

	Page
Granny Knot Direct	42
Great Gully	58
Green Groove Finish	94
Green Light	179
Grey Corner	147
Grey Rib	147
Grondle Grooves	111
Grooves Superdirect	128
Grooves Traverse	128
Grouter, The	181
Guns	165
Gurt Gardin Stuff	175
Gwynne's Chimney	69
Gymslip	185
Half Moon	62
Hang the Gallows High	165
Hanging Corner	138
Hanging Knotts	148
Hardup Wall	26
Harrison Stickle	83
Harristickorner	83
Haste Not	46
Haste Not Direct	46
Heartsong	81
Heather Groove (White Ghyll)	38
Heather Groove (Stickle Barn Crag)	52
Heather Slab	55
Helm Crag	179
Herdwick Buttress	122
Hermann Goering	198
Hiatus	127
Hidden Pleasures	200
Hidden Secrets	200
Hidden Treasure	200
Highlander	173
Hitcher	43
Hobbit, The	59
Hobson's Choice	78
Hogweed Direct	86
Hold On	164
Hollin Groove	42
Holly Tree Crack	180
Holly Tree Direct	93
Holly Tree Traverse	92
Horror	47
Hotpot	100

	Page
Hubris	188
Hunted, The	198
Hyphen	119
I Crashed a Vulcan Bomber	85
Idle Breed	190
Iguana	197
Imagination	188
Inertia	129
Inferno	38
Interlude	121
Intern	123
Into the Light	27
Introduction	122
Intruder's Corner	161
Ivory Wall, The	197
Jaundice	98
Jagged Edge	149
Jericho Wall	106
Jerusalem	107
Jingo	101
Joas	122
Jocker's Slab	104
Jolly Corner	166
Jolly Roger	166
Judith (Lightning Crag)	160
Judith (Side Pike)	171
Junction Arête	37
Jungle Wall	102
Juniper Buttress	130
Kalashnikov	94
Karma	44
Katie's Dilemma	161
Kettle Crag	158
Kipling Groove	120
Kneewrecker Chimney	97
Kudos	78
La Wally	138
Langdale Cowboys	123
Langdale Cowboys Continuation	123
Langdale Ferrets	86
Last Corner, The	164
Last Tango	184
Laugh Not	39
Ledge and Groove	145

	Page		Page
Left Chimney	52	Mindprobe	141
Left Wall	52	Minor Slab	159
Leningrad	167	Mithrandir	150
Lichen Groove	116	Monkey Puzzle	190
Lightning Crag	159	Monkey the Needle	165
Limbo	184	Moon Shadow	135
Limpet Grooves	170	Moss Wall	41
Little Corner	66	Mother Courage	77
Little Gully	58	Muscle Crack	98
Long Scar	161	Muscle Wall	98
Looking Howe Crag	199	Musgrave's Traverse	117
Longhair	39	Mussolini	198
Lower Scout Crag	31	Mythical M.M.	100
Madonna	33	Nadir	93
Maggie's Farm	65	Nazareth	107
Main Wall Climb	110	Naztron	44
Main Wall Crack	53	Neckband Crag	148
Main Wall Left-Hand	52	Neckband, The	153
Main Wall Rib	52	Neckband Crag	148
Main Wall Scoop	53	Nectar	153
Major Slab	159	Needle Arête	164
Mamba	101	Needle, The	164
Man	165	Nelli Kim	169
Man of Straw	39	New Girdle, The	191
Marginality	30	New Partnership, The	31
Margot Fonteyn	170	Nineveh	106
Marilyn 60 Today	85	No Big Cigar	171
Marilyn Monroe Please	100	No Flange for the Poor	195
Marrawhack	170	No Rest for the Wicked	195
Mary Ann	135	Nocturne	130
Massiacasm	154	Nod Off	163
Men at Work	103	Noddy	163
Mendes	89	North Buttress	139
Mendes Traverse	90	North Gully	148
Merlin Slab	133	North-West Arête	124
Meson	27	Not Again	38
Mice	163	Not Much	37
Middle Scout Crag	32	Nutcracker Cleft	96
Middlefell Buttress	87		
Middlefell Buttress	89	Oak Howe Crag	172
Middlefell Buttress	87	Oak Howe Needle	174
Midnight Movie	124	Oak Tree Wall	92
Militant Tendency	29	Obelix and Co.	199
Millbeck Crag	53	Oberon	158
Mind of no Fixed Abode	164	Obscured by Clouds	66
Mindbender	141	Offcomers Slab	196
Minder	173	Oh Heck Direct	31

	Page
Old Holborn	162
Old Man's Crack	54
Olga Korbut	168
Oliverson's Variation and Lyon's Crawl	117
Olympus	27
Orchid	56
Original Route, The	93
Ornithology	103
Out from the Darkness	28
Paladin	47
Paleface	131
Palestinians, The	41
Pallid Slabs	131
Pam's Wall	197
Panatella	171
Party Animal	29
Patella Pinch, The	91
Pathfinder	181
Pavey Ark	57
Pearls Before Swine	189
Peascod's Route	107
Peccadillo	187
Pendulum, The	184
Perfect Head	88
Perhaps Not	44
Pianissimo	105
Pianola	105
Pike O'Stickle	133
Pillar, The	52
Pink Panties	104
Plaque Route, The	143
Platt Gang Groove	161
Pluto	94
Poacher	119
Poacher Right-Hand	119
Pocket Crack	162
Pocket Way	162
Poker Face	68
Pollster	30
Porcupine	28
Porkers' Parade	51
Porphyry Slab	83
Porridge	173
Potluck	100
Potty	101
Power of Imagination, The	90

	Page
Prelude	114
Press Gang	169
Pretty in Pink	190
Prey, The	198
Private Affair	157
Private Dancer	156
Private Eye	157
Private Investigations	156
Prophet, The	160
Proportional Representation	29
Protus	27
Prow, The	164
Public Convenience	156
Question Not	42
R'n'S Special	95
Ragman's Trumpet, The	60
Rainbow	181
Raindancer	199
Rainmaker, The	65
Rake End Chimney	72
Rake End Wall	72
Rambler's Hangover	35
Rampant Finish, The	47
Ramrod	102
Raven Crag	83
Raven Crag, Walthwaite	25
Raven Crag Buttress	91
Raven Girdle	97
Razor Crack	151
Razor's Edge	153
Real World, The	163
Reckless Necklace	43
Recount	30
Rectangular Rib	70
Rectangular Slab	69
Red Groove	77
Red Slab	159
Return of the Giant Hogweed	86
Revelation	97
Rhythm Killers	29
Rib and Wall	56
Rib Pitch, The	73
Rib, The	71
Riboletto	140
Right of Peascod's Route	108
Right Wall Eliminate	146

	Page		Page
Right-Hand Chimney	53	Shower of Vegetation	90
Right-Hand Wall	146	Shroud, The	105
Right-Hand Wall Traverse	146	Siamese Chimneys	140
Risus	78	Side Pike	169
Riverboat Gambler	29	Sign of Four	104
Rock Around the Clock	74	Simon Says	194
Rope Not	43	Sinister Footwear	197
Rope Up	164	Sinister Slabs	143
Rothay Bridge Crag	176	Sinistral	59
Rough Ridge	170	Sixpence	79
Roundabout	66	Skinhead	32
Roundabout Direct	67	Slab, The	31
Route 1 (Gibson Knott)	182	Slabs, Route 1, The	49
Route 1 (Raven, Walthwaite)	26	Slabs, Route 2, The	49
Route 1 (Tarn Crag)	56	Slanting Grooves	51
Route 1 (Upper Scout Crag)	34	Slape Stones	192
Route 1.5	34	Slapestone Edge	192
Route 2 (Gibson Knott)	182	Slaphead's Groove	85
Route 2 (Raven, Walthwaite)	26	Sleep on my Pillow	162
Route 2 (Tarn Crag)	55	Slip Knot	40
Route 2 (Upper Scout Crag)	34	Slip Knot Variations	40
Route One	154	Slipshod	163
Rowan Tree Groove	102	Slowburn	136
Rubicon Groove	144	Solaris	136
Rudolf Nureyev	170	Solstice	78
Runner Wall	48	Something Stupid	161
Russet Groove	37	Sooty	54
		Sorbo	195
S.S. Scoop	199	South-East Lower Traverse	113
Sahara	39	South Wall Buttress	171
Sally Free and Easy	60	Speckled Band	102
Salmon Leap	35	Spectrum	180
Sam's Saunter	161	Spider Crack	171
Samaritan Corner	124	Spider Monkey	194
Samarkand	107	Spiny Norman	176
Savarnake	96	Sport For All	85
Scabbard, The	142	Spout Crag	175
Scoop, The	169	Spring Bank	118
Scout Crags	30	Stalag	68
Scout's Belt	35	Stars and Bars	79
Second Chimney	155	Startrek	82
Semerikod	159	Stephen	160
Sexpot	100	Stewpot	100
Sharni Slab	192	Stickle Barn Crag	52
Sherlock	105	Stickle Grooves	74
Shivering Timber	41	Stickle Slab	134
Shizen Groove	103	Stiletto	184
Short Man's Route	32	Sting, The	174

	Page
Stoat's Crack	75
Stony Buttress	59
Stop Showing Off	164
Subsidiary Ridge	104
Sun Street	87
Sunshine Crack	135
Supernova	80
Swastika	142
Sweeney	173
Sweeney Todd	149
Sweep	53
Swine Knott	51
Swine Knott Buttress	51
Swine Knott Chimney	51
Swing to the Left	29
Swing to the Right	29
Sword of Damocles	141
Take it to the Limit	187
Tapestry	45
Tarn Crag	55
Tattered Banners	154
Tenderfoot	33
Terrace Crack	155
Third Chimney	155
Thrang Quarry	30
Three	163
Time After Time	168
Tinning's Move	172
Titania	158
Titus Groan	41
Tonsor	152
Tonsure	152
Too Bleeding Hard	193
Too Excess	167
Tower Climb	170
Trambiolina	88
Trilogy	95
Troll's Corner	68
Twain Cracks	154

	Page
Twin Cracks Right	162
Two Star Red	181
Upper Scout Crag	33
Upper Spout Crag	176
Variation Girdle Traverse	50
Virgo	152
Wailing Wall	63
Walk Tall	88
Wall End	131
Waller's Crack	83
Walthwaite Chimney	26
Walthwaite Crack	26
Walthwaite Gully	28
Warlock	106
Warrior	47
Waste Not, Want Not	39
Watch, The	94
Watson Wall	104
West Buttress	55
West Raven Crag	87
West Wall	160
Whit's End	118
Whit's End Direct	118
White Ghyll Chimney	48
White Ghyll Crag	36
White Ghyll Eliminate	46
White Ghyll Traverse	50
White Ghyll Wall	44
White Rabbit	87
Why Not	42
Wilkinson Sword	149
Yellow Fever	163
Zebedee	53
Zero Route	35

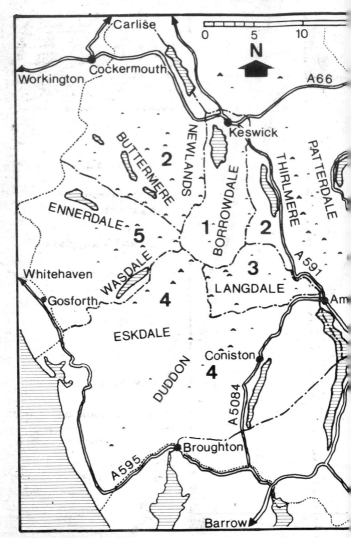